JOSÉ DONOSO'S HOUSE OF FICTION

Latin American Literature and Culture Series

JOSÉ DONOSO'S HOUSE OF FICTION

A DRAMATIC CONSTRUCTION
OF TIME AND PLACE

Flora González Mandri

WAYNE STATE UNIVERSITY PRESS
DETROIT

Library of Congress Cataloging-in-Publication Data

González Mandri, Flora María.
José Donoso's house of fiction : a dramatic construction of time
and place / Flora González Mandri.
p.   cm. — (Latin American literature and culture series)
Includes bibliographical references and index.
ISBN 0-8143-2526-2 (alk. paper)
1. Donoso, José, 1924–   —Criticism and interpretation.
I. Title.   II. Series.
PQ8097.D617Z63 1995
863—dc20   94-36956

Designer: Mary Krzewinski

*To my father who
died in a foreign land,
and to my mother from whom
I learned the pleasure of reading*

CONTENTS

ACKNOWLEDGMENTS

This book had its inception in the mid-eighties when I travelled to Chile under the auspices of a Tinker Foundation travel grant from the University of Chicago. I owe a debt of gratitude to David Benavente and José Donoso who offered me their hospitality and who facilitated meetings with people in the world of theater, film, and video in Santiago de Chile. These include actors, directors, and filmmakers who had collaborated with Donoso in various productions: José Pineda, Eugenio Guzmán, Bélgica Castro, Delfina Guzmán, Carlos Flores, Silvio Caiozzi, and the ICTUS experimental theater. The lengthy conversations I had with them and with José Donoso helped define the ideas that would eventually produce this work. I thank them for their generosity and time.

The writing of the manuscript became a possibility through a course release and several research grants from the Graduate Dean's Office at Emerson College. I appreciate the dialogue about my work with fellow Emersonians William Elwood and Joan Brigham. I am indebted to the technical help of Gregory Payne and William Gilligan, who made their computer facilities available for the preparation of the manuscript. The editorial advice of Robert Arney and Joseph Roman was invaluable. I wish to thank several colleagues and friends who read portions of the manuscript at several stages: James Redfield, Carlos Alonso, Jaime Concha, and Blanche Linden-Ward. Their support was most welcome.

I am grateful to the editors of *Revista de Estudios Hispánicos, Revista Hispánica Moderna,* and *Revista Canadiense de Estudios Hispánicos* for permission to reprint my discussions of *El jardín de al lado, La desesperanza,* and "Taratuta." Special thanks go to the former Instituto del Teatro de la Universidad de Chile, now Teatro Nacional Chileno, for their permission to reprint the program of the stage production *Coronación,* staged in Chile in 1966.

Finally, I wish to acknowledge the unflagging support of my professional colleagues and friends Jill Netchinsky and Alicia Andreu and of "mi compañero," Saul Slapikoff, who was there from beginning to end.

The author and publisher would like to thank the following institution and publishers for their permission to reprint and quote from copyrighted material:

Instituto del Teatro de la Universidad de Chile, now Teatro Nacional Chileno. *Coronación.* [Program from the stage production.] Santiago de Chile, 1966.

José Donoso. *Coronación.* Barcelona: Seix Barral, 1968. © José Donoso, 1968.

―――. *Coronation.* Trans. Jocasta Goodwin. New York: Knopf, 1965.

―――. *El lugar sin límites.* México: Joaquín Mortiz, 1966. © José Donoso, 1968.

―――. *Hell Has No Limits.* Trans. Suzanne Jill Levine and Hallie D. Taylor. In *Triple Cross. Carlos Fuentes, José Donoso, and Severo Sarduy.* New York: E. P. Dutton, 1972. Translation © 1972 by E. P. Dutton. Used by permission of Dutton Signet, a division of Penguin Books USA, Inc.

―――. *Este domingo.* Barcelona: Seix Barral, 1976. © José Donoso, 1965.

―――. *This Sunday.* Trans. Lorraine O'Grady Freeman. New York: Knopf, 1967.

―――. *El obsceno pájaro de la noche.* Barcelona: Seix Barral, 1970. © José Donoso, 1970.

―――. *The Obscene Bird of Night.* Trans. Hardie St. Martin and Leonard Mades. New York: Knopf, 1973. Translation © 1973 by Alfred A. Knopf, Inc. Reprinted by permission of the publisher.

―――. *Cuentos.* Barcelona: Seix Barral, 1971.

―――. *Charleston and Other Stories.* Trans. Andree Conrad. Boston: David R. Godine, 1977. Reprinted by permission of David R. Godine, Publisher, Inc.

―――. *Historia personal del "boom."* Buenos Aires: Sudamericana/Planeta, 1984. © José Donoso, 1972.

―――. *Casa de campo.* Barcelona: Seix Barral, 1978. © José Donoso, 1978.

―――. *A House in the Country.* Trans. David Pritchard with Suzanne Jill Levine. New York: Knopf, 1984. Translation © 1984 by Alfred A. Knopf, Inc. Reprinted by permission of the publisher.

————. *El jardín de al lado.* Barcelona: Seix Barral, 1981. © José Donoso, 1981.

————. *The Garden Next Door.* Trans. Hardie St. Martin. New York: Grove/Atlantic, Inc., 1992. Reprinted with permission.

————. *La desesperanza.* Barcelona: Seix Barral, 1986. © José Donoso, 1986.

————. *Curfew.* Trans. Alfred MacAdam. New York: Grove/Atlantic, Inc., 1988. Reprinted witih permission.

————. *Taratuta/Naturaleza muerta con cachimba.* Madrid: Mondadori, 1990. © José Donoso, 1990.

————. *Taratuta/Still Life With Pipe.* Trans. Gregory Rabassa. New York: W. W. Norton, 1993. Translation © 1993 by Gregory Rabassa. Used by permission of W. W. Norton & Co., Inc.

Flora González. "The Androgynous Narrator in José Donoso's *El jardín de al lado.*" *Revista de Estudios Hispánicos* 23.2 (1989): 99–113.

————. "Masking History in Donoso's 'Taratuta.'" *Revista Canadiense de Estudios Hispánicos* 17.1 (1992): 47–62.

————. "Political and Personal Transformation in José Donoso's *La desesperanza.*" *Revista Hispánica Moderna* 45.2 (1992): 210–24.

Note on Translations

In compliance with editorial policy, titles and quotations from primary sources are given in Spanish; English translations follow. Pagination after quotations refers to Works Cited. For quotations from secondary sources the translations are mine and pagination refers to Works Cited.

Introduction:
Entering Donoso's House of Fiction

Like many non-Chilean readers of Donoso, I first encountered his work with the novel *El obsceno pájaro de la noche* [*The Obscene Bird of Night*]. I was a lecturer at Dartmouth College in the early seventies, and Donoso spent a summer there teaching a course on the Latin American novel. In subsequent years I became a Donoso aficionada—including the Chilean writer as part of my dissertation work, and traveling to Chile to see the context from which all his literature sprang.

Gradually, I began to understand that I was fascinated by Donoso because of his ever present nostalgia for things lost, a nostalgia I shared as a Cuban exile in the United States. Donoso's fixing of this nostalgia in the domestic structure of the house became a concrete experience to me when I returned to visit my family home in Cuba after eighteen years in exile. I walked into the house that had been the hub of the Mandri family, my maternal side. The furniture was the same, it had not moved at all from the positions fixed in my mind; but the interior garden was overgrown with weeds, the fountain was silent, and the armoires were laden with material goods left by Mandri after Mandri as they abandoned the country during the sixties. Only my oldest aunt had remained, and the house had become a repository of all the objects that laid unused for almost two decades. As I walked from room to room, letting my eyes touch all the memories that were left behind, I was comforted by the recognition that this space resembled the space of Donoso's labyrinthine convent in *El obsceno pájaro de la noche.*

Now, twenty years after my first encounter with this novel, I feel that I have, in effect, moved through all the full yet unpopulated rooms of Donoso's world. The effect of this analytic enterprise is not unlike that of my heightened emotional response when faced with the empty rooms of the Mandri house. Emotions pent up in the spaces of exile found themselves portrayed in Donoso's work. His brush strokes created an image of my forgotten, melodramatically conjured past. Like all critical voyages, this one has returned a reader home.

In 1964, José Donoso and his wife, María Pilar Serrano, left Chile at the invitation of Carlos Fuentes to attend a writers' conference in Mexico, ending a period of alienation he felt in his country from the beginning of his professional writing career.[1] Although he had already published a book of short stories, *Veraneo y otros cuentos* (1955) [Summer Vacation and Other Stories], and had received the Municipal Short Story Prize in 1956, he was having difficulties getting the stories reprinted. *Coronación* [*Coronation*], his first novel, was published in 1957 with the agreement that only if he did much of the distribution himself would the press publish the book. He was also frustrated by the fact that even his most sophisticated readers refused to appreciate a novel that clearly transcended "the great tradition of Chilean realism."[2] Influenced by Alejo Carpentier's theory that "the baroque, the distorted, [and] the excessive could all increase the possibilities of the novel" (paraphrase by Donoso, *Boom* 29), Donoso established in *Coronación* a mode of narration based on dramatically etched visual scenes in which characters express themselves through mute gestures. It was with *El obsceno pájaro de la noche* (1970) that Donoso finally broke all ties to the realist novel. This novel brought him international notoriety and Donoso began to be considered one of the privileged writers whose name was included on the list of the Latin American "Boom."

Although there are countless definitions of what constituted the "Boom" and who should be included, Donoso himself defines it as a group of writers whose works abandoned a mimetic desire to represent the geography and idiom of their individual countries.[3] Because they felt an absence of a literary tradition worthy of their respect, they turned to North American and European models. With the "Boom," Donoso contends, the Latin American writer began to produce an international novel. By this he means not only that novelists were turning away from parochial concerns but also that they were open to the influence of "other arts such as film, painting, or poetry, the inclusion of numerous dialects, forms of slang, and the mannerism of social groups or specialized sects" (*Boom* 19). These Boom writers, including Gabriel García Márquez (Colombia), Julio Cortázar (Argentina), Carlos Fuentes (Mexico), Mario Vargas Llosa (Peru), Guillermo Cabrera Infante (Cuba), and Donoso, all became internationally known during the sixties and early seventies. Manuel Puig (Argentina) and Miguel Barnet and Reinaldo Arenas (Cuba) belong to a younger generation whose works claimed world renown in the seventies.

The Boom period of the sixties and early seventies produced novels that minimized plot and contained a critical, literary, political, or cultural metadiscourse. Included in the work was the story of how the novel itself was written, and the author often represented himself as subservient to the laws of language and literature. Besides Donoso's *El obsceno pájaro de la noche,* prime examples of Boom novels include Julio Cortázar's *Rayuela* (1963) [*Hopscotch*], Carlos Fuentes's *La muerte de Artemio Cruz* (1963) [*The Death of Artemio Cruz*], and Guillermo Cabrera Infante's *Tres Tristes Tigres* (1967) [*Three Trapped Tigers*].[4] Of the Boom writers, only Gabriel García Márquez and Mario Vargas Llosa redefined the meaning of the Latin American novel in mythical and cosmopolitan terms, while remaining faithful to the traditional narrative form in their works *Cien años de soledad* (1967) [*One Hundred Years of Solitude*] and *La ciudad y los perros* (1962) [*The Time of the Hero*]. In keeping with Donoso's definition, however, they did write novels that were influenced by North American and European models and reached out to an international audience through a wide distribution of translations. Even for those novelists who subscribed to the Boom impulse in which plot was minimized, there was a return to storytelling. In the early eighties the novelists explored autobiography, narrativity, and parodies of popular genres such as the romance novel, the detective story, and the erotic novel.[5]

In 1978, Donoso published *Casa de campo* [*A House in the Country*], a novel that combines both the self-reflexive games of the Boom years and a consciousness of a historical context in Latin America that could no longer be ignored: the wave of military dictatorships across the southern tip of the American continent. In Chile and Argentina, especially, the growing number of missing persons (the politically active who dared confront the military establishment and "disappeared") attracted world attention. After a long tradition of democratically elected governments, Chile was seized by the 1973 military dictatorship of Augusto Pinochet, which lasted until 1990. Writing and living in Spain, Donoso first recorded the fall of Salvador Allende and the military repression of Augusto Pinochet in *Casa de campo.* He then evaluated the role of the exiled Latin American writer in the face of military repression in *El jardín de al lado* (1981) [*The Garden Next Door*]. His response was not unlike that of other Latin American writers who recorded the wave of "dirty wars" that swept through the continent from the midseventies to the late eighties.[6]

After the publication of this latter novel, Donoso returned to Chile. With *La desesperanza* (1986) [*Curfew*], Donoso fashioned a new narrative, indebted to the myths of the southern Chilean landscape and attentive to the needs of a national readership that began to look to him for a more politically committed message. In his novella "Taratuta" (1990), Donoso, conscious of a shift in his literary voice, reevaluated the role of the writer and his narrative in Latin America, and he accomplished in a fictional piece what *Historia personal del "boom"* (1972) [*The Boom in Spanish American Literature: A Personal History*] did in the essay form. After almost forty years of recognition as Chile's major novelist, Donoso reflected on his definition of literary voice as mask and disguise and shifted to a more accessible form of representation that embraced the language of the mass media and film.[7]

In a 1992 essay entitled "A Small Biography of *The Obscene Bird of Night*," José Donoso gives us his own portrait of the writer as an accomplished novelist: "I believe that quite often a literary voice is a mask or a disguise, adopted in order to make it act as go-between, a messenger from the writer to the public" (19). This proposed contract between writer and reader via the mediation of disguise or mask (narrative voice) establishes a comfortable distance between the two and allows the writer to play a game of magical substitutions that demands the undivided attention of the reader or audience. Donoso's mastery as a writer lies in his ability to continually transform his disguise, to exchange one mask for another, and to focus on the language of theater as the most prolific of languages to represent and misrepresent the voice of the creator. If literary voice is a disguise for the hidden voice of the author, then there is an implied understanding that the mask will most likely deliver a necessarily ironic message.

Continuing to look at literary voice as mask or disguise as the guiding metaphor for all of Donoso's fiction, the reader is faced with the paradoxical definition of voice as image. In very literal terms, Donoso accomplishes as a writer the same feat that a ventriloquist does by disguising and multipliying his voice through the mask of a wooden dummy. A single voice refracts into two or perhaps more, once the possibility is granted for the proliferation of masks or dummies. Dialogue flows naturally from a singular source and theatrical performance results from the gestures that accompany spoken dialogue. But clearly, Donoso's definition of narrative voice as mask or disguise is much more complex than the performance of a ventriloquist. At the most obvious level of literary discourse, the writer speaks through the mask of many characters, just as the voice of the ventriloquist can speak through the mask of many dummies. Yet, because Donoso literalizes his metaphor of voice as mask, his character Mudito actually wears a giant papier-mâché head when he pretends to be Don Jerónimo in *El obsceno pájaro de la noche;* there is the possibility of a multiplicity of voices that can hide behind the mask. There is then a proliferation of masks as well as of voices: a singular voice can speak through many masks or many voices can speak through one mask. The result is that Donoso's definition of literary voice allows for a constant displacement, not only of masks but of voices as well.

Once we accept this multifaceted explanation of the metaphor of voice as disguise, we must also accept the notion of voice as performance, and, by extension, of performance as theatrical expression. Donoso's literary voice multiplies as it constantly finds refuge behind the illumined and grotesque faces of his monstrous creations. But when Donoso constructs a mask, he also provides for it the spatial dimension of an ever changing stage. So as to be able to distinguish one mask from another on Donoso's dramatic scene, the characters who wear the disguises express themselves with grandiose gestures. The notion of voice as mask has transformed into a mode of expression that favors the visual over the spoken and that defines the visual as a stage set where actors communicate through a gestural language. By taking the metaphor—voice as image in its literal sense—Donoso multiplies its possibilities for significance.

At this juncture I pause to suggest that José Donoso's statement of voice as mask be transposed to read "narrative voice as melodramatic expression." Melodrama as theatrical form found its fullest manifestation in eighteenth-century France, whereas Donoso is writing in the second half of the twentieth century. His short stories appeared in 1955 and 1956, his first novel *Coronación* was published in 1957, and the last novellas to date are *Taratuta/Naturaleza muerta con cachimba* [*Taratuta/Still Life with Pipe*], published in 1990.[8] Throughout his work, which spans nearly forty years, Donoso plays with the surface of theatrical expression, a surface that displaces one mask and disguise after another. This displacement seemingly evades but also finally arrives at a significance rooted in cultural contexts that need to be scrutinized and recast by the magnifying glass of the writer. Donoso's magnifying glass is that of melodrama, a theatrical genre that dwells on the conflict of polarized values that are "*spectacularly* acted out" (Brooks, *Melodramatic Imagination* 93, emphasis mine). Melodrama as form emphasizes conflict through grandiose gesture, a mode of expression that delays the unveiling of meaning behind the gesture through the proliferation of plots, characters, and other heightened vehicles of representation.[9] In the popular manifestations of melodrama in the twentieth century—serial novels and soap operas—the audience attentively awaits a resolution of the conflict that never seems to come. Attention to gestural language in theatrical and cinematographic terms and the spectacular mechanisms of postponement with the intent of displacing significance define Donoso's literary voice.

As we shall see in this study of Donoso's production of a melodramatic idiom, that which remains constant is the fixation on spectacular staging techniques. What gets displaced, postponed, and finally scrutinized is the cultural context that favors and encourages melodramatic expression. José Donoso is not the only Latin American writer who has perceived that the language of melodrama weaves in and out of Latin American cultural expression, at the elitist as well as the popular levels of society. Manuel Puig's entire oeuvre, representing the Argentine cultural landscape, is the best case in point because he brings into focus the use of melodrama as form in epistolary, cinematographic, and even academic languages. But there are many others—from Clarice Lispector in *Hora da estrela* (1984) [*The Hour of the Star*], Brazil, where the power of advertisement is made to define and destroy women's self images; to Guillermo Cabrera Infante in *Tres tristes tigres* (1967), Cuba, where cinematographic, theatrical, and literary conventions are parodied to expose how it is that culture appropriates such conventions for its own designs; to Mario Vargas Llosa in *Tía Julia y el escribidor* (1977) [*Aunt Julia and the Scriptwriter*], Peru, where the plots of radio serials are reproduced in the lives of intellectuals and the upper classes; to Gabriel García Márquez in *Crónica de una muerte anunciada* (1981) [*Chronicle of a Death Foretold*], Colombia, where life mimics the gestures of classical tragedy brought down to a melodramatic level; and to Luis Rafael Sánchez in *La guaracha del Macho Camacho* (1976) [*Macho Camacho's Beat*], Puerto Rico, where lyrics from a popular song expose the melodramatic plots of people's individual tragedies. Common to all of these narratives is an exploration and scrutiny of classical as well as popular manifestations of melodramatic expression in theater, dance, radio, film, television, and music with the express purpose of exposing the uses and misuses of melodrama by those in power to control and define the tastes and values of an entire culture.

When these writers, and Donoso in particular, exploit the limitless possibilities of melodrama as manipulative representation, they are not concerned with the resolution of basic conflicts of good versus evil within society, rather, they endeavor to question the pervasiveness of melodrama in Latin American behavior and culture. If melodrama postpones meaning, to what ends does it do so? As an artist who understands the power of rhetorical conventions, what better way to dismantle those cultural structures than to assume their form and then dislodge their rigid skeletons piece by piece? If read as a melodramatic text, most of Donoso's oeuvre unfolds as the process of construction of a complex melodramatic theatrical stage, wherein cultural manifestations of melodramatic expressions are highlighted and exposed. It is only in the later works that there is a move away from melodramatic forms and a redefinition of the artistic enterprise as a vast field, rather than a stage, where multiple languages can coexist and dialogue.

If Donoso sees Latin American culture through the prism of its melodramatic representations, let us examine how this Chilean novelist con-

structs his own dramatic structure. Let us return to the image of the magnifying glass that exposes cultural contexts. The concrete image of a glass
that distorts is clearly an ancient metaphor for the artistic enterprise. Donoso, in particular, conceives this glass as a series of windows that open
onto the world, which is seen as a conglomerate of culturally determined
performances. These windows also allow the reader to look into the house
that represents the writer's creative imagination. All readers of Donoso
are quick to acknowledge the prominence that houses have in his works.
Family houses define the physical space in *Coronación, Este domingo*
(1966) [*This Sunday*], and *Casa de campo*. A brothel is the center of the
action in *El lugar sin límites* (1966) [*Hell Has No Limits*], a convent in
ruins serves as the stage for *El obsceno pájaro de la noche,* and a fashion-
able apartment in Madrid becomes the watchtower from which to view
the action in *El jardín de al lado.*

I suggest that we view the house in Donoso's novelistic world in a
theatrical sense, the "house" as the space that accommodates both the
stage and the audience who will participate in the melodramatic experience. Before going on to set up the stage production as Donoso constructs
it, let us begin by defining the writer as observer and creator of that production, an observer who "sees" through the many windows of his house
of fiction.

In novelistic terms, Donoso's houses allude to a consistent literary
dialogue that the Chilean writer maintains with Henry James. Although
there is no intention here of tracing the American writer's influence on
Donoso, it will be useful to begin with James's own concept of the house
of fiction. In the preface to *Portrait of a Lady,* literary form is conceived
of in terms of an aperture that opens up, not to reality, but to an individu-
ally created vision—a figure stands behind the window and focuses on a
subject with an artificial device, field glasses. Artistic consciousness depends upon vision, and, more precisely, upon the ability to manipulate the
focus on that which is being seen. So as not to limit the scope of vision,
the house of fiction has not one window, but a million, thus insuring a
multiplicity of perspectives upon the subject observed. The one who observes stands protected by the window, distanced and unseen, yet is active
in the formulation of the human experience. According to James, literary
form consists in the framing, through a window, of a scene beyond. In
Donoso's novelistic world, windows will often serve as that glass through
which an ordinary, fantastic, or grotesque world is created. Although in
the short story "Santelices" Donoso actually has the character create a
scene through field glasses, in most novels, windows—a double glass window in *El jardín de al lado*—become the prism through which a narrator
envisions a scene.

Also following a Jamesian tenet, Donoso as artist creates a dramatic scene, a vision that carefully directs the movements of the subject as if on a stage. The dramatic vision, because of its imposed limitation in scope, is constructed as a provisional scene, one that will no doubt have blind spots and be discarded for an alternative scene. Each of Donoso's narratives is equivalent to a myriad of dramatic scenes that continuously displace each other with the purpose of eventually getting at the full picture. Since both the observer and the subject are presumably in motion as well, Donoso's creative process becomes a constant adjusting of the theatrical frame.

While nineteenth-century novels focus on the human subject in all its complexity, the subject for Donoso, working in the latter half of the twentieth century, becomes the creative process itself. Entering into any of Donoso's novels therefore means entering into the active formulation of a very specific, yet constantly changing vision. This study will proceed by formulating Donoso's use of a theatrical vision based on a melodramatic form of expression, a form that heightens quotidian and domestic reality. If the characters of classical tragedy are noble beings who are faced with internal conflicts of universal proportions, the characters of a domestic melodrama are faced with the conflict of holding on to values that clash with an increasingly invasive society that no longer distinguishes between the public and the private. In Donoso's novels, characters respond to society's invasion by retiring to the privacy of their enclosed houses. Their emotional response to the public attack finds appropriate expression in the heightened gestures of the melodramatic mode. Social and political issues are processed in personal, emotional terms. In Donoso, quotidian, personal conflicts become magnified and expressed in hyperbolic gestures.

This reliance on an expressionist form undergoes many transformations during the span of more than thirty years of the author's production (1955–90), and Donoso's houses become the stage on which both he and his readers may reflect upon the novelistic process. In order to better discern that process, we resort to another literary paradigm that also draws on a visual metaphor. M. M. Bakhtin views the analysis of the novelistic genre as an illumination of different languages as they come into contact and dialogue with one another. "The novelistic hybrid," maintains Bakhtin, is "an artistically organized system for bringing different languages in contact with one another, a system having as its goal the illumination of one language by means of another, the carving-out of a living image of another language" ("Discourse in the Novel" 361). The purpose of this study will be to carve out a dramatic image of Donoso's idiom as it moves from one stage set—and culturally determined language—to the next. While Donoso's predominant theatrical model is that of melodrama, he is not restricted to it. Ultimately, what consistently claims our attention is the motion of displacement of one language in order to make room for another, with the effect of creating the richest spectacle possible. As one language upstages another there is a confirmation of the notion that the novel as house of fiction can accommodate as many languages as arise in the human experience. Most often, Donoso brings into focus the language of theater and the plastic arts, but with the advent of mass media, more popular forms of expression get inducted into the system. Radio, film, and television reach out with a linguistic proclivity toward the vernacular; the latter novels in particular focus on an incorporation of the world of popular culture.

The paradigm I propose, that of dramatic scene and of dialogic discourse, acts as a structure that may serve many artistic purposes—to confront the ideologies of social classes, to synthesize feminine and masculine aspects of artistic voice, or to arrive at an aesthetically conceived language that illuminates a historic or political context. In this book I will commence by positing the house as the structural model for the novelist's primal scene (the discovery of the artistic idiom) in *Este domingo.* I will follow by setting the scene with *Coronación,* that is, by formulating the process by which the novelist first conceived the expressionistic language used throughout his career. After analyzing the works—"Santelices," *El lugar sin límites,* and *El obsceno pájaro de la noche*—that posit the creative process as the product of a controlling gaze, we will see that *Casa de campo* serves as a starting point for the political concerns that lead Donoso to question the exclusively aesthetic dialogue within his house of fiction. As these considerations get played out, there is a parallel move away from the use of the house as a lookout point from which to decipher a vision of time and place. The eighties trilogy of the Pinochet years (*Casa de campo, El jardín de al lado,* and *La desesperanza*) raises many questions regarding novelistic language. Finally, "Taratuta," the last of Donoso's works that I will consider, is a novella that also centers around the ever present relationship between history and fiction, and it provides us with new insights into Donoso's field of vision.

1

SETTING THE SCENE:
FROM *CORONACIÓN* TO *EL OBSCENO PÁJARO DE LA NOCHE*

With his early novels, *Coronación* (1958) [*Coronation*], *Este domingo* (1966) [*This Sunday*], and *El lugar sin límites* (1967) [*Hell Has No Limits*], José Donoso begins to define his idiom of the drama of domesticity. The domestic scene becomes the stage where conflicts between the personal and the public get played out. From the onset of his career, the Chilean novelist structures˙his works as a series of dramatic scenes that function as an exteriorization of a world within. This expressionism, defined here as the articulation of the repressed and the ineffable through posturing and the projection of imagined scenes, is developed at different levels. In the novel *Coronación,* for example, the middle-aged protagonist, Andrés Avalos, constantly divulges his inner struggle in conversations with his friend Carlos: he is a man unable to fully participate in life because of his fear of death. The reader is overburdened by the expression of this angst, which never gets resolved in any socially acceptable way. But more significant than a character's constant clarification of his inner life is that, with this novel, Donoso develops a technique of dramatizing interior struggles in exterior scenes through theatrical means. This technique finds expression through the donning of masks and disguises, the staging of tableaux in which exaggerated gestural language gives signification to a social or moral conflict, or the imagining of projected scenes that enact the character's desires. The final scene in *Coronación,* in which Misiá Elisa is dressed like a queen, constitutes a first rehearsal in the development of an expressionist dramatic language that will become a constant in all the works to come.[1]

The first stage of this ongoing formulation of dramatic form follows the definition of the melodramatic genre with its emphasis on the heightened manifestation of a moral polarization.[2] Even though Donoso uses

23

melodrama as a shell of exaggerated or grotesque expression in which to encase his novels, he does so in an ironic manner so that the polarized struggle of moral imperatives that characterizes the eighteenth-century theatrical genre disappears, and the form serves as an expressionistic medium to convey twentieth-century novelistic concerns.[3] Donoso effectively appropriates the discourse of melodrama, with its exaggerated gesturing and its simplification of moral values, in order to expose the rhetorical posturing that both upper and lower classes in Chilean society assume to influence others. Misiá Elisa, for example, is the nonagenarian who has raised her grandson, Andrés Abalos, and who now lies incapacitated in a bed that symbolically becomes her throne. From her seemingly powerless position, she controls her entire household by making excessive moralistic pronouncements that ultimately predict other people's actions (she accuses her grandson Andrés of lusting after the servant Estela, and he subsequently falls in love with the young girl).[4] Donoso projects the character of the grandmother as a grotesque caricature of the upper class's inability to exert power beyond a limited sphere. This propensity to control others through melodramatic language also becomes a weapon of destruction in the hands of the household maids, who through silent, theatrical postures, much like tableaux vivants, cause the death of Misiá Elisa at the end of the novel. Their ability to wield power like Misiá Elisa's is circumscribed within the confines of the house. By placing melodramatic language in the hands of both upper and lower classes, Donoso points to the pervasiveness of its rhetorical power in Latin American society, however limited that power may be. Furthermore, since in *Coronación* the exaggerated gesturing of melodrama appears as just that, a gesturing, Donoso gives us the outline of his form: melodrama in all its theatrical, cinematic, and mass-media manifestations.

In *Coronación* and *Este domingo,* characters are lost in a world where a new morality has begun to be defined individualistically and where self-definition and salvation must be fashioned in a spiritual void. Transcendence can only be possible in a phantasmagoric, fictional world. In order to project this search and transformation, the novels resort to stylized scenes that are representations of the passage from one world to another. From these first novels on, the house is the privileged space for transformations and transgressions. The family house marks the meeting place of masters and servants and the testing ground for efforts to transcend middle-class values.[5]

In *Este domingo,* the grandmother's house is the playground in which cousins run freely and play out their wildest fantasies. The agent who paves the way for licentious behavior is Chepa, the grandmother. Whereas in *Coronación* the grandmother represents the manipulating female, in *Este domingo,* she is the nurturing adult. Her house becomes the stage where the narrator as child first discovers the magical powers of the creative imagination. Chepa encourages the child's propensity toward the theatrical and provides the space and the tools for its development. In her absence at the end of the novel, the house stands in ruins, a shell that encases the memories of the narrator, and becomes the embodiment of her eclectic spirit. The narrator fashions a memorial to his grandmother with the following passage:

> *Me gusta que esos niños se refugien allí, como si esa casa que era prolongación del cuerpo de mi abuela viviera aún: la cornucopia derramándose todavía. Cuando entreguen la casa a los demoledores abrirán las puertas y las ventanas. La luz volverá a entrar como antes. Encontrarán la casa despojada de puertas y zócalos y jambas y guardapolvos y parquets, un cascarón que caerá a los primeros golpes de la picota hecho un montón de escombros en el jardín enmalezado.*
>
> *Pero me gustaría más que terminara incendiada por esos niños, una animita gigantesca encendida en su memoria.* (192–93)

> *I like the idea of those children taking refuge there, as if the house which was an extension of my grandmother's body were still alive: the cornucopia continuing to spill out. When they hand the house over to the wreckers they will open the doors and the windows. The light will come in as it did before. And they will find the house despoiled of doors and panels and door jambs and baseboards and parquets, a husk which will fall at the first blows of the pick into a pile of ruins in the garden overrun with weeds.*
>
> *But I would prefer it to end in a fire set by those children, a gigantic animita lit to her memory.* (177)

Houses in Donoso's novelistic world are thus much more than architectural constructs; they are living structures that protect, give in abundance, and warm the body and soul. Ultimately, they are mythic spaces that allow for growth, undergo organic changes, and retain the spirit of all those who encouraged the development of the fantastic within them. At the end of *Este domingo,* the shell of a house, which Chepa's grandson hopes will be burned by the homeless children who now live in it, presents a contradictory image of decay and abundance and stands as the symbolic structure of all of Donoso's works. In the first two novels, houses and grandmothers become indistinguishable, with the house and grandmother in *Coronación* acting as the stifling agent, and the house and grandmother in *Este domingo* as the nurturing one. The end of the latter novel recalls the image of the horn of plenty, which is linked early on with the grandmother (21–22; 13). *Este domingo* opens and closes with the image of this house, the nurturing body and place for the children's theatrical and linguistic games.

For the narrator, the grandmother's house provides the stage for that moment when the child passes into the realm of the symbolic—the moment of mastery over written language. The announcement of such an accomplishment goes ignored by the father but is praised and accentuated by the grandmother:

> *Nunca se da cuenta de nada [el padre]. Ahora no se dio cuenta de que mi interés no fue llamarle la atención sobre el fenómeno de encontrar el nombre de mi tío Roberto Matta escrito en una baldosa de la calle. No vio que estaba ansioso por demostrarle otra cosa: que yo ya sabía leer, que sin que él ni nadie me enseñara aprendí en los titulares de los diarios, y que sabía muy bien que esa baldosa rojiza no era la lápida de un gnomo sino que decía Roberto Matta, Constructor. A mi abuela, eso sí, yo le contaría que bajo el acacio de la vereda había encontrado una tumba diminuta. Juntos, en el calor de su cama el domingo en la mañana, muy temprano para que mis primos no hubieran acudido aún a meterse también entre las sábanas olorosas de pan tostado del desayuno mi abuela y yo abordaríamos sobre el asunto de la tumba del duende.* (14)

> *He* [the father] *never realizes anything. Just now he didn't realize that I was not calling his attention to my uncle's name, Roberto Matta, written on a street tile. He didn't see how much I wanted to show him something else: that I already knew how to read, that without him or anyone teaching me I had learned myself from the headlines in the daily papers, and that I knew very well that the reddish tile wasn't the gravestone of a gnome, that it said Roberto Matta, Contractor. Yes, I would tell my grandmother that under the acacia on the sidewalk I had found a little tomb. Together, in the warmth of her bed on Sunday morning, very early so that my cousins would not have come in yet to get between the sheets that smelled of her breakfast toast, my grandmother and I would embroider the story of the elfin tomb.* (6)

The quoted passage must be read as the narrator's dramatization of the oedipal scene. The grandmother pays tribute to his reading skill and encourages the acknowledged flight of the imagination. These two milestones in the child's life become fused in the moment of rejection of the father figure and in association with the mother, here displaced by the person of the grandmother. In Donoso, the dramatization of the oedipal scene coincides with the birth of a creative mind that has discovered the mechanism of displacement.

Such a mind was further nurtured by the grandmother's interdiction of any traditional board games within the confines of the house. The children's imaginary games generally took place in the late hours of Saturday night, when the cousins were free of the parents' rational control, and in a space filled with costumes, props, and old furniture. That room became the theater where nothing would happen unless the children invented it:

"Pero no pasaba nada si no lo inventábamos nosotros" (99) [*But nothing ever happened if we did not invent it ourselves* (87)]. Besides giving life to a mythic character, Mariola Roncafort, as well as scenes from her life and history, the children invented a language reserved for the fantastic character they had created: *"Su esencia estaba en nuestras palabras, en nuestras conversaciones"* (95) [*her essence remained in our words, our conversations* (83)].

The children's scenes are a paradoxical version of theatricality (a character in the limelight) narrated through language (*"her essence remained in our words"*). This fragment captures the nature of Donoso's novelistic enterprise, in which the narrator fabricates a language pregnant with the heightened signification of a character always seen as if bathed in intensified light, a character to which a special kind of language must be accorded.[6]

In *Este domingo,* the intensified character is Chepa, the grandmother. But first it is important to deal with the grandfather, who stands as the measure against whom the grandmother is fashioned. The novel is divided into five sections, three of which are narrated by the grandson and appear in italics, and two more extensive sections narrated by an omniscient narrator and entitled "Primera parte" [Part One] and "Segunda parte" [Part Two]. These two sections are dedicated to the grandfather Alvaro and the grandmother Chepa, respectively. "Primera parte" contrasts significantly with two of the three sections narrated by the grandson: *"En la redoma"* [In the Fishbowl] and *"Los juegos legítimos"* [Legitimate Games]. "Primera parte" concentrates on the grandfather's coming of age as a sexual being, while the other two sections highlight the scene of reading and of creating extraordinary characters as the significant rite of passage for the grandson. This contrast between the grandfather and the grandson places the latter in the limelight.

The grandfather, "La Muñeca" [The Doll] as the children call him, is a perfect figure of the bourgeois gentleman: he succeeds in life after acquiring a law degree, spends most of his time at his men's club, and came of age sexually in the bed of Violeta, the young maid assigned to care for him one summer when he was catching up on his math studies. The roles of young master and maid are neatly prescribed for them; Violeta knows to expect nothing from the sexual encounters with Alvarito and makes sure that she will not become pregnant by him. She is involved with a country boy with whom she will have no sexual relations so that he will marry her. Alvaro, on the other hand, goes out dancing with high society girls and then returns to Violeta, releasing the tensions the *pitucas* (society girls) arouse in him. The arrangement is preordained and leaves each member of the pact safe and sound:

27

[E]ntre ellos no existía otro vínculo que este compromiso de la piel sobre la piel bajo el calor de las sábanas, y el gozarse en los olores y roces mutuos. Era maravilloso porque así, a pesar de la intimidad, ambos quedaban intactos—poniéndose un límite, señalando un porte para las cosas, uno quedaba a salvo. Ella lo usaba y él la usaba, y ambos los sabían. (70)

[T]here wasn't any other tie between them but this compromise of skin on skin beneath the warmth of the sheets, and the pleasure of the touches and the smells they shared. It was marvelous, because this way, in spite of their intimacy, they both remained intact—by putting a limit on it, by giving a size to things, you were safe from them. She was using him and he was using her, and they both knew it. (59)[7]

Chepa, on the other hand, has lived beyond the prescribed limits of society: she has neglected her own children and dedicated her entire life to caring for the poor in the marginal towns. Her position between these two worlds makes her a hybrid who is neither accepted by her children, who berate her for not playing her role of respected society lady, nor by her women friends, who think that her commitment to the poor goes beyond the requirements of noblesse oblige. Her friend Fanny anticipates that her obsession with helping release a prisoner on good behavior will get out of hand. Chepa is quite conscious that her commitment to the poor, and now the obsession to liberate Maya, have little to do with humanitarian impulses, but rather with her own need to constantly mother and be needed by others:

> —Me siento tan culpable de no haber sido nunca buena mujer de Alvaro ni buena madre de las niñitas. Tú sabes que nunca me interesaron . . . , no, no creas que soy un monstruo. Pero dejaron de necesitarme tan luego. (117)

> "I feel so guilty for never having been a good wife to Alvaro or a good mother to the girls. You know they've never interested me. . . . No, don't think I'm a monster, but they stopped needing me so soon." (104)

It is precisely that she is seen by others as a monster that makes her attractive to the grandchildren and propels her into uncharted territories.[8]

Chepa stands in limbo between the security of her upper middle-class upbringing and stable marriage to Alvaro, and the dangers to be encountered as she comes into closer contact with Maya, a violent, dominating, and uncontrolled character. Chepa stands between two men who symbolize opposite poles in both the social strata and in the moral bourgeois scale.

Like all evil, Maya represents the unknown, and that is very attractive:

> ¿Por qué tenía Maya esa forma tan cuidadosa de hablar? Gangosa, como sacristán. . . , algún curita que le enseñó a pronunciar bien las eses y las

des. Y esa mancha en el labio que se mueve poco cuando habla de esa manera tan plana . . . sólo cuando sonríe, el lunar baila y descubre sus dientes grandes, fuertes. Claro. Roto nortino. Calcio. Tanta mina. . . . La sonrisa de Maya es sencillamente encantadora. (118)

Why did Maya have such a curious way of speaking? Nasal, like a sacristan's . . . some chaplain who taught him to pronounce his s's and his d's carefully. And that blotch on the lip that moves so little when he speaks in that flat way of his . . . . Only when he smiles does the mole dance and reveal his large, strong teeth. Of course. He's from the north. Calcium. So many minerals. Maya's smile is simply charming. (105)

In this description there is a mix of disdain and prejudice, coupled by a fascination with the Other. The beauty mark close to his lips can dance and be attractive, or it can stand for all the evil that lurks within his being and possesses him. While still in jail, Maya suffers from episodes he terms the "black hand," during which he lies in bed, completely disconnected from the outside world. After he is liberated from jail, he cannot control his gambling, all his desires are defined by excess, and his behavior swings from subservient dependency to inhumane defiance. Although Chepa does not stand for an example of selflessness, Maya follows the stereotypic role of the evil character ready to corrupt innocence. Because of the complexity of Chepa's character, Donoso's *Este domingo* transcends the melodramatic model in which good struggles against the influence of evil and emerges triumphant.

Like the character who is possessed by the forces of evil, Chepa is marked by her obsession with Maya. This obsession is closely tied to her insatiable desire to mother: "[E]lla siente ese remezón de placer, como si Maya fuera su guagua y ella le diera su seno repleto de leche y él chupara porque su hambre era inagotable y chupara más y más" (124) [She feels that tremor of pleasure, as though Maya were her baby and she was giving him her breast bursting with milk and he was sucking because his hunger was insatiable and he was sucking more and more (111)]. Both desires, to nurture constantly and to be nurtured without end, are here described in excess so that both characters become enslaved: "Lo peor es que mi mamá tiene esclavizado al pobre Maya. Lo vigila igual como nos vigilaba a nosotras. Y la Violeta es su espía" (148) [The worst is that Mother has enslaved poor Maya. She watches over him the same way she watched over us. And Violeta is her spy (134)]. A traditional stereotype, that of the selfless mother, is here presented in inverted terms so that she becomes the devouring mother: "[I]gual a usted, que las dos queríamos comerlo, tragarlo" (158) [just like you, that we both wanted to eat him, to swallow him (143)].[9] The relationship between these two extreme characters is sustained by Chepa's constant surveillance. She is not satisfied unless she feels that the uncontrolled character, Maya, is under her visual scrutiny. This obsessive power relationship will be further developed in Donoso's works in the character Peta Ponce (in *El obsceno pájaro de la noche*), for example, but with this novel, the essential elements are already present.

The dynamics are set up in terms of one character's dominance over the other under a controlling gaze. Maya's life transpires as if on a stage: "Ahora voy a tener que irme de aquí. No quiero que usted me siga vigilando" (153) [Now I'll have to get away from here. I don't want you to keep on spying on me (138)]. Maya feels controlled, yet Chepa's surveillance turns his menial tasks into dramatic representation. This relationship is detrimental to both. Because Maya cannot live independent of the gaze, he is doomed to fail. He eventually kills Violeta so that he can be taken back to prison, where he can count on predictable, though impersonal boundaries. The relationship as controlled by the gaze is unequal at the beginning, with one character controlling the other, but by the end of the narrative, roles are reversed and the subservient partner drives the other beyond her safe territory to an uncharted space of madness and moral destitution. At the end of *Este domingo,* Chepa goes into the marginal towns looking for Maya, gets lost, is attacked by children, and loses consciousness. In this final scene, she wanders the streets watched, she feels, by unseen eyes that hide behind every slanted door. Later, safe at home, she spends the remainder of her days in a state not all that dissimilar from Maya's "black hand," in which the subject neither observes, nor is observed.

In a reversal of preordained roles, rather than engulfing her offspring, Chepa has been swallowed up by the indigent children of the marginal towns. She lives the fate that she supposedly would have inflicted on others.[10] The end of "Segunda parte"—the demise of the grandmother at the hands of the children in the marginal town—gets repeated in a symbolic manner at the end of the novel, when the narrator desires that homeless children burn the house (which has been established as an extension of the body of the grandmother) in memory of Chepa. The repetition of this scene in which children overpower the admired grandmother was already foreshadowed in *"Los juegos legítimos"* ["Legitimate Games"], in which the child narrator takes joy in seeing that his mother and aunt have punished the grandmother for not behaving properly: *"Estábamos contentos, pero callados, porque mi madre y mi tía Meche la [Chepa] castigaron, como a veces nos castigaban a nosotros"* (98) [*Of course, we were happy, even though quietly, because my mother and my Aunt Meche had chastised her [Chepa] the way they chastised us so often* (86–87)]. Soon after this pronouncement in which the children welcome the defeat of the grandmother, they retire to their dramatizations, where they, rather than the adults, are the ones capable of defining action. The scene at the table is seen by the narrator as a bit of family drama. Having witnessed it as a passive agent, he goes on to derive energy from the grandmother's defeat and to actively create his own representation: *"[N]o pasaba nada si no lo inventábamos nosotros"* (99) [*But nothing ever happened if we did not invent it ourselves* (87)].

The novel has represented three versions of a similar scene: The first, in which children observe the grandmother being scolded by her own two daughters, the second, in which children who are strangers physically attack and down the grandmother in the mud, and the projected third, in which homeless children burn the grandmother's house (body). In all three, the all-giving, all-powerful figure of the grandmother is subjugated in dramatic scenes that are increasingly symbolic in the narrator's eyes, and the figure of the child narrator is increasingly absent from the scene. In the first, he is a passive observer; in the second, he narrates, through the voice of an omniscient narrator, a scene that he did not see but overheard or perhaps even imagined; and in the third, he is the adult narrator returning to the scene of the first childhood event. The dramatization of the beating of the grandmother by an omniscient third-person narrator (presumably the adult grandchild) establishes a narrative distance that will ultimately result in erasing the grandmother from the center of attention in the novel. In the closing scene of the novel, both the child and the grandmother have been displaced by an adult grandson, the writer of the story we now read. This narrator, distanced in time from the events and from his contradictory feelings, can now pay homage to a deceased grandmother. Thus, in this dramatic shift from passivity to activity, the narrator plays out his ambivalence regarding his rejection of his grandmother as a powerful figure and his indebtedness to her for his creative accomplishments. She is both monster and cornucopia.

Even though there is a prescribed polarity of good and evil, of right and wrong, of propriety and impropriety in Donoso's world, the incursion into impropriety and destitution does not necessarily carry a negative charge. Although the grandmother loses her charm as the grandchildren grow, the narrator remembers her as the light in his life that permitted him to enter into the imaginary, the world of dramatization. The thematic link with the traditional struggle between the forces of good and evil in melodramatic aesthetics loses its hold here, and it becomes evident that melodrama is used by Donoso as a heightened dramatic structure devoid of its moral didacticism. Like the grandmother's house, melodrama becomes a shell that will be useful in any novelistic discussion of the creative process itself. In the grandmother's life it is important that she was capable of going beyond her society's limits, not that she was psychologically deranged at the end of her life. Unlike Alvaro, who always lived encased in a cocoon dictated by what was proper, Chepa was capable of transgression.

31

Madness represents the thrilling danger the characters risk when transgressing society's limits. It is this movement away from the norm and toward the monstrous that interests Donoso throughout his career. At the formalistic level, the movement from central to marginal character (mother or father to grandmother) in a gesture of displacement becomes the essence of Donoso's novelistic process. In order to illumine this shift from center to margin, his narrative develops more and more complex forms of dramatic expression, a form that will always be linked to the labyrinthine structures of his multiple houses. The body of his work, made visual in the metaphor of the house, always returns to that primal scene in *Este domingo,* where reading (mastery over the letter) and the flight of the imagination (ability to create dramatic scenes) converge under the protection of the grandmother's gaze.[11]

After having posited *Este domingo* as the novel that dramatizes the initial scene of reading, and then writing, for the young narrator, we retrace our steps and concentrate on the first novel, *Coronación,* in which the melodramatic agenda at the thematic level and the use of a complete array of theatrical signs at the dicursive level will be presented as the clearest example of the melodramatic imagination in Donoso's works.

Coronación comes complete with what at first appear to be stereotypic characterizations of good (Estela, the young, innocent maid who enters the Abalos household) and evil (René, a younger version of Maya in *Este domingo*). Somewhere in between these two, we find the protagonist, Andrés Abalos, a neurotic, middle-aged, self-supporting bachelor who collects walking sticks as a hobby, and his lower-class counterpart, Mario, Estela's boyfriend, a delivery boy who strives to rise out of his class. These two men desire Estela and see her as the innocent girl from the country who will, because of her naivete, help the men rise out of lethargy and destitution, respectively. Misiá Elisa Grey de Abalos, Andres's grandmother, serves as a transmogrifying mirror to the young Estela; she clings dearly to a very strict set of moral and sexual standards that she feels are violated by all those who surround her. Misiá Elisa requires the constant care of Estela, who acts as her personal nurse, and Lourdes and Rosario, longtime, faithful servants.

Because this novel first presents itself as a record of the desacralization of bourgeois moral values in Chilean society, it begins by following the very traditional format of melodrama, with its idealization of innocence and its subsequent corruption. Estela arrives at the Abalos mansion with her aunt Lourdes and is immediately perceived by Andrés, who occasionally visits the grandmother, as

Alguien a quien no iba a ser necesario explicar nada de lo trágico de la situación [la abuela está loca], porque eso sólo la confundiría. En esta

muchacha adivinaba esa capacidad de aceptación muda de los campe-
sinos, esa entrega a cualquier circunstancia, por dura que fuera y por
eso no sufriría como las demás cuidadoras. Estela era un ser demasiado
primitivo, su sensibilidad completamente sin forma. (18)

Someone to whom he need not explain the tragic situation [the grandmother is crazy]—because to do so would only bewilder her. He sensed
in this girl all the traditional capacity of a peasant for dumb endurance,
the unquestioning submission to the realities of a situation, however
harsh. Because of this, she would not suffer as the other nurses had. Estela
was too primitive a being, her ego was still quite amorphous. (12)

Estela represents the stereotype of the good savage, completely unaware
of the corrupting forces of society and civilization. She is the clean slate
from which Andrés, as master of the house, will hope to fashion the selfless
servant. Along with her lack of worldly knowledge, Estela comes with a
sensual transparency that Andrés finds disturbing: "[L]a palma era unos
tonos más clara, un poco rosada, como . . . , como si estuviera más des-
nuda que el resto de la piel de la muchacha" (17) [(T)he palms were several
shades lighter, and pinkish, almost as if they were more naked than the
rest of her body (11)]. Andrés interprets her innocence and her awkward,
shy behavior as a sort of nakedness; she is someone who has not been
forced to fabricate disguises to protect her sense of self. It is important to
note here that Estela's characterization as the innocent, sensual being is a
projection of Andrés's desires and does not constitute a true portrayal of
the young woman, who, as we shall see later, is capable of contradictory
desires and emotions. At the beginning of the novel, by virtue of being the
only young member of the household, Estela exists as a function of other
people's expectations. In the Abalos mansion, she becomes the mirror that
reflects Misiá Elisa's madness: "[S]u rostro parecía haber despertado, ad-
quirido vida al reflejar como un espejo las expresiones del rostro de la
anciana, siguiéndola a los mundos y momentos que su voz antiquísima
evocaba" (40) [Her normally expressionless face awakened and came to
life as it mirrored the old woman's expressions and followed her into the
times and places her aged voice conjured up (41)].

In her madness, Misiá Elisa projects all her repressed obsessions onto
the young servant. These inspire accusations of stealing and licentious
sexual behavior, and a contrasting religious devotion that borders on the
macabre. The old woman's strong words in turn constitute a mirror for
Andrés whose life wanders aimlessly and purposelessly:

Yo mando en mi casa, no tú, que no eres más que un pobre solterón que
no sirves para nada. ¿A ver, que has hecho en toda tu vida que valga la
pena, ah? A ver, dime. Dime, pues, si eres tan valiente. ¿Qué? Nada. Te
lo pasas con tus estupideces de libros y tus bastones, y no has hecho nada,

33

no sirves para nada. Eres un pobre solterón inútil, nada más. Y eres malo, malo, porque le tienes miedo a todo, y sobre todo a ti mismo; malo, malo. Yo soy la única santa." (52)

This is my house and I give the orders here—not you! You're nothing but a pathetic, useless old bachelor. What have you ever done, eh? Why don't you tell me, since you've gotten so brave and bold all of a sudden? What have you done? Nothing! You just fritter your life away with your stupid walking sticks and books. You've never done anything, you're no good to any one, you're just a poor old useless bachelor. And a wicked one too, because you're afraid of everything, most of all yourself! You're wicked, wicked! I'm the only good person here. (56)

In this fragment, Misiá Elisa, as supposed director of what transpires in the household, sets up the basic polarity at the heart of her own narrative, with the passive male agent classified as bad while the female is attributed with sainthood and mastery. In the nonagenarian's life, the roles have been reversed, and rather than be the object of her husband's silent admiration, she accuses all others in the household. Unable to define himself, Andrés Avalos is compulsively drawn to his grandmother's house, where he rediscovers his youth in the person of Estela and truth in the words of his grandmother. The two women become for him the contrasting poles of life and death, an ambivalent mirror in which he can see himself reflected.

The novel marks the trajectory of Andrés's self-definition in a series of scenes within the house in which his empty life becomes progressively threatened by the grandmother's madness: "Esta casa, en cambio, de viejas maderas impregnadas en la voz de la enferma, era la peor amenaza para la cordura de Andrés" (43) [Whereas this house, where the very woodwork was permeated with the sick woman's voice, represented a serious threat to Andres's mental equilibrium (44)]. As in *Este domingo,* house and grandmother become indistinguishable. Lourdes, who readied the house by cleaning it from top to bottom for the occasion of Misiá Elisa's birthday, has the knack of resurrecting it from its deathlike state: "[E]ra como si el rubor de la vida invadiera el cadáver de la casa" (48) [(I)t seemed as though a faint flush of life was stealing back into this cadaver of a house (50)]. In this somber atmosphere, Misiá Elisa seems to be the character who brings the place to life with her "scenes" (22; 17). Her language becomes virulent, and she narrates scenes of sexual excess, especially between Andrés and Estela. Further, she accuses the female servants of stealing her most prized possessions. When creating these scenes, Misiá Elisa's tone intensifies and becomes sarcastic and domineering (49–53; 51–58). The opposition between good and evil, which the old woman sets up with respect to her grandson, is more accurately described as one of mastery and subservience, with Andrés losing all control over the situation:

La mente de Andrés no le obedecía, su abuela bloqueaba por completo su pensamiento, impidiendo el paso de toda emoción menos esto, esto nuevo, que parecía querer transformarse en terror. No hallaba manera de dominar la farsa macabra. (51)

Andres's mind no longer obeyed him, his grandmother was blocking his thoughts, preventing the passage of any emotion save this, this quite novel one, which threatened at any moment to become stark terror. He could not check the macabre farce. (55)

Andrés, the only male member of the household, has lost all control over the grotesque drama unraveling within his grandmother's house.

To counteract the insidious effect these scenes have on him, Andrés finds refuge in reading about marginal historical characters and in fabricating a world of Omsk, where the prevailing tonality is unmitigated sadness and singular beauty. Omsk becomes a sign, "una clave para aludir a ciertas cosas de la ciudad que ambos amigos encontraban dotadas de una peculiar tristeza, de una peculiar hermosura" (66) [a sort of code word denoting aspects of the city that seemed to them imbued with a special pathos and beauty (74)]. But even this idyllic world of the imagination does not help the bachelor against Misiá Elisa's insinuations that he is having an affair with Estela behind her back. Misiá Elisa's powerful words invade his imagination; he now daydreams about what at first he rejected:

Andrés se puso de pie. En lugar de Tenchita veía a Estela, envuelta en el chal que él había regalado a su abuela . . . , y Estela despertaba en el lecho junto a él. El calor joven de la muchacha, su cuerpo levemente humedecido por el sueño tibio, lo tocaba. Tenía vivo en la nuca el aliento de Estela al ayudarlo a ponerse el abrigo, y ante sus ojos se hallaba abierto el peligro desnudo de sus palmas. (113)

Andres stood up. He saw not Tenchita but Estela, wrapped in the shawl he had given his grandmother. . . . Estela waking up beside him in bed. He felt the girl's young warmth and the slight dampness of a body warmed by sleep. He felt Estela's breath sharp against his neck as she helped him with his coat, and the naked danger of those palms flashed before his eyes. (132–33)

In this projected scene, Andrés, like his grandmother, is terrified by naked, sensual contact and reacts by fleeing from the person who touches off his imagination. As he rejects any real contact with Estela, Andrés begins to create a scenario not unlike those of the *radio novelas* (radio serials) that fill Lourdes and Rosario's empty afternoons (34; 33). Since Andrés cannot bring himself to lust for Estela, he imagines he is in love with her: "[V]io claro que no era sólo deseo lo que sentía por Estela, era amor, sí, amor cuya certeza lo clavaba" (117) [He now realized . . . . It was

35

not simply desire he felt for Estela but love, yes love, and this knowledge sliced through him like a knife (137)]. With such a genteel emotion as love invested in the young girl, Andrés creates the prototypic melodrama of the lofty gentleman who falls in love with a lowly maid. She lifts him out of his lethargy, and he lifts her out of social degradation. Thus, the grandmother's house becomes the stage where Andrés plays out his conflicting desires, using Estela as the character who will realize his unfulfilled dreams. With Andrés as the creator of the scenes that we witness as readers, Donoso—given the ironic distance established by the omniscient narrator—effectively exposes the upper class's penchant for the melodramatic.

But melodramas can never develop without countless complications, and in *Coronación,* one complication bears the name of Mario. Mario is the delivery boy who frequents the Abalos household and who falls in love with the young Estela. He is protected by the cook and housekeeper who enjoy having him around the kitchen and who trust him to court Lourdes's niece. Unlike Andrés, who is much too old for the girl, Mario is an appropriate partner; he comes from the same class, has a steady job at the grocer's, and impresses her with his experience in the city when he takes her to the movies. But Mario's life is on the margin of stability: his older brother, René, is the neighborhood thief and all-around manipulator. The younger brother constantly struggles to remain outside the elder's influence, to keep a job, stay honest, and not be touched by the miserable living conditions in which René and his wife and children subsist.

After realizing that he loves Estela, Andrés goes back to the house in search of new possibilities in his life. Instead, he finds the couple kissing outside the house gate and switches into the same scenario that Misiá Elisa had predicted for Estela: "Sí, su pobre abuela tenía razón, Estela era una corrompida, casi una prostituta. ¡Su pobre abuela no estaba loca, eran estos jóvenes los locos, los sucios y envenenados!" (118) [Yes, his grandmother was quite right, Estela was definitely bad, practically a prostitute! His grandmother wasn't mad at all, it was these young people who were mad, rotten, corrupt! (139)]. Andrés goes into the kitchen, accuses the young people of being irresponsible, and berates the older maids for leaving the grandmother unattended. With this scene, Andrés enters into the same world of lunacy that possesses Misiá Elisa.

Since the world in *Coronación* is structured—at least according to Misiá Elisa's narrative—around the binary opposition of good and evil, the character Andrés searches for self-definition outside of that opposition, in a territory of the imagination. Andrés's willful act of creating dramatic scenes fills the empty, silent spaces of his life. He begins by repeating his grandmother's morality play, but also listens to the voice of reason as expressed by his friend Carlos Gross, who brings Andrés's existential tragedy down to the level of melodrama:

> En esa simplísima dificultad estriba toda esta gran *tragedia folletinesca* que estás tratando de vivir. Estás celoso, nada más. Y te aferras a esta dificultad para fabricarte *una tragedia de amor imposible*. . . . (132, my emphasis)

> This whole *grand tragedy* you are trying to get going boils down to one hugely simple problem: you are jealous, nothing more. And so you clutch on to this problem and you construct yourself a *tragedy of unrequited love*. . . . (155, my emphasis)

The voice of Carlos Gross stands not only for the voice of reason, but it also forms what will be in later novels (*Casa de campo,* for example) the voice of an omniscient narrator who constantly interrupts the flow of the narrative to point to the fictional strategies used in the structuring of the novel. With this quote, it becomes clear that the staging of melodramatic scenarios by several characters at different levels becomes the central architectural design in *Coronación.*

The danger that Andrés Abalos faces on a daily basis is the lack of differentiation between being master of his life and going mad. The protagonist of the novel associates strong feelings with living a full life; Carlos Gross interprets his friend's outbursts as a form of excess pertinent only to madness and to melodramatic expressionism (hyperbolic articulation of emotions and desires through theatrical means). Even as Andrés listens to his friend's advice, he has already begun to cross over into the realm of lunacy. "—Mi abuela loca es la única persona que conozco que es capaz de percibir verdades, tú ni siquiera te acercas a ella con tu razón fría y tus pasiones acartonadas" (133) ["My mad grandmother is the only person I know who is capable of perceiving the truth. You don't come anywhere near it with your cold reasoning and compartmentalized passions" (157)].

This erasing of boundaries between one form of reality and another also manifests itself at the social level within the confines of the house. In *Coronación,* the boundaries that define the domains of the different classes and their spheres of influence begin to break down. Certainly Rosario and Lourdes belong to the lower sphere of the servants' class; they know their place and seldom see fit to trespass their limits. Estela's case is a bit more ambiguous; at least in the mind of Misiá Elisa she dares to entertain emotions that would involve her with the master of the house. Even though these prescribed relationships are acceptable as long as there are no expectations of crossing class lines, such as the one between Alvaro and Violeta in *Este domingo,* Andrés violates all codes of class propriety by imagining he is in love. Carlos Gross makes it very clear that it would be all right for Andrés to have a fling with the maid if she were willing, but conceiving of love between two such players would be completely out of the question. The violation of boundaries also occurs on the physical level of the house. Mario's entrance into the kitchen is perfectly permissible in the eyes of Rosario and Lourdes, yet, when René enters the family living room to make accusations on behalf of his brother concerning Estela's pregnancy, Andrés immediately reacts:

> La insinuación de que él, y no Mario, era el padre de la criatura de Estela demoró en penetrar con toda fuerza en el cerebro de Andrés. Pero cuando se hizo sentir, lo colmó de asco por haber permitido que siquiera rozara la orilla de su mundo este otro mundo de acusaciones viles, de extorsiones y vicios. ¿Cómo se atrevía este roto a violar los límites tan cuidadosamente preservados por varias generaciones de la familia Abalos? (186)

> René's insinuation that he, not Mario, was the father of Estela's child, sank in. But when it did, he was overwhelmed by abhorrence for this world of vile innuendo, extortion and vice which he had allowed to brush against his own. How dare this broken creature overstep the limits which had been so scrupulously upheld by generations of Abalos? (220)

Even though he shuts the door on the evil intruder, the master of the house cannot stop René from violating his space. René notices that all the family silver is laid out on the table to be cleaned. After this scene of intrusion, the novel closes at a precipitous pace. René forces Mario into trying to steal the silver with the help of Estela. By the time the robbers arrive, however, the silver has been safely locked behind doors in anticipation of a party to be given in Misiá Elisa's honor, and Andrés is still in the house. Mario forces Estela to act out a scene in which she pretends to seduce Andrés while he and René open the cupboard with a key secured by her. The girl, still basically honest, cannot follow through with the plan and announces to Andrés that people are stealing the silver. The men flee into the city streets, carrying no silver prize, but having sequestered the gem of the household. As in a melodrama, evil has overpowered good but has not touched its moral fiber. As she is taken from the house, the still innocent Estela harbors some hope that she can build a future with Mario and her expected child: "Pero en el fondo de las tinieblas de su dolor físico había una chispa que podía transformarse en claridad, una certeza fiera de su triunfo" (211) [But deep down in this dark night of physical pain there was a spark that might suddenly be kindled into light, the proud knowledge of her victory (252)]. The language in this quotation points to the clear opposition between the forces of darkness and light, and to the triumph

38

of the latter. It also calls attention to the rhetoric of melodrama that Donoso has appropriated to expose its simplistic binary oppositions.

The melodrama of the lower classes ends here, a few pages before the end of the novel.[12] The rest of the book follows the fate of the members of the upper classes, Misiá Elisa and Andrés Abalos. If the melodrama of the working class as seen by Misiá Elisa sets up the opposition between good and evil, then that of the bourgeoisie vacillates between madness and reason. For all of them, however, the central issue is that of power, and who exerts it over the members of the opposing camp. Mario and Andrés are the two characters who experience the most difficulty in wielding power. Mario feels he is controlled, both by his brother who reminds him of his social fate within a highly stratified society, and by his lover Estela, who, when she becomes pregnant, imposes on him the obligations of parenthood. Mario is driven to despair by these two unrelenting forces and crumbles under the pressure. Andrés, on the other hand, acknowledges no social and biological pressures; he does not even allow his lust for Estela to control him for very long. His insecurity stems from his grandmother's madness and her control over the events within the Abalos mansion. Andrés is lost amid the forces of an inherited propensity for lunacy and his own incapacity to control the servants and the outsiders who intrude in his family home.

At the end of the novel, when Andrés loses all control because of violations perpetrated against the proper limits set by generations of one Abalos after another, he opts, in a conscious way, to slip into a fantasy world where he has meticulously set the scene. While the brothers are robbing the china cupboard, Estela is in the library with Andrés. When she realizes she is being used, she decides not to participate in the robbery, bites Andres's lip, and flees to warn the others. Frightened by her unexpected entrance, Mario and René drop their booty with a loud crash and flee. Andrés follows, picks up all the silver pieces one by one, and puts them back into place. Terrified by his disillusionment regarding Estela and by his lack of control over his surroundings, Andrés pretends that nothing has transpired. "Esto del robo es una alucinación mía" (213) [The robbery was a hallucination on my part (255)].[13] Soon after, when his friend Carlos Gross arrives, Andrés decides to cut all ties with reality and tells him to go into the study to see Estela lying on the sofa, waiting for him. Then he instructs him to go look at the empty cupboard. Carlos realizes that his friend is crazy and patiently concurs with the now imaginary events:

Diciendo estas palabras Andrés sintió el placer de cortar sus últimas amarras con la realidad. Si era capaz de convencer a la gente, y sobre todo a Carlos que era médico, de que él estaba loco, entonces, simplemente, lo estaba, y en ese caso ninguno de sus dolores era efectivo, y todos los acontecimientos de esa noche, ficción. (215)

As he said this, he felt a distinct pleasure in cutting his last ties with reality. If he could succeed in persuading everyone, and particularly a doctor like Carlos, that he was mad, well then he would be mad, and none of those horrors could touch him and nothing which had happened that night was real. (257).

Andrés first lies to himself that nothing has happened, then alters reality (puts the silver back in the cupboard) so that his lies can be confirmed. He turns around and creates another fiction by making an assertion (the cupboard is empty) that is contrary to reality. The first lie helps him distance himself from his own painful emotions, the second breaks the links between verifiable physical reality and his verbal construct. In both cases he has produced fiction. His third step away from a reasonable world is a claim that his grandmother is not crazy, but rather, the only person who holds the truth: "Pero sabes muy bien que no está loca, que es la única persona que sabe la verdad" (216) [But you know quite well she's not mad, she's the one person who knows the truth (258)]. Andrés becomes the self-appointed narrator, divulging his way of proceeding as he goes. In doing so, he rewrites his grandmother's melodramatic script and purports to define his reality. One character usurps narrative voice from another in order to gain the reader's attention. With this, his first novel, Donoso has entered into the realm of the self-reflexive novel even though he has chosen to hide it under the shell of a seemingly transparent structure: melodrama.

Although our analysis has centered around the character of Andrés Abalos and his passage from the real to the fictional, we must return to Misiá Elisa, "la única persona que sabe la verdad" [the one person who knows the truth]. If an analysis of the coronation scene, which gives the novel its title, is to reveal the truth about *Coronación,* we must seek the agent or agents of mastery who engineer the novel's closing scene.

Misiá Elisa alternately claims to be a queen and a saint. When Andrés brings her a pink shawl for a present, she rejects it and gives it to Estela:

—¡Pruébate tu chal! ¡Pruébate tu chal rosado, que a ti te lo trajo de regalo! Si me lo trajo a mí sería un insulto, porque es un chal de puta, sí de puta, no para una señora que merece una corona de santa y de reina, como yo. (51)

"Let's see you try on this pretty pink shawl he's brought you. He wouldn't have chosen a shawl like that for me—it isn't the sort of thing you give to a lady with the virtue of a saint and royal blood in her veins. It's a whore's shawl, a whore's shawl, do you hear? Go on, you slut, try it on!" (55)

When Misiá Elisa begins to show signs of arteriosclerosis, she becomes obsessed with the fact that she is a descendant of royalty. She even has her husband subscribe to European magazines that will keep her abreast of the latest gossip (24; 19). Lourdes and Rosario become accustomed to hearing her talk about it. The old woman rants and raves when people come to see her and often mixes accusations with a defense of her status. In her mind, as a queen and saint she is endowed with the ability to dictate the fate of those around her. This obsession protects her from the insecurities she feels with her husband's family as a first-generation Chilean:

> —y Ramón se reía de mí porque creía que eran todas mentiras, pero yo sé que me tenía envidia. ¿Cómo no, si soy pariente de todos los reyes y los nobles de Europa? Aquí en Santiago me miraban en menos porque mi papá no era chileno y decían que Ramón se había casado con una desconocida. ¡Claro, desconocida aquí, en este país de indios! Cuando era chiquilla mi mamá fue a un baile en el palacio de no sé quién, en Europa y bailó toda la noche con un príncipe. Ella tenía puesta una corona, a la que tenía derecho porque era noble, como yo también tengo derecho. (149)

> ". . . and Ramón laughed at me because he thought it was all lies, but I know he envied me secretly. Well, naturally, since I was related to all the kings and nobles of Europe. They looked down on me here in Santiago because my father wasn't a Chilean and they said Ramón had married a foreigner. Who wouldn't be a foreigner in this country of Indians? When my mother was a girl, she went to a ball in someone's palace, I can't remember whose, but it was somewhere in Europe and she danced all night with a prince. She wore a crown too, being of noble birth, as I am too, of course." (176)

Misiá Elisa's monologue exposes a dying ideology. As a grotesque character, this aging lady can only define herself as she degrades others ("este país de indios" [this country of Indians]). In a highly stratified aristocratic society, or in the upper-middle-class society in Chile, the symbol of one's status is all important. For Misiá Elisa that symbol becomes the crown.

Even though Misiá Elisa madly "dictates," it is Rosario and Lourdes who are capable of transforming the house for parties and celebrations, and they remain unaffected by Misiá Elisa's and Andrés's ups and downs. In the final analysis, Rosario and Lourdes are the unconscious puppeteers who manipulate the strings of unsuspecting characters in the Abalos household. They have no particular stake in believing or disbelieving Misiá Elisa's deranged accusations. Her stories, however, can serve to enrich their own. Lourdes, for example, spends a great deal of time preparing a present for Misiá Elisa's saint's day, which consists of a crown and a dress that were safely stored away in the attic. The mistress provides the verbal script, and Lourdes interprets it dramatically by seeking out the necessary props.[14] The maids are unconscious masters of a creative intermingling of voices.

A close analysis of the conversation between Rosario and Lourdes yields a weaving of fictional and daily reality in an indiscriminate manner:

—Le estoy haciendo un regalo a misiá Elisita.
—Mire, Lourdes, que la señora las va a reconocer y va a creer que usted se las robó.
—No creo. Estoy haciéndole una coronita, una coronita de flores de plata para regalársela el día de su santo, que ya está acercándose. ¿No ve que ella siempre dice que es reina de Europa, y además que merece una corona de santa por lo buena que ha sido? También voy a regalarle este vestido de gasa, tengo que arreglarlo con mucho cuidado porque está hecho un harnero. Y se lo voy a regalar todo para su santo . . .
—Poca gente irá a venir.
—¿Será la hora de la comedia?
—La bonita ya pasó qué rato.
—Ay, qué pena. Sí, poca gente . . .
—Dicen que don Emiliano se quedó muerto en la tina de baño.
—¿De qué?
—De repente.
—Sí, pues, así dicen.
—Pobre. Tan diablazo que era.
—Y mucho más joven que la señora.
—No, no mucho. ¡Qué salud la de la señora! Va a ver no más, nos va a enterrar a toditos . . .
—Harto bueno que sería, digo yo, tan santa que es la pobre. Y se pone cada día más diabla y más habilidosa. Y como es tan moral para sus cosas, bueno sería que durara un ejemplo como el de ella.
—Así no más es.
—Y tiene noventa y cuatro.
—Mm . . .
—¿O noventa y seis?
—Mm . . .
—No, noventa y . . . , no me acuerdo. ¿Se acuerda usted?
Rosario se había dormido porque estaba realmente extenuada. (147)

"I'm making a little present for Misiá Elisita."
"But the señora will recognize them, Lourdes, and think you stole them."
"I don't think she will. I'm making her a little crown, a little crown of silver flowers for her saint's day, which is coming soon. You know how she calls herself the Queen of Europe and says she should have a saint's crown for having been so good always? I'm going to give her this gauze

dress too, but first I have to mend it very carefully because it's full of holes. And I'll give her all these presents on her saint's day."

"There won't be many people."

"Is it time for the serial yet?"

"It was over ages ago."

"What a shame! No, there won't be many people . . ."

"Don Emiliano died in his bath they say . . ."

"What of?"

"He just died suddenly."

"Ah well, that's the way to go . . ."

"Poor soul. He was such a devil."

"And much younger than the señora, too."

"No, not much. How strong the señora must be, though! She'll see us all into the grave, you mark my words."

"Well, she deserves to, poor good lady that she is. And here she is, getting perkier and cleverer every day! A good person like her ought to live a long time so she can be a good example for the world."

"That's right."

"And she's ninety-four."

"Mmm."

"Or is it ninety-six?"

"No, it's ninety. . . . I've forgotten. Can you remember?"

Rosario had dozed off. She really was worn out. (174)

This conversation clearly illustrates how, in conceiving their daily reality, the maids weave elements from Misiá Elisa's fictional world (she is a queen and a saint), and the radio-serials (Emiliano has died in the tub) into the factual but not very accurate world of their reality (Misiá Elisa is younger than Emiliano). They compare the ages of Emiliano and the lady of the house as if they both belonged to the same world, acknowledge the fact that they are quite forgetful about real facts (the lady's age), and, in a deadpan manner, create humorous scenarios based on wordplay:

—Dicen que don Emiliano se quedó muerto . . .
—¿De qué?
—De repente.[15] (147)

"Don Emiliano died in his bath they say . . ."
"What of?"
"He just died suddenly." (174)

This play on words highlights the authorial presence, alerting the reader to linguistic games that are meant to create a humorous effect rather than communicate information or meaning. Further, this fragment of the novel weaves different languages into the fabric of the text precisely because of the women's propensity to displace one subject with another. This technique of subject displacement in the trajectory of a narrative will find its ultimate expression in the *dicen* (they say) of *El obsceno pájaro de la noche.* Donoso's novels will increasingly reflect this metaphorical weaving of many languages by agents who forget to speak in a straight line. Later on in the conversation, Lourdes states that Misiá Elisa is a saint, but she is getting to be a devil in her old age. She regards the lady as exemplary, but having inadvertently described her both as a saint and as a devil, the contradictory statement makes her an ambivalent moral example. Linguistic play in this dialogue subverts Misiá Elisa's moral agenda, in which good triumphs over evil, and sets up a paradigm that celebrates both good and evil. Because of their forgetfulness and lack of precision in the way they think and speak, the maids become perfect vessels for a textual interweaving of languages—of the "real" (Misiá Elisa's words) and the "melodramatic" (plots from the *comedias* [serials]).

The actual coronation scene becomes a melodrama itself, complete with music played on an ancient record player: "[U]n pobre hilo de melodía en medio de una maraña de chirridos y rasmilladuras" (201) [(A) frail thread of melody almost swamped by scratching and chirruping noises (239)].[16] The maids create a theatrical scene as they arrange flowers and lamps to highlight the figure of the ancient lady: "La luz hizo incorpórea la figura de misiá Elisa Grey de Abalos, aislándola como en un nicho rodeado de flores en medio de la oscuridad de la habitación" (200) [The lighting made Misiá Elisa look unearthly, isolating her in an illuminated niche of flowers in the midst of the darkened room (238)]. The intense light creates the right atmosphere while the lady is asleep, before the presentation of all the gifts takes place: "Y como los mercaderes orientales de las leyendas, las sirvientas desplegaron a los pies de la reina los resplandores de sus presentes" (201) [Like the legendary merchants of the East, the maids laid their magnificent gifts at the queen's feet (239)]. The scene borrows elements from the legendary as well as from classical mythology. The maids cannot agree on who will help Misiá Elisa into her dress and crown; they fight, and in doing so, begin to express the vengeance of the Furies.[17] Already drunk, they decide to give the old lady a drink against her will:

> La festejada se negaba a abrir la boca. Rosario, introduciéndole un dedo en la boca para abrirla, logró verter un buen vaso de ponche en el gaznate de la nonagenaria, que se quejaba como un niño. En vez de animarse, la anciana desfalleció por completo. (202)

> The object of these ministrations refused to open her mouth. Only by inserting a finger into her mouth and forcing it open could Rosario manage to tip a good part of the contents of the glass down the lady's throat,

44

while she struggled and whimpered like a child. Instead of reviving, though, she passed out. (240)

After the coronation, they leave her "con la cabeza volcada hacia adelante y la corona de plata chueca sobre el rostro pintarrajeado, parecía haber perdido el conocimiento" (203) [with her head slumped forward and her silver crown askew above her painted face, apparently unconscious (241)]. As Furies, the maids avenge the lady's insistence on demarcating levels between social classes. By pouring liquor down her throat as if she were an animal ("el gaznate de la nonagenaria" [the old lady's throat]), they literally shut her up so that she can no longer dictate her royal pronouncements.[18] Such a scene incorporates all the necessary elements for a good melodrama: old-fashioned music, exaggerated makeup and gesture, abundant props, contrasting light, and grotesque appearances.[19]

In this final coronation scene, the main character is given an elaborate theatrical role that contrasts heavily with her ordinary constrained existence. As the character moves from ordinary life to theater, a distance is established so that a liberating change can take place. When, much later, Misiá Elisa wakes up from her stupor, she believes that she has died and gone to heaven. She later dies surrounded by sequins and lights that she believes to be stars:

> [A]l ver luces remontando por los regueros de mostacillas del suelo hasta los brillos de su vestido de gran aparato, pensó que también eran estrellas del firmamento y que la envolvían entera. Suposo, entonces, que ya había muerto, y que iba subiendo entre tanta y tanta estrella, subiendo muy suavemente camino directo al cielo. Después cerró los ojos. Estaba tan agotada que no se dio cuenta de que sólo en ese instante moría, y no antes, cuando creyó ver a todas las constelaciones rodeándola. (219)

> [S]eeing nothing but sparkling lights all the way up from the showers of spangles on the floors to the brilliants on her coronation crown, she thought that these were stars too and that she was surrounded by them. Then she supposed that she must already be dead and that she was ascending very gently through the firmament straight to heaven. She closed her eyes. She was too exhausted to notice that it was when she died and not before when she saw herself surrounded by constellations. (262)

By centering on melodrama and its illusory, often grotesque aspects, the Chilean novelist creates an ironic distance between the social content being depicted (there is a contradictory gesture of crowning at the same time that the "queen" is bereft of all her powers) and the theatrical form, which becomes the focus of signification in the narrative.

The focus of mastery over language has been displaced from Misiá

Elisa, who insists on perpetuating the stratification of a class society by constantly voicing her status as queen and saint, to the two maids, who by exclusively theatrical means wield their power over the household and redefine the social roles within their limited stage. Their mode of melodramatic expression has been borrowed directly from the *comedias* they hear on the radio. By transposing a popular form of expression from its verbal, radial dimension to a dramatic representation, they in fact "dethrone" their mistress's class rhetoric.[20] Popular dramatic language displaces empty, high-class pronouncements. Misiá Elisa, positioned in a privileged space at the end of the novel, wears a grotesque grimace that allegorizes the death of a decaying class. With *Coronación,* Donoso creates a theatrical frame that will be used to different ends throughout his novelistic career. A close analysis of the concepts of social role and theatricality in this novel, and of the dialogic function of diverse languages within narrative discourse to heighten the ordinary, has served to place Donoso's oeuvre on the threshold of two modes of narration: the socially committed and the polyphonically conceived.

While in the first two novels just discussed, there is a marked emphasis on scene setting and on the individual character's desire to gain mastery over dramatization, it is with "Santelices" that Donoso begins to associate theatricality with the control of the gaze.[21] If in *Este domingo,* Chepa constantly spies on Maya through the eyes of Violeta, and in *Coronación* all events in the household seem to be closely monitored by Misiá Elisa as if the walls had eyes, there is a role reversal and a loss of control on the part of these characters that is represented by their lack of vision when they enter a sphere beyond their immediate class conceptions. In the short story "Santelices," less emphasis is placed on polarized oppositions based on class differences than is placed on the expression through visual means of a character's repressed desires.

The story is built around Santelices's obsession with the yellow gaze of wild cats whose pictures he has been collecting for years. This middle-aged single man, a hard worker and a good tenant, has kept these cutouts in the bottom drawer of his dresser. One evening he dares to tack them up on the walls of his boarding room, an action that the landlord describes as perverse and almost crazy. Santelices is compelled to action in a compulsive manner:

> [E]sos largos ojos amarillos, esas patas acolchadas, esos cuerpos suntuosos en el letargo caldeado de otros climas, estaban prisioneros, planos en el último cajón de su cómoda. Era como si los hubiera oído dar alaridos desde allí y no pudo resistirse. (260)

Those long yellow eyes, those padded feet, those bodies sleek in the warm lethargy of other climates, were prisoners, laid out flat in the bottom drawer of his bureau. It was as if he heard them howling in there, and he couldn't resist. (155)

For Santelices, these visual images represent "la peligrosa presencia de la belleza, con la amenaza que acecha desde la gracia y la fuerza" (264) [the dangerous presence of beauty, . . . the threat contained in grace and strength (158)]. The pictures of wild cats are charged with a sense of beauty, a sense of menace fashioned out of grace and power. These are all qualities that are completely absent in the protagonist's life. In order to recapture that feeling of the exercise of graceful power, Santelices identifies with the wild beasts, that, in his eyes, possess the qualities that he must bring out in himself: "El pecho de Santelices palpitaba junto con la víctima, y para salvarse del pánico, pegaba sus ojos al agresor para identificarse con él" (266) [Santelices' heart pounded with the victim's, and to save himself from panic he fixed his eyes on the aggressor (160)]. His passage from the role of victim to that of aggressor is imagined via the identification with the beautiful and wild.

All that has been neatly repressed for years surfaces with the help of a visual aid: there is an exchange of gazes in which the libidinal forces (within the hidden drawers of his mind) look at him, and Santelices answers with another look, a look that transforms him from victim to aggressor. This initial step, the exteriorization of repressed forces, allows Santelices to go beyond the walls of the boardinghouse where he feels trapped and conceive a dramatic scene that exists independently of himself but contains the uncontrolled forces within him. To control those forces, Santelices secures a set of field glasses with which to distance his gaze from the scene that he safely demarcates with a window frame and focuses five stories below his office (the space where he can control his environment):

Se sentó en su escritorio y se volvió a parar. Desde la ventana miró el estrecho patio de luz cortado en dos por los rayos oblicuos, las nubes que se arrastraban en el cielo terso de la mañana allá arriba, y la muchacha rubia que jugaba en el fondo del patio, cinco pisos más abajo. (270)

From the window he looked down into the narrow patio bisected by the slanting rays of light, the clouds dragging themselves across the clear morning sky, and at the blonde girl playing down in the patio, five stories below. (165)

For Donoso this demarcated scene—framed by the window, kept at an allowable distance, and limited to the perspective of the changing focus of a pair of field glasses—provides a metaphor for the creative process, a metaphor that he adopts early in his career and will develop to its ultimate conclusion in *El jardín de al lado*.

Looking out his office window, Santelices sees a young woman doing her daily chores and playing with a female cat. The girl represents an ideal (she is blond, young, and enclosed in a gardenlike space) that contrasts strongly with the only woman Santelices knows, his landlady Bertita:

> La Bertita estaba en cama todavía, incorporada en medio de lo que parecía un mar de almohadones gordos en la inmensa marquesa. Sobre la mesa del velador había una caja de polvos volcada, una peineta con pelos enredados, pinches, bigudíes, horquillas. Junto a ella vigilaba don Eusebio, con una escoba en la mano y un trapo amarrado a la cabeza. (267)

> Bertita was still in bed, sitting up in the midst of what looked like a sea of fat pillows. On her night table there was an overturned box of powder, a comb with tangled hair, rollers, hair clips, bobby pins. Next to the bed, keeping guard over her, was Don Eusebio, a broom in his hand and a rag tied around his head. (162)

Bertita, an old maid who controls Santelices by cooking for him and by encouraging his complacency in life, contrasts strongly with the young girl, who is distanced and accompanied by a tamed feline. The old maid is surrounded by a disordered, decadent frame, and her figure is flanked by her father, who, by virtue of holding a broom and wearing a rag around his head, represents the emasculated male.[22] This is the oedipal scene that Santelices desperately wants to displace and substitute with the framed picture of the girl with her cat.

"Santelices" is really about the transformation of the scene outside the window as the character focuses the field glasses:

> Cuando llegó a la oficina se fue derecho a la ventana, pero le costó encontrar el foco preciso. El ansia trababa sus manos y lo hacía pensar que siempre podía haber un foco mejor. Por fin quedó satisfecho. (277)

> When he got to the office he went straight to the window, but it was a struggle to focus the binoculars. Anxiety confused his hands and made him think he could always find a sharper focus. Finally he was satisfied. (170)

What he experiences on this second viewing is a projection of pent up feelings ("El ansia trababa sus manos" [Anxiety confused his hands]), as seen through a mechanical set of eyes that can be adjusted to obtain the desired effect. He sees the same blond girl, but now she is delicate, "con una fatal cifra de melancolía en el rostro que parecía decir que no pertencía a nadie ni a nada" (277–78) [a fatal sign of melancholy in her face seemed to say she didn't belong to anybody or anything (170)]. Santelices's controlled gaze has the power of possessing what he sees: since the girl does not appear to belong to anyone, he could certainly fill in that gap. The female cat has had kittens, but, rather than the tame animal that he first saw, it is now an enormous cat, surrounded by many other cats that the smiling girl pets. The once tame scene has been transformed into a new, wilder version, not unlike the pictures of wild animals that he previously kept hidden in the drawers.

The transformation continues in subsequent viewings, but in a gradual and subtle way so as to slowly accommodate the pent up feelings of the agent who creates it. The changes mark his attempt at creative mastery in which affect is expressed through increasingly complex dramatic scenes, as if in a recurring dream. Each new vision incorporates a less censored version of the repressed content. If at first the cats surround the girl, at least she is capable of petting them and thus controlling them; later scenes multiply the number of animals and she becomes less and less defined while the feelings of the observer become more and more evident:

> Las sombras se hundieron, cayendo bloque sobre bloque en el patio exiguo, iluminado por el fulgor de ojos verdes, dorados, rojos, parpadeantes. Santelices apenas divisaba las formas a que pertenecían con la ayuda del anteojo. Los animales eran docenas, que circulaban alrededor de la muchacha: ella no era más que una mancha pálida en medio de todos esos ojos que se encendían al mirarla codiciosos. (280)

> The shadows sank, falling on the tiny patio, lit by the brilliance of green, gold, red, blinking eyes. Even with the binoculars, Santelices could barely make out the shapes the eyes belonged to. There were dozens of animals circling around the girl: she was nothing more than a pale spot in the midst of all those eyes that lit up as they watched her greedily. (172–73)

His lust for the projected female figure masks the lust for Bertita, an object that he cannot bring himself to desire. So as to deny himself the appropriate expression of his feelings, he contrasts the vision of Bertita's bedroom with an imagined jungle scene that calls for his heroic intervention. The multiple sets of eyes threaten to devour the girl, and he must return their gaze and thus save her.

In the final scene, the intensity of the jungle as vision corresponds to the compulsion that first surfaced when Santelices hung all the figures on the wall:

> En la oscuridad se allegó a la ventana y la abrió de par en par; enorme ventana que descubrió sobre su cabeza toda la oscuridad de un cielo desteñido, en que la luna caliente, roja, de bordes imprecisos, como un absceso, parecía que ya iba a estallar sobre las copas de los árboles

gigantescos. Ahogó un grito de horror: el patio era un viscoso vivero de fieras, desde donde todos los ojos—amarillos, granates, dorados, verdes—lo miraban a él. (282–83)

In the darkness he approached the window and opened it wide: an enormous window exposing over his head all the darkness of a discolored sky, in which the hot, red moon with imprecise contours like an abscess looked ready to burst over the tops of the gigantic trees. He strangled a cry of horror: the patio was a viscous den of wild beasts, from which all the eyes—yellow, red, gold, green—were watching him. (175)

The description of the scene has now reached hyperbole; the window frame is about to swallow him, the moon and the trees have gained gigantic proportions, and the patio, now a veritable jungle, is filled with brightly colored eyes that stare at him. Santelices fashions himself as the hero who must save the girl from the beasts' attack. If in the boardinghouse scene he was attracted by the power of the yellow eyes, in this scene the girl is being swallowed by the intensity of the jungle, and he is the agent who will protect her from the wildcats. In the first scene, he is scolded like a child for decorating the walls of his room. He could only respond in a passive way, by retreating to the safety of his office. By creating a new scene outside his office window, he places himself in a position of active participation: he sees the girl in danger and must protect her. In a leap of heroic gesture, he jumps to his death to save the girl.

If the garden five flights down stands for the exteriorization of a world within, the figure of the girl is a picture of Santelices who is surrounded by the beasts of desire that he does not control. When he leaps from the window, he meets the sensuous life that he had so far rejected (as represented by the jungle and the cats), but he also meets his death. This final moment is a moment of self-recognition in which he sees himself in the image of a being that is the diametrical opposite of himself. The series of scenes in "Santelices" dramatizes the steps in Freudian psychoanalysis. These scenes represent the return of the repressed (the cats on the wall), the overdetermined enactment of the repressed in a dreamlike scene (the girl with the large cat), the conception of conflict in terms of a struggle between life and death (the girl with the wildcats), and finally, the attainment of the moment of self-recognition and the move to fuse the two selves (the leap into the garden).[23]

What is at stake in the repetition and transformation of scenes is not so much a clarification of meaning (the lust that finally surfaces in the eyes of the beasts) but an increased control over the expression of the lust that has been repressed. If at first Santelices could only "represent" his lust through displaying another's photography, now he is the creator of the dramatic scenes that truly represent his emerging self. Mastery is a function of the manipulation of the field glasses. If we are to follow the argument that Santelices's scenes describe the creative process, it must be concluded that plot development follows a progression from repression of image (the pictures in the drawer) to an increased expressionism that goes from subtle statement (the initial scene of the blond girl with a single cat) to fantastic hyperbole (the threatened white figure surrounded by wild animals). The complexity of the scene is dependent on an increased exaggeration of detail and gesture and an erasure of individualization. All of these mechanisms correspond to a melodramatic imagination in terms of the visual construct. Unlike melodrama, in which good triumphs over evil, or vice versa, in Donoso's heightened scenes there is an effort to maintain the ambivalence between opposites: "No le importaba nada, porque la selva crecía dentro de él ahora, con sus rugidos y calores, con la efusión de la muerte y de la vida" (281) [Nothing mattered to him, because the jungle was gowing inside him now, with its roars and heat, with its effusions of death and life (174)]. The triumphant character transcends his poor reality because he integrates the forces of life and death in a visual dramatization that gives him mastery over the deadly conflict. And mastery is gained as the result of a theatrical process in which the powerful gaze of the public (the cats) is returned by the agent of the action to evoke the illusion of self-presence. In the distorted mirror of the projected scenes, one can see oneself as actor.

With "Santelices," Donoso's narrative has effected a leap in the formulation of his dramatic scene. If in *Coronación* Andrés is conscious of his entrance into the sphere of madness, and if in *Este domingo* the narrator recreates his memory in order to have control over the influence that his grandmother has exerted over him, there is as yet no discursive strategy in these novels that consciously demarcates a scene that is to be privileged as a fictional projection. With the use of the window as frame, there is an emphasis on the process of transformation as effected by the viewer's manipulation of point of view. Since thus far in Donoso's work the viewer who is capable of mastery is often a male, an association is established between the one who gazes and the female object of the gaze, who is transformed and made into the object of the spectacle.[24] The male is literally driven by the obsessiveness of the female he has created (the grandmothers in both novels and Bertita in the short story), and he is propelled into a creative process that will allow him to take control of his life by inverting the image of the devouring mother into that of the helpless damsel in distress. This process of mastering as a result of the manipulation of the gaze is but a step in scene setting. At the end of "Santelices," the agent discards the field glasses and enters into the frame in an effort to become part of the representation and to be swallowed by it. In the end, there is no differentiation between creator and creation. When Santelices discards

51

the field glasses and enters into the picture, he is no longer the agent of the look, but is now being seen.[25] He is an actor in the theatrical frame he has created.

In *El lugar sin límites,* dramatic scene becomes spectacle. The character under the lights is La Manuela, a homosexual caught between his biologically determined role as the father of La Japonesita, the owner of the house of prostitution in which he lives, and his erotic role as transvestite: "Ella no es más que la gran artista que ha venido a la casa de la Japonesita a hacer su número" (112) [She's just the great artist who's come to Japonesita's house to do her number (212)]. Before going on to delineate the complex character of La Manuela, it is important to describe the socially determined scene that gives structure to the novel.

La Japonesita and La Manuela live in El Olivo, a run-down, desolate town that is characterized mainly by its absence of electricity. El Olivo is on the edge of a vast vineyard, owned by Don Alejandro Cruz, the prototypically powerful male figure. El Olivo has no electricity because Don Alejo has willed it so. His hope is that the town will disappear so that he can extend his vineyards into that land. As landlord, he is the agent of darkness, a regional senator whose power goes beyond his reach, most dramatically in the figures of his fierce black dogs. The only characters who resist his commands are La Japonesita, who refuses to sell the whorehouse to him, Pancho, a bastard son who was raised on the grounds of the Cruz's estate, and Octavio, Pancho's brother-in-law.

Don Alejo's only hold over Pancho is the money that the young man has borrowed from him to buy his red pickup truck. Pancho, who knows he will be humiliated by Don Alejo every time he comes in to pay his monthly debt, withholds the monthly payments so as not to have to show up in town and be degraded by the old senator. When he does return, he is in fact humiliated in public. Octavio, who comes to the rescue of Pancho by lending him the money to repay Don Alejo in full, defines the man's power in relationship to money and nothing else:

> —Esto es lo que vale, compadre, no sea leso: la plata. ¿Usted cree que si uno tuviera no sería igual a él? ¿O cree que don Alejo es de una marca especial? No, nada de cuestiones aquí. Usted le tiene miedo al viejo porque le debe plata nomás. (90)

> "That's all that counts, buddy, don't be a jerk: money. Don't you think you'd be as good as him if you had it? Or do you think don Alejo is something special? No, no two ways about it. You're afraid of the old man because you owe him money, period." (199)

Octavio's confrontation with Don Alejo is signified by his ability to meet and hold the old man's gaze without having to deflect it: "Octavio sosteniendo la mirada del senador durante un instante" (98) [Octavio meeting the senator's eyes for an instant (204)]. The novel represents all power relationships in terms of control over others with one's look:

> Don Alejo se acercó a la mesa. Con sus ojos de loza azulina, de muñeca, de bolita, de santo de bulto, miró a la Manuela, que se estremeció como si toda su voluntad hubiera sido absorbida por esa mirada que la rodeaba, que la disolvía. ¿Cómo no sentir vergüenza de seguir sosteniendo la mirada de esos ojos portentosos con sus ojillos parduzcos de escasas pestañas? Los bajó. (75–76)

> With his delft blue doll's eyes, the earnest eyes of a saint's statue, he looked at la Manuela who trembled as if all her will power had been absorbed by the gaze that surrounded and dissolved her. How could she help feeling ashamed of meeting those marvelous orbs with her grizzly little eyes and skimpy lashes? She lowered them. (190–91)

Power is here defined in terms of race; Don Alejo's blue eyes represent his European ascendancy, while La Manuela, with brown eyes, supposedly belongs to a lower order. La Manuela is enthralled by the senator's gaze, and translates that into love:

> No recordaba haber amado nunca tanto a un hombre como en este momento estaba amando al diputado don Alejandro Cruz. Tan caballero él. Tan suave, cuando quería serlo. Hasta para hacer las bromas que otros hacían con jetas mugrientas de improperios, él las hacía de otra manera, con una sencillez que no dolía, con una sonrisa que no tenía ninguna relación con las carcajadas que daban los otros machos. (76)

> She couldn't remember ever having loved a man as much as at that moment she loved Congressman don Alejandro Cruz. Such a gentleman. So suave, when he wanted to be. Even when he made jokes the others made, with their thick, gross lips, he made them another way, with an artlessness that didn't wound, with a smile far removed from the guffaws of the other men. (191)

With this passage, love translates as an unequal relationship; this time there is a difference in class, because Don Alejo, as the possessor of social manners, has an ability to manipulate through language and gesture and he can condescend in a gentle manner. Moreover, he is a male capable of disguising blatant laughter with a smile. The novel thus defines Don Alejo in terms of four forms of privilege: money, race, gender, and class.

Positioned at the other end of the spectrum is La Manuela, who defines himself in entirely ambiguous terms. He is a man, but uses the feminine when referring to himself: "—Es que me gusta ser reina de la fiesta" (72) ["I like to be the belle of the ball" (188)]. This ambiguity dominates the novel from its outset, as the figure of La Manuela begins to awaken. All adjectives in the first few pages point to the definition of a female character, but soon after, the reader is aware that La Manuela is "really" Manuel.[26] In addition to assuming a female character through language and manner, La Manuela adopts the theatrical role of a flamenco dancer with a stylized body and a mastery of step. As a female he is put in a subservient role (in relation to Don Alejo and Pancho), but as a performer he is in the position of controlling his own space: "—Si me trajeron es porque querían verme, asique . . . Si no quieren show, entonces, bueno, me pagan la noche y me voy . . . (73) ["They brought me here because they wanted to see me, so . . . if they don't want the show, fine, pay me for tonight and I'll go" (189)]. As a dancer, La Manuela has a prescribed role that he performs in a professional manner; his employment ensures that he will be seen and that he has a place and a time within the structured society of the brothel he joined when he came to El Olivo.

El lugar sin límites vacillates between two time periods: the present, a time when El Olivo is a forgotten town and the house of prostitution is a house in ruins; and the past, when El Olivo held the promise of a bustling town and the brothel was at its center. La Manuela's role in the house was defined when La Japonesa, La Japonesita's mother and madam of the brothel, was still alive. By virtue of having been Don Alejo's favorite prostitute in her younger years and a friend during the years of his most active political life, La Japonesa was able to build a booming business in the town. La Japonesa brought La Manuela and other flashy prostitutes for a special celebration in honor of Don Alejo's successful senatorial election. The prostitutes left, but La Manuela stayed. Eventually, Don Alejo bet La Japonesa that she couldn't get La Manuela to make love to her. La Japonesa answered that she could, but that she wanted ownership of the house if she won the bet. La Japonesa convinced a reluctant La Manuela by promising to give him a partnership in the business. La Japonesa won the bet, and La Japonesita was born of that union. Out of the arrangement, La Manuela gained the security of having his own place, of being his own boss, of not having to roam aimlessly from town to town looking for shows: "y así, proprietaria, nadie podrá echarla, porque la casa sería suya. Podría mandar" (87) [and that way, as a proprietress, no one could throw her out, because the house would be hers. She could give orders (197)].

La Manuela's security is grounded in his ability to perform contrasting roles: male-female, father-transvestite. The male role is one that he chooses not to play, it has been imposed on him by Don Alejo's controlling gaze. In order to ascertain that La Japonesa would not fool the senator, he insisted on watching the lovemaking scene through a window:

[D]on Alejo mirándome, mirándonos, nosotros retorciéndonos, anudados y sudorosos para complacerlo porque él nos mandó hacerlo para que lo divirtiéramos y sólo así nos daría esta casa de adobe, de vigas mordidas por los ratones, y ellos, los que miran, don Alejo y los otros que se ríen de nosotros, no oyen lo que la Japonesa Grande me dice muy despacito al oído, mijito, es rico, no tenga miedo, si no vamos a hacer nada, si es la pura comedia. (107–8)

Don Alejo watching me, watching us writhe, knotted together and sweating to humor him because he ordered it and this is the only way he'll give us this adobe house with its rat-gnawed beams, and those watching, don Alejo and the others who are laughing at us, don't hear what Big Japonesa is slowly saying in my ear, this is so sweet, honey boy, don't be afraid, we won't do anything, it's just an act. (209–10)

La Manuela's self-definition in a partnership where he shares as much of the profit as the other member, La Japonesa, is based on pure theater, on being the object of the gaze of someone who will pay dearly to see this particular show (Don Alejo was quite sorry to have to give up his house).

All social relationships in El Olivo are based on terms of inequality. La Manuela's partnership with La Japonesa favors the latter; not only is she the madam of the brothel but she also bases the arrangement with the transvestite on deceit. When trying to convince La Manuela to participate in the bet, La Japonesa insists that he does not have to perform sexually, that they just have to deceive the men who are watching from a distance. But when the time comes to perform in bed, she actually seduces him by playing the male role and encouraging him to accept a female role: "[Y]o te estoy haciendo gozar porque yo soy la macha y tú la hembra" (109) [I'm making you like it because I'm the man and you're the woman (210)]. La Japonesa has acted like a director in a play and solicited a masterful performance on stage. Like an actor, when La Manuela assumes the female role, he forgets himself and performs as a man. For La Manuela, "la pura comedia" brings him back to his rejected self so that he literally puts on an act when his male sexuality surfaces. La Manuela's life is a constant performance, and much more so when he is called to act as a man and a father.

When La Japonesita calls on him to play the protective role of the father against Pancho's threats, La Manuela first recoils, but then resurfaces as the accomplished performer that he is. Evasion of one role forces the donning of another. Pancho has come back to town threatening to violate both La Japonesita and La Manuela. Even though Don Alejo advises him to leave them alone, Pancho defies his command after having paid the debt. Throughout the novel, because of Pancho's penchant for violence, both father and daughter fear for their lives. Eventually, the daughter asks the father to protect her: "—Usted me tiene que defender si viene Pancho" (49) ["You have to protect me if Pancho comes" (174)]. At moments like that, La Manuela loses his aplomb, and the poor reality that he inhabits comes tumbling down on him and transforms the supposedly beautiful flamenco dress into a pile of rags:

> Porque cuando la Japonesita le decía papá, su vestido de española tendido encima del lavatorio se ponía más viejo, la percala gastada, el rojo desteñido, los zurcidos a la vista, horrible, ineficaz. (50)

> Because when Japonesita called him father, the flamenco dress over the washstand looked older, the percale threadbare, the red faded, the stitches showing, horrible, inane. (175)

When Pancho approaches, La Manuela runs the other way, but the memory of her conception brings him back from the chicken coop where he had retreated. He comes to the rescue of his daughter by assuming his feminine dancing persona:

> La Manuela avanza a través del patio entallándose el vestido. Tan flaca, por Dios, a nadie le voy a gustar, sobre todo porque tengo el vestido embarrado y las patas embarradas y se quita una hoja de parra que se le pegó en el barro del talón y avanza hasta la luz y antes de entrar escucha oculta detrás de la puerta, mientras se persigna como las grandes artistas antes de salir a la luz. (112–13)

> La Manuela walks across the patio smoothing her dress against her body. So skinny, dear God, no one's going to like me especially with my stained dress and muddy feet and she removes a vine leaf clinging to the muck on her heel and goes toward the light and before she goes in she hides behind the door, listening, while she makes the sign of the cross as all great artists do before walking into the light. (212–13)

As he advances, there is a transformation of the character so that the ugly reality of his body and dress becomes annulled and the gesture of making the sign of the cross, like a true artist, brings out the actor in him. The two scenes of conception and sacrifice are juxtaposed, the former appearing as a flashback, to bring out the contrasts between the two.[27]

In order to perform like a father, La Manuela must once again assume a female role. If the transvestite was able to conceive his daughter only because La Japonesa had brought out the female in him, now he will be able to save his daughter, and literally save her life, by becoming the feminine victim himself. This time, the aggressor is played by Pancho and not by a female:

Pancho, de pronto, se ha callado mirando a la Manuela. A eso que baila allí en el centro, ajado, enloquecido, con la respiración arrítmica, todo cuencas, oquedades, sombras quebradas, eso que va a morir a pesar de las exclamaciones que lanza, eso increíblemente asqueroso y que increíblemente es fiesta, eso está bailando para él, él sabe que desea tocarlo y acariciarlo, desea que ese retorcerse no sea sólo allá en el centro sino contra su piel, y Pancho se deja mirar y acariciar desde allá . . . el viejo maricón que baila para él y él se deja bailar y que ya no da risa porque es como si él, también, estuviera anhelando. Que Octavio no sepa. No se dé cuenta. Que nadie se dé cuenta. (126)

Pancho suddenly becomes quiet watching la Manuela. Watching that thing dancing in the center of the room, all eye sockets, hollows, spasmodic shadows, that thing which is going to die despite its cries, that incredibly repulsive thing that, incredibly, is the party, and dances for him, he knows he aches to touch it and caress it, he doesn't want that writhing thing to be alone there in the center but against his skin, and Pancho lets himself watch and caress from a distance that old queer who is dancing for him and he surrenders to her dance, and now it isn't funny anymore because it's as if he too were gasping for breath. Octavio mustn't know. He can't know. No one must know. (220–21)

The dance floor turns La Manuela into an object of Pancho's gaze ("eso que baila" [that thing dancing]), into an object of desire and an object of wrath ("eso que va a morir a pesar de las exclamaciones que lanza" [that thing which is going to die despite its cries]). But that object of desire dares to look back, and the gesture of looking back objectifies Pancho and puts him in a problematic space. If Pancho is desired by La Manuela, and he in turn desires La Manuela, he too is a homosexual, a possibility that scares and threatens him: "Que nadie se dé cuenta" [No one must know]. This exchange of the gaze makes them equals, two subjects free to transcend sexual boundaries, and that is not acceptable in El Olivo. Octavio notices that Pancho is being receptive to La Manuela's advances:

La Manuela se inclinó hacia Pancho y trató de besarlo en la boca mientras reía. Octavio lo vio y soltó a la Manuela.
—Ya pues compadre, no sea maricón usted también . . .
Pancho también soltó a la Manuela.
—Si no hice nada . . .
—No me vengas con cuestiones, yo vi . . . (129)

La Manuela swayed toward Pancho and tried to kiss his mouth while he laughed. Octavio saw it and let go of la Manuela.
"Come on, pal, don't you be a fag too . . ."
Pancho also let go of la Manuela.
"I didn't do a thing . . ."
"No excuses, I saw . . ." (222–23)

To allow a transgression of the masculine code is tantamount to being an accomplice, at least from Octavio's point of view. The act of seeing, on Octavio's part, reinstitutes a polarity between men and not-men that had been erased during the performance. If in the scene of conception, La Manuela had easily adopted the female role to perform the male sexual act, he had done it in a much safer frame of reference; after all, La Japonesa was a woman, even though she played the role of the man in the seduction. Ultimately they were a man and a woman together in bed performing for the pleasure of others. In this scene, however, the sexual equality of the actors presents a violation of clearly prescribed male roles in a highly stratified society. Within this context there is no room for transgression. La Manuela's trespass was to have dared to look back, and in so doing, he made Pancho into an object of desire, thus robbing him of his male subjectivity. As a result, La Manuela, as female, is violently raped by the men and left to be ravaged by Don Alejo's dogs.

For La Manuela, "el lugar sin límites" is the scene of performance, the only place and time where, through the exercise of returning a gaze, he can become a subject. For Donoso, the scene of sexual performance becomes the scene of novelistic conception in which, for the first time, gender and subjectivity become confused and interchanged so that what is being highlighted is not individual integrity, but rather the dispersal of individuality through loss of pronominal fixation:

> Yo [La Manuela] soñaba mis senos acariciados, y algo sucedía mientras ella me decía sí mijita, yo [La Japonesa] te estoy haciendo gozar porque yo [La Japonesa] soy la macha y tú la hembra. (109)

> I [La Manuela] dreamed about my breasts being caressed and something happened while she [Big Japonesa] was saying, yes little girl, I'm [Big Japonesa] making you like it because I'm [Big Japonesa] the man and you're the woman." (210)

The confusion of sexual roles at the theatrical level is mirrored at the grammatical level in a game where one subject can easily be lost in the other. The personal pronoun *yo* loses its specificity and erases all differences. This loss of differentiation is allowed within a scene neatly demarcated by a window frame and explicitly defined as the spectacle of

58

entertainment. What transpires within that frame, inside a house of prostitution, stands as symbolic of Donoso's act of representation itself, a time and a place, which like hell, has no limits.[28] In Donoso's novel, hell is used as a paradoxical metaphor. A dramatic scene under the watchful eye of a powerful audience (Don Alejo), and with the prescribed limits of La Japonesa's bedroom (the site of prostitution), allows for multiple transformations within the frame of licensed behavior (licensed because prescribed). Under the light of spectacle, transgression is sanctioned; La Manuela can play both male and female sexual roles and not pay with his life. Outside that frame, he is exposed to society's unrelenting rules.

Because La Manuela dares to play the games of sexual nondifferentiation outside the confines of the house, of the theatrical space, he exposes himself to Octavio's interpretation based on the prevalent social mores. Outside the scene of dramatic representation, there is in this novel a space that still serves to expose the enduring, rigid social system of a landed elite. *El lugar sin límites* records a small victory of the working class over the power of the landowner. Octavio dares to look back at Don Alejo and in doing so allows Pancho to act as an agent in his own life, rather than as a subservient object. The novel ends with a defeated and dying Don Alejo. Before he is ready to succumb, however, he unleashes the power of his black dogs. The violence inbred in these animals contaminates Pancho and Octavio as they perpetuate the same male dominance with the persistence of the controlling gaze.[29] Because Octavio saw a forbidden exchange that implicated a male participant (Pancho), there had to be an object of victimization, a scapegoat. In victimizing La Manuela, Octavio merely perpetuates Don Alejo's gesture of humiliation over Pancho. If a character like La Manuela is to transcend, he will do so only under the dramatic light of ambiguous performance. Within the clearly demarcated space of theatrical scenes there is room for boundless transformation, but the context of social stratification endures outside those boundaries with its rigid definitions of gender and class. Ultimately, *El lugar sin límites* stands out as the first novel in which Donoso has made an unambiguous statement about class confrontation while simultaneously upholding a sexually ambiguous dramatic representation.

In *El lugar sin límites* the gaze is a controlling function of the ruling class and the patriarchal system, in *El obsceno pájaro de la noche* (1970) it is also the sign for existential definition and the creative process. Identity in this novel is contingent on being seen. Mudito, the deaf-mute narrator of most of the novel, starts as a nonentity based on his lack of visibility:

No me mirabas. No me veías. Estoy acostumbrado a ser una presencia sobre la que los ojos se resbalan sin que la atención encuentre nada en qué fijarse. ¿Por qué me seguías, entonces, si ni siquiera me ibas a conceder existencia con una mirada? (76)

You never looked at me. You didn't see me. I'm used to eyes sliding over me without finding anything to fix on. Why did you follow me, then, if you didn't mean to acknowledge my existence by so much as a glance? (58)

Although in this particular quotation, the protagonist wishes to be noticed by Iris Mateluna, the only person in the convent who is capable of procreation, it is in relation to the patriarchal figure of Don Jerónimo that Humberto Peñaloza (later to become Mudito) wishes to define himself.[30]

Don Jerónimo is a desirable model because he is from the upper class, appears often in the tabloids, and by virtue of his name, commands respect in political circles. All through his childhood Humberto's father had pointed out to him the figures of high society so that his son could emulate them: "[M]e enseñó a reconocer a esos caballeros bigotudos reclinados junto a damas fabulosas que para mis ojos de niño eran manchas fugaces bajo sombrillas rosa o color limón" (103) [He taught me to recognize those mustachioed gentlemen reclining alongside fabulous ladies who, to my childish eyes, were fleeting blurs beneath pink or lemon parasols (79)]. At a young age, the child was taught the art of looking, of envying a position that would probably be out of reach. One day, Humberto picked out the figure of Don Jerónimo from the crowd and his life became determined:

> Entonces, al mirarlo a usted, don Jerónimo, un boquete de hambre se abrió en mí y por él quise huir de mi propio cuerpo enclenque para incorporarme al cuerpo de ese hombre que iba pasando, ser parte suya aunque no fuera más que su sombra, incorporarme a él, o desgarrarlo entero, descuartizarlo para apropiarme de todo lo suyo, porte, color, seguridad para mirarlo todo sin miedo porque no necesitaba nada, no sólo lo tenía todo, sino que era todo. (104–5)

> Then, as I watched you, Don Jerónimo, a gap of hunger opened in me and I wanted to escape through it from my own puny body and merge with the body of that man who was passing by, to become part of him, even if I were only his shadow, to merge with him or tear him apart completely, to dismember him and appropriate everything of his—his bearing, his coloring, the self-assurance with which he looked at everything without fear because he needed nothing, because not only did he have everything but he was everything. (80)

Don Jerónimo, the possessor of all that is enviable, could be appropriated by the certainty of the gaze, a gaze that the child does not control, but that he recognizes as the defining factor in being that "all" that Don Jerónimo represents.

If the first step toward becoming is the recognition that one must possess a self-assured gaze, the next must be to acquire it. And since Humberto Peñaloza lacks all the attributes—ancestry, wealth, beauty—that ensure that acquisition, he must become Don Jerónimo himself. Humberto is hired to write a chronicle of the Azcoitía family, and as a consequence, he is constantly by the side of Don Jerónimo. Keenly aware that "being somebody" depends on one's ability to see and be seen, Humberto Peñaloza robs his master of his identity when the secretary is confused with Don Jerónimo by a crowd of voters. In a northern region of the country where the candidate could not count on the radical vote, the ballots are stolen, and Don Jerónimo has to go in front of a hostile crowd: "Se quedó mirándolos desde lo alto de las gradas" (198) [He stared at them from the top of the steps (160)]. The people, who keep demanding to know about the ballots, cannot believe that the candidate would appear before them and pretend that all is normal. The crowd becomes uncontrolled, and Don Jerónimo and Humberto Peñaloza flee through the church door, knowing a car will be ready for them if they climb the rooftops on the other side of the church. Humberto climbs ahead, and seeing the opportunity to act as the supposed brave candidate facing the crowd, he stands up on the roof and begins to scream at them; a shot rings out, and Humberto falls wounded. The crowd believes that Don Jerónimo has fallen. The would-be senator later maintains this illusion when he walks out into the square as if he had been shot:

La crónica no registra mi grito porque mi voz no se oye. Mis palabras no entraron en la historia. Pero alguien me señaló. Mil ojos vieron a don Jerónimo de Acoitía sobre el tejado. Sonó el disparo. Mil testigos me vieron encogerme con el dolor de la bala que me rozó el brazo justo aquí, Madre Benita, en el lugar donde años antes me había rozado el guante perfecto de don Jerónimo. La cicatriz se me pone dura como un nudo, sangrienta como un estigma. ¿Cómo no va a quedarme la marca que me recuerda que mil ojos, anónimos como los míos, fueron testigos que yo soy Jerónimo de Azcoitía? Yo no me robé su identidad. Ellos me la confirieron. (204–5)

There's no historical record of my shout, because my voice made no sound. My words didn't pass into history. But someone pointed me out. A thousand eyes saw Don Jerónimo de Azcoitía on the roof. The shot rang out. A thousand witnesses watched me double up with pain from the bullet that grazed my arm right here, Mother Benita, on the spot Don Jerónimo's perfect glove had grazed years before. The scar's getting hard like a knot, bloody like a stigma. How could I still not bear the brand that reminds me that a thousand eyes as anonymous as mine were witnesses that I'm Jerónimo de Azcoitía? I didn't steal his identity. They conferred it on me. (166)

For once in his life, Humberto Peñaloza is the recipient of an admiring gaze; he can speak the words that important people speak, even if they are not heard; he can nurse the wound that marks that moment of stardom that will never be repeated:

> La gran pena de mi vida, Madre Benita, es que el único momento estelar, el único en que he sido protagonista y no comparsa—ese breve momento en que don Jerónimo y el párroco rajaron mi manga y curaron mi herida—, lo pasé inconsciente. (205)

> The great sorrow of my life, Mother Benita, is that my only starring moment, the only one in which I was the lead and not an extra—that brief moment when Don Jerónimo and the parish priest ripped my sleeve and treated my wound—occurred while I was unconscious. (167)

Humberto Peñaloza's stellar moment is not a conscious one, he could not even be present when Don Jerónimo and the priest treated his wound and smeared his blood on the master's arm so that the candidate could be the one to appear wounded. By virtue of standing in for Don Jerónimo, Humberto Peñaloza becomes the senator. Conversely, by virtue of robbing him of his blood, Don Jerónimo becomes intermingled with him. Characters interchange identities in a melodramatic reversal, and a grand, silent gesture before an observing public brings a lowly figure the status of the greats. But only Humberto Peñaloza knows of this theatrically ochestrated reversal. Always ready to seize a good opportunity, Don Jerónimo masterfully plays the role of the brave, and now wounded, victim. Even though Humberto was capable of playing the role of his master, he was soon upstaged by his more experienced counterpart who went on to win the elections because of a convincing, compelling performance.

Since Humberto Peñaloza cannot be the object of the public's gaze for very long, he effects a reversal and describes himself as the possessor of the gaze: "[L]os testigos son los que poseen la fuerza" (254) and "[M]e redujo a lo que soy, apoderándose del ochenta por ciento y dejando el viente, reducido y enclenque, centrado alrededor de mi mirada" (332) [(W)itnesses are the ones who have power (205)] and [He also reduced me to what I am, confiscating eighty and leaving twenty percent, shrunken and decrepit, centered on my look (263)].[31] In order to hide the insignificance of his being and emphasize the power of his gaze, the defeated Humberto Peñaloza disappears in the convent as a deaf-mute; his new persona cancels the voice that he knows to be ineffective and concentrates on his power to define personality via the dramatization of the gaze. The scene that best exemplifies this subsuming of voice to the power of the gaze is when Mudito wears the papier-mâché head of the Giant in order to enjoy the services of Gina, the neighborhood prostitute, who is also

Iris, an orphan at the convent where Mudito resides. The Giant's head allows for the interchangeability of all who wear it and is instrumental in Mudito's ability to perform a role, such as that of a dandy, which permits him to make love to Iris. Many critics have already noted the importance of this passage regarding the emptying out of pronominal referents in the novel.[32] What concerns me here, however, is that when Mudito wears the mask there is a coincidence of voice and gaze so that the two become one:

> Me la pones por encima, ritualmente, como el obispo mitrado coronando al rey, anulando con la nueva investidura toda existencia previa, todas, el Mudito, el secretario de don Jerónimo, el perro de la Iris, Humberto Peñaloza el sensible prosista que nos entrega en estas tenues páginas una visión tan sentida y artística del mundo desvanecido de antaño cuando la primavera de la inocencia florecía en jardines de glicinas, la séptima bruja, todos nos disolvimos en la oscuridad de adentro de la máscara. No veo. Ahora, además de carecer de voz, no tengo vista, pero no, aquí hay una ranura en el cuello del Gigante, por donde tengo que ir mirando. A nadie se le va a ocurrir buscar mis ojos en la garganta de este fantoche de cartonpiedra. (90)

> You put it over me, as if going through a ritual, like a mitered bishop crowning the king, eradicating with this investiture each of my previous existences, every one of them: Mudito; Don Jerónimo's secretary; Iris's dog; Humberto Peñaloza, the sensitive prose writer who offers us in these simple pages, such a deeply felt and artistic vision of the vanished world of yesterday, when the springtime of innocence blossomed in the wisteria gardens; the seventh witch. All of us dissolved in the darkness inside the mask. I can't see. Now, besides lacking a voice, I'm sightless, but no, there's a slot here in the Giant's neck to see through. No one will think of looking for my eyes in this papier-maché puppet's throat. (67)

Being, with its multiple manifestations (he is the deaf-mute, the secretary of Don Jerónimo, the servant of Iris, the seventh witch, and Humberto Peñaloza, the producer of melodramatic narratives), is here represented by the Giant's mask, a persona that stands for male potency of performance, as well as for the male sexual organ itself.[33] Behind its exaggerated countenance, this mask offers the possibility of producing a voice through visual means and of translating insignificant reality into heightened representation. By allowing this coincidence ("mis ojos en la garganta" [my eyes in this ... throat]), the novel offers that moment of royal initiation ("como el obispo mitrado coronando al rey" [mitered bishop crowning the king]) when a male power figure becomes the producer of a visual voice. The hollow head is a perfect metaphor for novelistic language, allowing multiple sources of identification to occur at the same time that it is projecting narrative voice through visual forms of representation.

Mudito, the deaf-mute and now self-appointed creator of a multiple persona, has achieved mastery by fashioning a voice out of his ability to manipulate the gaze. His mastery points to a limited capacity to displace the central character in a drama (Don Jerónimo) and replace him with a marginal one (Humberto Peñaloza). But for such a substitution to have permanence, it must be clothed in hyperbole (the Giant's head), a fragile yet useful countenance under which either a marginal character such as himself or a principal actor such as Don Jerónimo can have sexual inter-course with Iris Metaluna, the neighborhood prostitute (96–97; 72–73). Like *El lugar sin límites,* this novel creates a scene of grotesque sexual performance that depends on masks, role reversals, and an audience. When Don Jerónimo dons the head of the Giant and tries to make love to Iris, he finds himself impotent. It is not until the gaze of Humberto Peñaloza, the servant, enters the scene through the window that Don Jeró-nimo succeeds in his performance:

> Hoy sí, porque yo le permito que vea mi rostro encuadrado en la venta-nilla del auto, y el dolor de mis ojos mirándolo, el dolor que sigue habi-tando mis pupilas: Por eso [Don Jerónimo] pudo hacer aullar de placer a la Iris Mateluna. (98)

> Today you can, because I allow you to see my face framed in the window of the car, to see the torture in my eyes as I watch you, the torture that still inhabits the pupils of my eyes; that's why you were able to make Iris Mateluna scream with pleasure. (74)

This scene is not unlike the scene in the house of prostitution in El Olivo where a monster, La Japonesita, ("Era un fenómeno" [She was a freak] translation mine) is conceived by the power of Don Alejo's gaze.[34] Here, however, the roles have been switched, inverted, so that now it is the lowly character, Humberto Peñaloza/Mudito, who lends his gaze to empower the senator.[35] The fruit of this sexual encounter will eventually be another incarnation of Mudito himself, an old man-child who will save the old women in the convent (see my discussion in the next chapter). This reversal of the observer, from powerful figure to subservient one, traces a spiral movement of displacement from one novel to the other, so that now the act of visual representation, coincident with that of sexual performance (still framed by a window), is under the supervision of a many-named creator. With this inversion of the power relations, Donoso gives birth to a narrator expert in the art of displacement and hidden under the mask of a monstrous production. The power of the gaze has now paradoxically been transformed into narrative voice: "mis ojos en la garganta" [my eyes in this . . . throat].

With *El obsceno pájaro de la noche* Donoso perfects narrative techniques that were instituted in his first novel. The most notable and persistent of these is the setting of a discrete scene that is clearly demarcated by an agent in order to establish a sense of mastery. But mastery is an elusive condition, a constant struggle that demands an ever changing point of view, so that the narrator must refashion new frames of reference and invariably readjust the focus of the gaze in order to go beyond the previously conceived scene.

The analysis undertaken thus far began by delineating the "primal" scene in Donoso's production: the scene of mastery over language and imagination. Mastery is based on the repetition of an original event with the purpose of transforming and transcending it via the establishment of a distancing process. In Donoso's works, distance is achieved through exaggerated gesture and the framing magnification of visual constructs, as clearly demonstrated in the study of "Santelices." At the thematic level, *Coronación* stands as an ironic rendering of a melodramatic plot. The novel transcends a series of dichotomies (master-servant, evil-good, reason-madness) by deviating from binary oppositions and ushering in scenes of displacement. Already in this novel, we find an alternative form of mastery as actualized by feminine agents of dramatization. This form of mastery, which emphasizes the play on words and a taste for the vernacular of popular melodrama, contrasts with a male ordering and patriarchal control that quickly loses leverage. Finally, as with *El lugar sin límites* and *El obsceno pájaro de la noche,* Donoso skilfully combines a presentation of social concerns that record the disintegration of a bourgeois mentality with its insistence on a unified sense of self and a morality based on hierarchical priorities, with a marked focus on the ambiguity inherent in narrative language and its capacity to represent a multiplicity of stances and points of view.

As I will demonstrate in the chapter that follows, Donoso's penchant for the framing of the gaze and the setting of scenes progressively erodes the traditional definition of the omniscient male narrator and his capacity to create his own scene of origins. Even though there is a strong relation between mastery and the male agent of the creative process, there are already signs that feminine attributes of the imagination are equally as essential to the formulation of narrative discourse. This concept of a feminine imagination is prevalent both in *Coronación* and *El lugar sin límites.* Donoso's idiom begins by setting up binary oppositions but always moves toward a synthesis and a transcending of polarities. Thus far, I have emphasized a drive to express and expose either the repressed or the forbidden through a heightened dramatic form of representation. Expressionism, as I have portrayed it in these works, moves toward revelation in its use of hyperbole and overstatement. At the same time, there is a countering force that veils and silences, displacing any real possibility of discovering the "truth" hidden behind the many stage curtains. The use of spectacle distracts from the production of meaning so that signification in the novel is constantly delayed by a repetition of scenes that culminate in a final gesture. The illustration of this process finds its ultimate realization in *El obsceno pájaro de la noche.*

2

Battles between Oral Tradition and Theatrical Representation in *El obsceno pájaro de la noche*

La Casa de Ejercicios Espirituales [The House of Spiritual Exercises] in *El obsceno pájaro de la noche* (1970) constitutes a chaotic space wherein characters forge their lives by telling stories that constantly discredit each other. All the characters involved tell lies in order to gain power in the hierarchy within the dilapidated convent and to overcome their own impotence and the sterile environment they inhabit.

In the first five pages of the novel, Donoso introduces three voices who will tell different versions of the legend of the girl-witch and the girl-saint: a third person omniscient narrator; a collective voice of a group of gossiping old women; and a first person singular narrative belonging to Mudito, the protagonist. The collective voice spins out stories and fragments in a continuous but disordered fashion while Mudito's mute "voice" is governed by a compulsion to order and make clear the contradictory stories of the women.[1] Mudito evolves into many forms. He is the attentive listener and observer who motivates the women to represent their stories in dramatic form within the confines of the house, under his direction. Concurrently, he records an original and comprehensible version of the tales that the women weave in a fragmented manner. His record, a culmination of listening, ordering, retelling, and dramatizing, produces a manuscript that is the synecdoche of *El obsceno pájaro de la noche.* This record is a story, not only of the servant's growth as a character from a lowly mute to a master of ceremonies but also of the growth of the narrative from a chaotic, contradictory beginning to an enduring and coherently written record.

The Casa, the metaphorical space in which all narration takes place, is itself contradictory in nature.[2] It was built as a convent in the nineteenth century by the Azcoitía family in order to house a female descendant of holy, but nevertheless questionable, character. Since then, many sections have been added to the convent so that its halls and floors resemble a complicated labyrinth that only Mudito understands:

> [E]ste edificio creció tanto y tan anárquicamente que ya nadie recuerda, y quizá sólo a la pobre Inés le interesa saber, cuál fue el sector inicial, los patios primitivos destinados a encerrar a la hija del fundador. (49)

> [T]his structure has grown so much and so erratically that no one remembers now, and perhaps only poor Inés is interested in finding out, which section went up first, which the original courts destined to confine the founder's daughter. (36)

At the same time that this house has grown uncontrollably through the centuries, it has stayed the same: "Sin embargo esta Casa se conserva igual, con la persistencia de las cosas inútiles" (53) [And yet, this place remains the same, and all the uselessness persists (39)]. The house, then, defines itself according to its ability to proliferate and its tendency to remain the same despite its many transformations. Like the house, Donoso's novel will expand, ruled by the anarchic multiplication of fragmented tales, and remain the same, as Mudito molds and directs those tales according to his own structuring design. *El obsceno pájaro de la noche* undergoes many transformations from beginning to end; this study will address those transformations at three levels: the physical level of the house itself, with Mudito as the keeper of the keys and master of it; the narrative level, which addresses the development of the oral tale surrounding the Azcoitía girl for whom the convent was built; and the textual level, which encompasses several modes of narration including the oral, written, and dramatic forms of representation.

The manuscript that Mudito hides under his bed consists initially of tales, bits of news, and gossip, which the women tell while sitting around the warmth of their kitchen stove. Already at the outset of the novel, the omniscient narrator describes the oral nature of the women's telling: "[L]a Madre Benita la llamó por teléfono para *contarle* que la Brígida había amanecido muerta" (11, emphasis mine) [Mother Benita called up *to tell her* that Brígida had died in her sleep (3, emphasis mine)]. An oral narration also necessarily implies an audience. At the beginning of the novel, Madre Benita speaks and Misiá Raquel Ruiz listens. This narrative includes the story of Brígida's death and funeral as told by Madre Benita, but it also tells of Misiá Raquel's fears about her death and her plans for her own funeral and burial. The conversation exchanges one death for the other as it alternates speakers, each presumably not listening to the other. Rather than dialogue, we have two women talking about the same subject but only addressing their individual experience of it. Madre Benita talks about Brígida's death and Misiá Raquel prepares for her own. Further, with these conversations that anticipate death and invoke the fears surrounding the event, Donoso foreshadows Mudito's death, a death that will close the novel.

Given the deteriorating nature of the Casa, the women within it constantly worry about carving out their own space that cannot be taken away from them. This obsession is even extended to the struggle for a physical space in which to be buried.[3] Before the servant Brígida dies, Misiá Raquel Ruiz promises that Brígida will be buried in the spacious Ruiz mausoleum. Misiá Raquel's supposed generosity merely hides the mistress's own fear of death. She wants Brígida's body to warm her niche so that her bones will not be cold and afraid:

> [P]ara cumplir con mi promesa le cedí mi nicho en el mausoleo para que ella se vaya pudriendo en mi lugar, calentándome el nicho con sus despojos para que los míos, cuando desalojen a los suyos, no se entumezcan, no sientan miedo. (15)

> [T]o keep my word, I gave up my vault in the mausoleum for her to start rotting in my place, keeping it warm for me with her remains so that when they take them out mine won't get numb, won't be afraid. (6)

Misiá Raquel uses her generosity to mask her fear that someone else in the family will steal her resting place. Since Brígida is a faithful servant, she will duly "relinquish" her place and Misiá Raquel's remains will ultimately reside in the tomb. One body displaces another just as one subject of conversation substitutes for another; the telling of Brígida's death loses importance and Misiá Raquel's fear of losing her resting place becomes the center of attention in its place. The ultimate issue, a space for death, closes the conversation.

The displacement of narrators that characterizes the women's stories creates a shifting narration that ignores syntactical ordering and passes freely from one topic of conversation to another. Such shifting often results in the confusion of pronominal referents[4] and constitutes an incessant play at the linguistic level interrupted occasionally by the third person omniscient narrator who replaces syntactical chaos with a well-ordered paragraph that describes the women's rhetoric as "la retórica anticuada pero conmovedora de la Madre Benita" (12) [Mother Benita's archaic but still touching rhetoric (4)].[5] Displacement permeates the novel at various levels. At the physical level, one body replaces another; at the pronominal level, one female voice substitutes for another; and at the syntactical level, varying subjects of conversation link metonymic chains to produce endless paragraphs. These forms of displacement persist always in relation to the women's narration. The male voice, represented by the omniscient narrator and by Mudito, orders, frames, and channels the women's seemingly endless chatter. The play of substitutions that opens the novel is stopped by Mudito's intervention. It is he who closes off the women's first scene of telling with an authorial gesture: "Yo cierro el portón con tranca y llave" (16) [I bolt and lock the outside door (7)]. The entire structure of the novel will consist in just such a play of substitutions of narrative voices, one usurping the other, until Mudito's ashes figuratively fill the last space in the novel. The uttering of any narrative voice thus results from a struggle to secure a space for death and "telling."[6] This activity warms the bodies of the women who listen endlessly around the kitchen stove in the Casa.

Just as the omniscient narrator serves the function of demarcating the women's conversation and commenting on the nature of their rhetoric, so Mudito serves the same purpose from the point of view of a first person narrator. Chapter two signals the moment when Mudito's voice appears so as to establish a new order and offer his commentary on the women's tale telling. He makes the situation clear: there are six old ladies and one orphan (Iris Mateluna) who sit around the kitchen table to gossip and tell stories. Mudito sits away from them to establish a distance between teller and listener: "Yo me sentaba un poco más allá en la misma mesa" (34) [I used to sit farther down at the same table (23)]. Mudito's supposed deaf-muteness and his distance immediately classify him as a privileged listener.[7] At the table he pretends to be deaf and asleep; because of that, he will hear more than the women would choose to utter in the presence of any other man. Mudito's listening constitutes a trespass upon the women's circle of narration. He stays outside yet penetrates that circle with a false silence that will allow him to hear the privileged telling and to appropriate it as his own. In chapter two, it is not the women who tell the story but Mudito as mediator, who tells it as he heard it: "Esa noche, no me acuerdo cuál de ellas, repetía más o menos este cuento" (35) [That night one of the women, I can't remember who, was telling a story that went more or less like this (23)]. The tale as told by Mudito consists of his own synthesis of the many versions that he has heard evening after evening; the structure of the tale follows the conventions of telling. It begins with the "Erase una vez" (35) [*Once upon a time* (23)], then goes on with a chronological description of the main characters placed in a specific time and place, and finally closes with a resolution of the problem posed in the telling. At the end, Mudito frames his story by repeating:

Dije que esa noche en la cocina, las viejas, no me acuerdo cuál de ellas, da lo mismo, estaban contando más o menos esta conseja, porque la he oído tantas veces y en versiones tan contradictorias que todas se confunden. (43)

I was telling how in the kitchen that night the old women were telling this story, *more or less.* I can't recall which of the women it was, because I've heard it so many times and in such contradictory versions that it becomes confused in my mind, but it's all the same. (30)

Mudito's task, then, is to order that which he considers to be contradictory and confusing.

Beyond the role of framing and ordering the narrative, Mudito serves as commentator and interpreter. He underlines the variant elements in the many tales and points out what is constant. He synthesizes a tale of a landlord who lived in the eighteenth century and had nine sons and a beautiful young daughter. Since the time of the mother's death at the last birth, the girl was cared for by an aging maidservant who became her constant companion. The landlord owned much land. When drought and sickness beset the region, rumors began that the child and her maid were the cause of all their tragedies. According to the stories, the girl's head flew through the sky each night, following the flight of an old yellow dog, who was the girl's maid. When the father found out about the rumor, he ordered his sons to help find the dog and skin her alive. The sons killed the bitch and the father went into his daughter's room and covered with his poncho a sight that terrified him. He then uncovered the body of the witch who lay transfixed on the bed. The sons tied the witch to a tree and flagellated her, but she did not die. She was then thrown into the river and pursued to the sea where she disappeared. The landlord took the daughter to the city and placed her in a convent, where she remained for the rest of her short life.[8] Several generations of the descendants tried to have the daughter canonized and she became the laughingstock of the city. The convent where the girl was placed is now the nearly condemned house where Mudito and the women live. Both stories converge in the space of Mudito's telling.

As narrator and interpreter, Mudito emphasizes the father's covering gesture (the poncho in front of the door), which creates a blank in the flow of events and allows a displacement. With this authorial gesture, the landlord places the blame on the witch rather than on the noble descendant of the Azcoitía family. The poncho covers the truth. The gesture of displacement turns the witch, an unworthy character, into the protagonist of the tale:

Sólo lo esencial siempre permanece fijo: el amplio poncho paternal cubre una puerta y bajo su discreción escamotea el personaje noble, retirándolo del centro del relato para desviar la atención y la venganza de la peonada hacia la vieja. Esta, un personaje sin importancia igual a todas las viejas, un poco bruja, un poco alcahueta, un poco comadrona, un poco llorona, un poco meica, sirviente que carece de sicología individual y de rasgos propios, sustitutye a la señorita en el papel protagónico de la conseja. (43)

Only the essential facts always stay the same: the father's huge poncho blocks a doorway and, under its discreet cover, he makes the noble daughter vanish, thus removing her from the center of the story in order to shift the attention and vengeance of the farmhands to the old woman. A person of no importance, like all other old women, somewhat of a witch, bawd, midwife, wailer, healer, servant, who seems to lack an individual psychology and characteristics of her own, she takes over the girl's leading part in the story. (30–31)

In the course of Donoso's novel, Mudito will mimic the father's authorial function so that in the space that the house constitutes, he, a nameless servant, will become the protagonist that will close the narrative. As distant listener, narrator, and finally protagonist of his own story, Mudito permeates the space of the novel at several different levels.

Just like Misiá Raquel at the opening of the novel, Mudito seems very concerned about securing spaces in which to voice his narration and in which to die. Mudito would risk his place around the kitchen table as listener if he disobeyed the women's commands. He must therefore remain silent and follow orders from the six women. His greatest fears are of the outside world where the walls of the house will not protect him. Mudito must secure his place free from the external forces outside his domain— the house constitutes his domain because he holds the keys to all the doors, and knows what lies beyond each one. The women, in turn, rely on his knowledge to ease their stay in the dilapidated convent.

In an inversion of the legend of the girl-witch, which was created to produce a scapegoat whose elimination would end the spell of doom over the Azcoitía domain, the women of the house create the child-savior. This infant will free them from the convent so that they may be transferred to a new location where, someone has told them, the city will house them in luxury. In the meantime, Mudito's role as the keeper of keys leads to his assignment of finding a secret place for the newborn savior. The job of finding a place for the child insures a privileged place for Mudito as he becomes the seventh witch in the circle of the six women around the table: "Sólo cuando les dije que había encontrado el lugar justo, un sótano, quedé aceptado y me permitieron ser la séptima bruja" (47) [Only when I told them I'd found just the right place, a cellar, was I accepted and allowed to be the seventh witch (34)]. At the end of chapter two, Mudito objects to a degrading task given to him by the women. Iris, the orphan, has just vomited, and he must clean up after her. They threaten him with expulsion and he consents to the task. The women fuss over the young girl, because according to their latest narration, she is to bear "el niño milagroso" (47) [the miraculous baby (34)] who will come and save them from the misery of their lives. The child will never come because Iris has, in fact, not even matured as a woman. After the telling of the tale of the girl-witch, the women confuse the event of Iris vomiting with the tale that has just been told and create the tale of the child-savior. Mudito suggests that he may be the father of Iris's child; the women laugh at him, yet it is he who secures for them a place in the basement to play out their fantasy.

Displacement is inherent in the women's oral narrative. Mudito notices this disordered linear progression, yet he fixes onto a central image, that of the nursemaid, an insignificant character as protagonist. His gaze, like that of the Azcoitía master, centralizes; the women's voices flow into myriad versions. Chapter two contains the narration of the tale of the girl-witch, introduces its contradictory version, the tale of the girl-saint, and presents the birth of the tale of the savior, a child to be born from the virgin Iris Mateluna. Mudito essentially becomes the director (an authorial father figure) of this tale as he appropriates the space for its production. Since Iris will bear no child savior, Mudito, the only man in the house, plays the protagonist son, now safely at the center of the space that he himself has provided. By listening and remaining silent, Mudito has taken an essential first step toward becoming a narrator. Neither he nor the women can claim to produce an original narration: the women rearrange previously heard facts; Mudito interprets and represents them. Thus far, narration in the novel falls into one of two categories. First, the women tell, and second, Mudito transforms that telling into dramatic representation. The women tell, Mudito shows. This activity of showing rather than telling places Mudito in various roles before the reader's eyes. Mudito merits the public's attention, not only as narrator, but also as protagonist and interpreter.[9]

To have a place from which to speak will entail a struggle: Mudito will not be displaced from the center as easily as Madre Benita was displaced by Misiá Raquel. Mudito is afraid ("¿Por qué mi temor, si yo tengo siempre en mi poder las llaves?" (138) [Why should I be afraid, when I always have all the keys on me? (108–9)]) because the young Iris Mateluna, who plays the virgin mother in the basement of the house (133–48; 104–16), and can be lured into the outside world by the many men who take advantage of her sexually, may reveal his other identity outside of the Casa. Iris threatens to reveal that he can hear and speak, and that he is a man with a name. Mudito's identity as a man threatens the women. They only accept him as the seventh witch as long as he is subservient to them and consents to their every wish. Any attempt on Mudito's part to exercise power necessarily constitutes a subversive action. His desire to manipulate the women's actions and tales must remain hidden from them. By knowing about Mudito's hidden desires, Iris controls him, yet he too exerts some power over her. Mudito restrains Iris from divulging his secrets because he holds the keys and allows her to go out as long as she will come back and play her role. He seduces her by offering her the possibility of a prestigious father for her son (Don Jerónimo, a greatgrandchild of the landlord's). His ultimate fear is that of bringing to light something not completed:

> Iris, te felicito, tu razonamiento me acorrala y me desnuda, exponiéndome a todo porque voy a tener que sacarlo todo de debajo de mi cama, mi voz, mi facultad de oír, mi nombre olvidado, mi sexo aterido, *mis manuscritos inconclusos.* (143, emphasis mine)

> Iris, congratulations, your deduction drives me into a corner and strips me bare, leaving me wide open because I'll have to drag everything out from under my bed—my voice, my hearing , my long-forgotten name, my lifeless sex organ, *my unfinished manuscripts.* (112, emphasis mine)

The manuscripts represent his life after he stopped being Humberto Peñaloza, a man who lived in the outside world, had an insignificant name, and worked for Don Jerónimo Azcoitía. Though merely perceived as a "humble" servant to the family, he was also its biographer. Mudito considers the biography worthless because it refers to the outside world and fails to include him at the center of the narrative. The tale of the child-savior will not only include him as the child but also as the begetter of the same: "Soy Humberto Peñaloza, el padre de tu hijo" (143) [I'm Humberto Peñaloza, the father of your son (112)], he tells Iris. Mudito's fight to remain at the center of the representation constitutes a conscious effort to give birth to his own self, authorial and otherwise. In effect, the tale becomes his fictionalized autobiography.

Why must Mudito remain with the women, within the house? He takes on the mask of the seventh witch because he recognizes the all-encompassing power of longevity that the women's oral tales possess:

> [D]icen, *siguiendo los meandros de los años y quizá los siglos* la repetición de la palabra dicen, quién sabe quién se lo dice y cuándo lo dice y cómo lo dice, pero de decirlo sí lo dicen. (135, emphasis mine)

> *[T]hey say, following the repetition of these words down the meandering years,* or perhaps centuries, that *they say,* who knows who or to whom or when or how, but say they do. (106, emphasis mine)

The women's telling knows no author, because their narration functions on the mechanism of the displacement of one teller by another. Mudito practices a more deliberate version of self-effacement. His voice, his name, his sex, his manuscripts, all lie underneath the bed, surreptitiously controlling and managing the telling and the actions of the women.[10] Only Iris, who represents the demanding reader, questions and sees beyond his masquerade. He becomes the seventh witch, not to be displaced, but rather to gain the central role as child-savior in a tale that he hopes will endure through the years and even perhaps the centuries in the form of his own written rather than oral narration. In the seclusion of the house, Mudito transposes the women's oral tales.[11]

The legend of the girl-witch centers around the father figure who hides an unutterable truth. In this sense, Mudito's muteness recalls the silence of the original authorial figure. In a moment of self-reflection, Mudito interprets what is missing with a question: "Me pregunto si no sería el parto de su hija lo que cubrió el poncho paternal al extenderse por encima de la puerta demasiado grande de la realidad" (359) [I wonder if the father's poncho, spread across the door of a reality that was superior to him, didn't cover his daughter in the pangs of childbirth (287)]. The covering gesture of the father obliterates the reality of a bastard son and replaces it with a legend that endures for two centuries. Mudito's gesture as interpreter of tales will consist in unveiling that reality and in bringing about a new kind of displacement. Mudito's displacement will not remove a character (the bastard son) as the landlord does; rather, he will replace the character of the displaced bastard son with himself. Further, Mudito will substitute his fiction in place of the landlord's. Rather than hide a nameless son to preserve the family name, the interpreter of tales will lose his name to inscribe a persona in the space provided by the father's poncho. So as not to be forgotten, Mudito will leave an image and not just a nickname in the blank left by the women's telling.

Having interpreted the oral, multiple tale, the silent narrator proceeds not with a telling, but with a theatrical representation of his own tale. His tale is of a self-effacement that yields self-begetting. The space for the representation is a site of ruins, a fragmented space. Mudito and the women regret that the auctioneers have emptied out the chapel of the convent, stripping it of its saints and even of its stained glass windows so that: "En los muros de la capilla con las puertas condenadas por cruces de madera quedaron cuatro boquetes enormes" (325) [Four huge gaps were left in the walls of the chapel, whose doors were sealed with crossboards (258)]. Yet it is in this empty space that the women stage the scene of the Virgin with her child. The emptied, condemned space of the chapel constitutes the stage on which the women will play out their fantasies directed by Mudito:

El Mudito insinuó que si el Arzobispo les quitaba sus santos, ellas podían fabricar otros, era el colmo que dejaran la capilla convertida en una barraca. Las asiladas se enorgullecían con sus hallazgos y con sus creaciones. Tuvieron mucho tiempo de entretenimiento en que casi olvidaron a la Iris con su niño, porque esto de armar seres, organizar identidades arbitrarias al pegar trozos con más o menos acierto, era como un juego, y una qué sabe, puede resultar un santo de verdad con estos pedazos que vamos pegando, pero qué importa, para eso está el Mudito que ahora no puede hacer trabajos pesados, él sabe, dibuja facciones en los rostros borrosos, sugiriendo combinaciones de trozos interesantes que a una quizá no se le hubieran ocurrido. (327).

Mudito suggested that if the Archbishop took away their saints, they could put together others, it was the last straw, leaving the chapel turned into a tumbledown shack. The inmates were proud of their finds and of their creations. This became such a pastime that they almost forgot Iris and her child, because putting beings together, assembling arbitrary identities by gluing together fragments that more or less matched, was like a game, and who knows, these pieces we're sticking together may turn out to be a real saint, but what's the difference, that's what Mudito's for, now that he can't do heavy work, he knows how, he sketches features on the blank faces and suggests combinations of interesting pieces that maybe we wouldn't have thought of. . . . (259)

It is not the act of piecing together fragments that gives integrity to the saint, it is rather Mudito's strokes that turn "rostros borrosos" [blank faces] into San Fidel, San Jerónimo, Santa Brígida, and so forth—characters in the women's and Mudito's experience and tales. The names come from different contexts: both exterior to the Casa and from the interior reality.[12]

As the silent narrator, Mudito delineates the characters and privileges each with a name. He transforms the undefined, fragmented bodies into entities capable of repopulating the convent's chapel. Mudito does so with a writing instrument, not just by telling a story about them (329; 261). The women's act of piecing together unlikely saints from all the dismembered ones is not unlike their composition of linear yet disordered tales, stringing together unrelated bits of gossip and old tales to create the tale of the child-savior. The women's tale telling, however, often bores Iris, and she threatens to tell Madre Benita, who would put an end to their games:

Ya pues, estuvo aburrida la fiesta esta noche. Miren cómo le corren los mocos a la guagua. Si no es más divertida la fiesta de mañana, las voy a acusar a la Madre Benita. Ya está bueno. Estoy cansada de pasármelo aquí con la guagua en brazos, vámonos para adentro. Tengo sueño. Quiero acostarme. (326)

That's enough. The party was such a drag tonight. Look at the way the baby's nose is running. If the party isn't a lot more fun tomorrow, I'm going to turn you all in to Mother Benita. I've had enough. I'm sick of sitting here all the time and holding the baby, let's go inside. I'm sleepy. (259)

Even the women are aware that Mudito's suggested dramatic games are a lot more interesting than their tales.

Mudito's sense of order limits him in one respect: he lacks the ability to conjure up "fantasías anárquicas" [anarchic imaginations]. In his own territory, "el patio de él" [his quarters], Mudito furnishes the women with the fragmented pieces and directs them in their disordered activity. He himself cannot enjoy the women's freedom in making combinations. In fact, Mudito became a seventh witch to appropriate the sense of anarchy he lacks: "[V]oy urdiendo algo nacido de la libertad anárquica con que funcionan las mentes de las ancianas de las cuales yo soy una" (138) [I plan something born of the anarchic freedom with which the minds of old women, of whom I'm one (108)]. Mudito's ability to plot entails a usurpation of the women's gift of free association.

After the women fashion their saints, and names are given to them, Mudito proceeds to create the scene originally narrated by the women:

> En el carro del Mudito van llevando sus creaciones para repoblar la capilla vacía, disponiéndolas alrededor de la Iris Mateluna entronada con el niño en brazos [Mudito], rodeándola con una corte apenas vislumbrada a la luz temblorosa de las velas que arden alrededor nuestro, protegido por un baldaquino que infla el viento al entrar por los cuatro boquetes de las ventanas. (329–30)

> They transport their patchwork saints on Mudito's cart and repopulate the empty chapel again, placing the saints around the enthroned Iris Mateluna, with the child in her arms, surrounding her with a court barely discernible in the flickering light of the candles burning around us as we're protected by a canopy that billows with the wind coming in through the four window openings. (262)

The original scene of telling around the warmth of the stove in chapter two is transformed into a theatrical representation under Mudito's silent direction in chapter twenty. He emerges from his marginal position at the table away from the stove by adopting several central roles: those of interpreter, director, and protagonist of the drama. The women's creations, the saints, standing in the semidarkness of the chapel, occupy a marginal space around the Virgin's throne. The candles burn around the figure of the Virgin (Iris) and her child (Mudito), creating a supernatural scene as the wind inflates the canopy where mother and child sit for all to adore.[13]

By displacing the act of narration with physical representation, Mudito repeats the landlord's original gesture by placing a once marginal, insignificant character at the center of the narrative. However, Mudito inverts the "concealing" gesture of the landlord by "revealing" the miracle of a virgin birth, thus exchanging the act of repetition for an act of transformation.

It is clear that narrative discourse in *El obsceno pájaro de la noche* describes an alternating movement of displacement in which modes of narration (telling and showing) exchange places within a chaotic space, the house—a ruined space now transformed into the site of representation. With this game of displacement, the novel erases distinctions between thematic and discursive levels and establishes the convent as a fluid space that will allow all types of anarchic combinations. But it is also true that in all of Donoso's works, houses afford the confined security inside of which the monstrous and the marginal can play out their fantasies. In *El obsceno pájaro de la noche,* there is a second such house: Don Jerónimo's La Rinconada, built to seclude his monstrous son from the outside world. Inside, Boy coexists with other deformed beings and concludes that he leads a normal existence. The character risks ridicule and death outside the house but "acts out" an illusory reality inside. Within La Rinconada, Humberto Peñaloza, Mudito's former self, attempts to record his own life, but is unable to do so. Living within Don Jerónimo's creation cripples and castrates the writer. He is surrounded by monsters such as the manager Emperatriz, who constantly invents tales with the explicit purpose of deceiving Don Jerónimo, the absent master. Since he is unable to control the fictions of Emperatriz and Don Jerónimo, Humberto Peñaloza suffers from writer's block and ultimately flees from La Rinconada to the Casa de Ejercicios Espirituales.

What concerns us here is Donoso's use of the house as a metaphor for the novel that we now read. In the opening paragraphs of "Paseo" ["The Walk"], an earlier short story by Donoso, the house represents a bound volume: "[N]uestra casa está de pie aún, angosta y vertical como un librito apretado entre los gruesos volúmenes de los edificios nuevos" (208) [But our house is still standing, narrow and vertical as a book slipped in between the thick shapes of the new buildings (75)]. If the Casa is the novel, the activities within it signify the modes of narration that characterize Donoso's fiction: telling as an oral account ruled by displacement, and showing as dramatic representation. But neither form is eternal.

The destruction of the house is imminent, and all its inhabitants must prepare for it, including Mudito. The only one who is ready to live outside the confines of the house is Iris, who is eventually thrown out by the women at Mudito's request. Once she has "given birth" to the child-savior (Mudito in his newest guise), Iris can be discarded and the bastard child can come into being. Eventually, even the unprepared orphans and the women will find a place elsewhere, but Mudito must fabricate a new space for himself. The fact that he bears a nickname facilitates his adoption of other masks, such as the seventh witch and the child-savior. But as a male, albeit a child, Mudito threatens the women with his sexuality. Like his name, his identity as a man must also be erased so that he may become the child-savior:

> Comienzan a envolverme, fajándome con vendas hechas con tiras de trapo. Los pies amarrados. Luego me amarran las piernas para que no pueda moverlas. Cuando llegan a mi sexo lo amarran como a un animal dañino, como si adivinaran a pesar de su disfraz infantil que yo lo controlo, no se vaya a saber lo que oculto, y me fajan el sexo amarrándomelo a un muslo para anularlo. Luego me meten en una especie de saco, con los brazos fajados a las costillas, y me amarran en una humita que sólo deja mi cabeza afuera. (335–36)

> They begin to wrap me up, swaddling me in bandages made with strips of old rags. My feet are tied up. Then they bind my legs so I won't be able to move them. When they reach my organ they tie it up like a dangerous animal, as if they guessed, despite its childlike disguise, that I control it—I hope no one even finds out what I'm hiding—and they truss my organ by binding it to my thigh, thus nullifying it. Then they stick me into a kind of sack, with my arms bound to my ribs, and they swaddle me tight, leaving only my head out. (267)

Symbolically, as well as practically, Mudito will lose his domain, and his role as keeper of the keys will vanish, with the disintegration of the house. The crumbling of Donoso's house of fiction coincides with the emasculation and ultimate death of the male, the authorial figure who has supervised all the transformations of its interior spaces.

Although Mudito periodically convinces Íris to untie him by telling her stories that entertain her (338–47; 269–77), he eventually desires to be the fetus that the women have fashioned:

> [Q]uiero ser un imbunche metido dentro del saco de su propia piel, despojado de la capacidad de moverme y de desear y de oír y de leer y de escribir, o de recordar si es que encuentro en mí alguna cosa que recordar. (433)

> I want to be an *imbunche* stuck into the sack of his own skin, stripped of the capacity to move and desire and hear and read and write, or remember, if I can find anything in me to remember. (346)[14]

Mudito desires self-effacement so as not to remember the writer's fears about impotence that plagued him when he was Humberto Peñaloza in

La Rinconada. If he is to reenter a creator's world when the walls of the house crumble, he must do it as a newborn child ("[Iris] Está muy gorda porque yo ya voy a nacer" (436) [She's very fat because I'm going to be born soon (348]).

For Mudito, the wrappings become the layers within Iris's womb: "[E]ste pequeño bulto que soy no tolera más el temor sin salida que lo comprime y me doy cuenta que ha llegado el momento inaplazable. Tengo que nacer" (448) [(T)his small bundle that I am won't be able to stand the terror that provides no way out and compresses it, and I realize that the undelayable moment has arrived. I must be born (358)]. The moment that cannot be deferred is the novel's end; Mudito's time of birth is also his time of death. The house is the place of refuge for Humberto Peñaloza, who isolated himself within its walls to listen to the women's tales—to listen, to write, and not to remember.

When Iris threatens to divulge Mudito's identity, it is the women who protect him and displace his identity once again by turning him into a bastard son:

—No tenís nada que ver con el niño, Iris.
—El niño es de nosotras.
—Lo vamos a esconder.
—Sí, mejor esconderlo.
—El niño nació en esta casa hace muchos años.
—Nadie se acuerda quién fue su madre.
—Y padre no tuvo.
—No, porque los hombres son cochinos.
—Y no puede contar quién fue su madre.
—Claro, porque es mudo. (514)

"You've got no claim on the child, Iris."
"The child's ours."
"We're going to hide him."
"Yes, better hide him."
"The child was born in the Casa years ago."
"Nobody remembers who his mother was."
"And he never had a father."
"No, because men are filthy."
"And he can't tell who his mother was."
"Of course not, because he's dumb." (413)

Mudito is twice the nameless child, because he knows no father and because he can utter no name. He found refuge in the house where he could abolish his name precisely to become the essence of writing:

No pudieron hablar con Humberto Peñaloza porque al oír ese nombre huyó por los pasadillos hasta el fondo de la casa, no existe Humberto

Peñaloza, es una invención, no es una persona sino un personaje, nadie puede querer hablar con él porque tienen que saber que es mudo. En una habitación remota abarrotada de fardos de diarios y revistas reblandecidas por la humedad se refugió su sombra vulnerable. (447)

No one was able to speak with Humberto Peñaloza because as soon as he heard that name he fled down the corridors into the depths of the Casa, Humberto Peñaloza doesn't exist, he's an invention, he's not a person but a character, no one can want to speak to him, because they must know that he's a mute. His vulnerable shadow took cover far away in a room cluttered with bundles of newspapers and magazines the dampness has made soft. (358)

First, Mudito wants to be born as a character, as the protagonist of a story; later, the mask becomes insufficient, and at the conclusion of the novel he is reborn as the metaphor for writing. Mudito has emerged as an authorial figure, the director, only to disappear later and be dispersed like ashes.[15] This closing metaphor takes the theme of self-effacement from the fictional level of Humberto Peñaloza's escape into the Casa as Mudito, to the discursive level, where fire metaphorically disperses the narrator's voice, and authorial stance, so that only writing remains.

Representing the role of a character necessarily assumes the availability of a space in which to act out the role. Writing also occupies a space, a blank space. Mudito undergoes many transformations; and with each one he sheds a different layer of narrative authority. In the last of these transformations, persona has been abandoned. Mudito finally becomes an object, the object of writing:

Soy este paquete. Estoy guarecido bajo los estratos de sacos en que las viejas me retobaron y por eso mismo no necesito hacer paquetes, no necesito hacer nada, no siento, no oigo, no veo nada porque no existe nada más que este hueco que ocupo. (537–38)

I'm this package. I'm hidden under layers of burlap sacks, the old women packed me in them and that's why I don't have to make other packages, I don't have to do anything, I don't feel, I don't hear, I don't see anything, because nothing exists except this hole I'm in. (434)

As interpreter of the tale in chapter two, Mudito sees the landlord's gesture, and specifically his poncho, as a space that he can occupy and a stance that he can repeat and transform. Likewise, at the beginning of the novel, the women's displacement has left open a niche. Mudito moves into the space warmed by Brígida's remains and dies in the most significant time and space in the novel, the end. In the opening pages, the omniscient narrator and the women describe all the events surrounding Brígida's death, yet "forget" to tell about the death itself. This missing fact creates a blank at the beginning of the novel that is later filled by Mudito's death by burning.[16] His ashes leave a smudge on the white rocks by the river, and so signify writing as the most enduring form of narration in the novel. Through his death by burning, Mudito becomes the writing that we now read as Donoso's novel. So that he can be seen as both the package burnt by the old woman and the book that we now read, the reader must link two instances of burning in the novel. The first burning is of Humberto Peñaloza's papers by Mudito just after entering the convent (153–34; 120–21), the description of which closely resembles Mudito's burning at the end:

> La vieja se pone de pie, agarra el saco, y abriéndolo lo sacude sobre el fuego, lo vacía en las llamas: astillas, cartones, medias, trapos, diarios, papeles, mugre, qué importa lo que sea con tal que la llama se avive un poco para no sentir frío. (542)

> The old woman stands up, she grabs the sack and, opening it, shakes it out over the fire, emptying it into the flames: kindling wood, cardboard, stockings, rags, newspapers, writing paper, trash, it doesn't matter what as long as the flame picks up a bit to fight off the cold. (438)

Mudito (Humberto Peñaloza) sought refuge at the Casa while being pursued by the police for the theft of the book about the Azcoitía family. The burning of that book erases his name and allows the production of a subsequent book whose author also disappears like smoke.

The novel closes with this second burning just after the house is shut. All the women leave the house for a better dwelling—except for one old woman, who drags out the sack with Mudito inside. Followed by an old dog, this woman is clearly reminiscent of the witch with her yellow dog in the tale of the girl-witch. The sack indicates the *imbunche,* or sewn-up child, stolen by witches and used as a source of entertainment (see chap. 2).[17] Mudito, as *imbunche,* serves as a metaphor for the novel and writing. The sewn-up package (novel) will now entertain its readers after having undergone the penultimate transformation in a series that began with the tale of the girl-witch. Now, the old woman sits by the river. She is cold and burns the package to warm herself. This scene recalls an earlier one in chapter two, when the women sit by the fire to gossip and weave tales, but here, there is no oral narrative to pass away the time. The woman is alone, and the only sounds are made by the fire and the wind. The contents of the package burn, and the ashes scatter in the river. As the girl-witch gave way to girl-saint, the child-savior gives way to bastard-son, *imbunche,* and finally smoke, flame, and ash.[18] The female teller is displaced by a male representation that disappears into the ashes, becoming writing, or a smudge left on the rocks.

82

In the legend of the girl-witch, the witch's body disappears into the sea, leaving but a speck on the horizon. Similarly, at the end of the novel, the ashes disperse and leave a black smudge on the stones by the river. Mudito has effected the displacement from listener to interpreter, to director, to protagonist, to the text itself. The final scene of death is at the same time one of birth.[19] Narration comes to its conclusion at the point of its fullest signification, the scattering of the ashes into time and space.

Mudito's "life" in the novel may be described as a process of the gestation of the narrative itself, a process culminating in the statement: "Tengo que nacer" (448) [I must be born 358]. His figure as *imbunche,* as package, becomes Donoso's metaphor for his own production of *El obsceno pájaro de la noche.* Mudito redefines death as the birth of a different mode of narration; his remains leave a mark that scatter into multiple possible readings. Although it arrives well after the women's "telling" of death in the beginning of the novel, Mudito's death enjoys priority over Brígida's which was entirely displaced by the subsequent narration. Mudito's transformation of death from a temporal to a spatial concept (displacement as a chain of substitutions in the telling yields the smudge as image of writing) allows him as character to become a representation of the self-effacement that characterizes the authorial stance in the modern novel. Mudito's struggle to create a definition of death that supersedes the women's points to Harold Bloom's statement that "artists create their precursors" (141).[20] As one of the narrators in the novel, Mudito appears to have given life to the women's tales by representing them on the stage of the chapel as well as by literally giving life to one of their characters by impersonating the child-savior. Mudito thus appropriates their telling and gives it greater significance: his presence as child-savior appears to have granted the women's wishes of displacement to a better "home." Mudito even supplants the God removed from the chapel when the local priest came and removed the sacred host.

At the metaphorical level, Mudito transforms telling into an act of self-reflection on the new narrative—the author has been displaced by the process of writing itself. In a much more global sense, Donoso has incorporated the novel's precursor: oral telling and the epic.[21] The women's oral narratives antecede the epic's development; their chatter follows a formulaic development (the "dicen" [they say]). But rather than secure historical memory for generations to come, the women's tales emphasize the art of forgetting.[22] National epics effect that monumental leap from the oral to the written, leaving behind the democratic and truly representational nature of the bard, who recites before a live audience. Like the art of telling before the birth of the epic, the women's chatter forgets the teller and emphasizes the telling. In *El obsceno pájaro de la noche,* Donoso portrays an agonistic confrontation between a male authoritative voice that endeavors to appear center stage and the persistent form of telling that forgets the teller and returns all to the process of telling itself. This labyrinthine work systematically retraces the novel's steps back to the moment before writing, when teller and audience occupied a common public space. Donoso's novel begins by remembering the scene of fractured tales, proceeds to incorporate the theatrical aspects of a public representation, and ends with that final rupture in which the art of telling is no longer associated with the presence of a public forum. By recalling the novel's historical development, the Chilean author places his novel at the birth of a genre.

Written in 1970, this novel marks a stage in the evolution of narrative form in Donoso's work; it also serves as a marker for a moment in Hispanic letters when Latin American authors were becoming internationally known, and consequently, establishing paradigms for world literature to follow. With *El obsceno pájaro de la noche,* Donoso synthesizes several prevailing literary tendencies: the disappearance of the author, the adaptation of universal myths within the fictional world, and the reincorporation of the oral into the written. These discursive practices find legitimacy at all levels in Donoso's novel, for the tale found in chapter two gets played at three distinct levels: the physical, in the space of the kitchen and the chapel; the thematic, as the narrator of the tale develops from passive listener to dramatic director and main protagonist; and the discursive, when the character-director becomes writing itself. This final transformation coincides with the destruction of the physical space that housed the original telling. Mudito had filled spaces by assuming an authorial stance and by becoming the protagonist of a dramatic representation of a tale. Ultimately he becomes the writing that arrests all narrative and gives way to the time of reading.

Donoso has populated this novel with voices: "The natural inheritance of everyone who is capable of spiritual life is an unsubdued forest where the wolf howls and the obscene bird of night chatters" (epigraph by Henry James, Sr. 10).[23] Narrative voice rises up as a constant act of displacement; one narrator replaces another, and showing occupies the place of telling. The process of narration takes place in "an unsubdued forest," where it is difficult to distinguish one vine from another and one voice from the next. In this respect, Donoso, like his contemporaries, emphasizes the genre's richness in its ability to encompass all forms of discourse, including its predecessor, oral telling. The chain of displacement set up by the first lines of the novel forces the final silence, when voices give way to image. By annulling the figure of the author through the force of fire, Donoso creates an agent that orders and centralizes, but ultimately disperses so as to remain, not unlike the phoenix who rises triumphant from its own ashes: "[L]a mancha negra que el fuego dejó en las piedras y un tarro negruzco con asa de alambres. El viento lo vuelca, rueda por las piedras y cae al río" (542–43) [(T)he black smudge the fire left on the stones, and a blackish tin can with a wire handle. The wind overturns it and it rolls over the rocks and falls into the river (438)]. This agent, presumably the wolf who howls from the epigraph, is forever linked to the chatter of the women, immortalized in the title of *The Obscene Bird of Night.*

3

Casa de campo:
Chile's History from Opera to Melodrama

With *El obsceno pájaro de la noche* (1970) Donoso joined other Latin American Boom writers in divorcing language from immediate social, political, and historical contexts. In the sixties and early seventies their novels became playgrounds for multiple linguistic manifestations, each always denying the other's claims of definitive authority. In *El obsceno pájaro de la noche,* several modes of expression vie for supremacy: women's undifferentiated gossip, theatrical representation within a religious context, and the male's single authorial written word, among others. The houses in this novel serve as arenas for combat and for the rapid transformation of authoritative voices. But faced with the task of responding to Chile's political tragedy in the seventies and eighties, Donoso wrote three novels that seriously reconsider the role that language plays in his artistic production. I will posit each one of these novels, *Casa de campo* (1978) [*A House in the Country*], *El jardín de al lado* (1981) [*The Garden Next Door*] and *La desesperanza* (1986) [*Curfew*], as a panel in a Chilean triptych that marks not only a historic trajectory of events in the country, but also traces a transformation in Donoso's novelistic development.[1]

Jorge Luis Borges, the master reader of his own fictions, wrote: "*The Garden of Forking Paths* is an enormous riddle, or parable, whose theme is time" (27), and "*The Garden of Forking Paths* is an incomplete, but not false, image of the universe" (28). I suggest that for "The Garden of Forking Paths" we substitute *Casa de campo* in order to find an interpretive opening into the complex labyrinth of Donoso's novel.[2] *Casa de campo,* like Borges's short story, must be read both as an incomplete yet true cipher of its author's universe (Chile during the early seventies) as well as a

86

discourse on the definition of the novel, a genre whose main preoccupation, at least according to Borges, lies in the nature of time and its multiple manifestations.[3]

Because the novel begins with an enigma, it raises questions of meaning and therefore of authority. From its first pages, *Casa de campo* poses two questions: Why did the parents leave? and Will they ever return? The second question is frequently asked by several of the thirty-three cousins who have been left unattended by both parents and servants in their summer estate, but it is the young protagonist Wenceslao who plants the seed of doubt on the third page of the novel: "Estoy convencido de que partieron con el propósito de no volver nunca más" (15) [I'm convinced their idea is to go away and never come back (5)]. The narrator makes clear that no one has bothered to ask the first (23; 10). As several critics have so aptly stated, the novel begins with the undermining of authority in the house in the country.[4] That authority was previously exerted by both parents and servants, especially the Majordomo, the nameless butler who imposes order at all costs. Now, in the parents' absence, with only the Majordomo and a skeleton crew of servants left in the house, several leaders arise: Casilda, Malvina, Arabela, Wenceslao, Mauro, and Juvenal. The first part of the novel outlines the intrigues of these children as they plot out divergent rebellions.

Casa de campo supplies no direct answer to the many questions or doubts that it raises; rather, the novel branches out in meandering paths. It is as if Donoso had set out to write a novel that uses Borges's "El jardín de senderos que se bifurcan" ["The Garden of Forking Paths"] as a narrative paradigm. Borges stresses that all stories begin in medias res, that they anticipate the end from their inception, and that they are built around a question or enigma that must be either resolved or abandoned in that end. Although narratives therefore impart a chronological sense of past and future, the process of creation occurs in suspended time (one must recall Borges's "El Milagro Secreto" ["The Secret Miracle"]). At the narrative level of "El jardín de senderos que se bifurcan" Borges subverts the direct flow of events from beginning to end by introducing the possibility of forking paths and by allowing for the coincidence of contradictory spacial and temporal dimensions.

Likewise, in Donoso's novel, the action begins in the Ventura's vacation home in the middle of the summer, just around the time when parents, children, and servants have grown weary of their daily routines. Parents start to question their children's unpredictable actions, and an unexpected sensation of terror arises:

¿Pero terror, en buenas cuentas, de *qué*? Eso era lo que se preguntaban los grandes al beber un sorbo de agua por la noche, despertando con la

87

garganta atascada de vilanos imaginarios, víctimas de una pesadilla de degüellos y navajazos. No. Absurdo. (21)

But terror, after all, of what? That was what the grown-ups asked themselves drinking their nightly sip of water, waking with their throats choked by imaginary thistles, victims in a nightmare of slashed throats and stabbings. No. Absurd. (9)

A communal nightmare experienced by the parents anticipates the asphyxiating atmosphere of the novel's end. But like the parents, the reader quickly brushes aside such premonitions and joins in the fantasy of the anticipated excursion meant to assuage fears and help eliminate boredom. The planned expedition seems to be just a diversion from the unexplained fears that will soon destroy the daily life of the Ventura mansion.

Because the adults in the novel deny any consciousness of reality and history, the narrator and the children fill in the blank space left by the parents' ignorance. In order to counteract this denial, the children subversively gather knowledge against the family's wishes. Their actions consciously break old family tabus, and their intrigues may be viewed as a manifest expression of the family's illicit desires. Thus, Arabela (the near blind librarian who recalls Borges in his library of Babel) "sabía todo lo que se puede saber" (27) [knew everything there was to be known (13)] even though the books she keeps are perfectly hollow; Malvina, the only bastard child in the Ventura family, turns into a spy who knows all that transpires in the house (213; 147); Casilda, the bookkeeper of all the wealth in the family, becomes the leader of "una cábala siniestra" (179) [a sinister plot (122)]; and Mauro, the rational child who aspires to become an engineer, leads his brothers in the secret task of digging all the lances that make up the fence around the house (chap. 3). Yet the habit of willful ignorance continues even in the parents' absence: Wenceslao unabashedly proclaims that the parents will not return, a fact that the children, and the reader as well, dismiss through a good part of the narrative. Wenceslao is wrong. But when the parents do return a year later, neither the house nor the children are the same. The encounter between the two generations after the long absence produces a shock—a lack of recognition—as sons and daughters confront their parents, each with their newfound knowledge. What is important, however, is that all these secrets, all these unspoken or blasted-out truths provide a point of departure for narratives that lead away from the usual story of life in the summer house. And these meandering plots mirror the substructure of the house itself—a labyrinthine basement that provides an alternative space and history from which to fashion fates other than those prescribed by the Ventura adults.

Prior to the departure, the flow of events in the Ventura family is meticulously organized by an army of servants headed by the Majordomo and trained by Lidia, one of the older aunts. Both history and order have been carefully orchestrated. Although the family supposedly comes to the country house to vacation, the real purpose is to maintain a close grip on the family gilding business:

> Existía un motivo práctico para el sacrificio de este largo período de aburrimiento anual: era la única manera en que podían controlar la producción del oro de sus minas en las montañas azules que teñían un breve segmento del horizonte. (54–55)

> There was a practical motive for the sacrifice of this long stretch of annual boredom: it was the only way they could control the production of gold from their mines in the blue mountains that dotted a brief span of the horizon. (32)[5]

Here in Marulanda, the Ventura clan is close to their gold and source of cheap labor, the natives or anthropophagi, as the Venturas prefer to call them. The elders, with the support of the servants, have terrorized the children with the story that the natives are cannibals and that to avoid being eaten, they must never cross the boundaries of the fence that surrounds the house.[6]

The only member of the adult generation that has dared to establish human contact with the workforce is Wenceslao's father, Adriano Gomara, a liberal doctor who married into the family. As the result of exposing his family to the natives' practices—he had them watch the slaying of a pig in his honor—one of his two daughters duplicates the action and slays her sister to prepare a banquet. The doctor goes insane at the sight of his sacrificed daughter and kills the second in a fit of rage. This hideous act takes place in the hidden basement of the house, away from the comfortable living spaces. Subsequently, the whole family relegates the anthropophagous event into the sphere of oblivion; no one is to mention that such a thing ever happened. What has transpired is repressed to the unconscious by Wenceslao and will later surface as legend. Adriano's liberalism and his respect for the natives' practices become the sin for which he must atone with the death of his daughters. Because he goes beyond the safe boundaries set by the Venturas, he is imprisoned. His screams from the tower are ignored by everyone in the house, except Wenceslao. It is no surprise, then, that soon after the parents leave for their excursion, it is Gomara's only surviving child who dispels the fiction of the cannibals:

> Los antropófagos no existen, de modo que no hay nada que temer. Son una ficción con que los grandes pretenden dominarnos cultivando en nosotros ese miedo que ellos llaman orden. Los nativos son buenos, amigos míos y de mi padre, y también de ustedes. (130)

The cannibals don't exist, so there's nothing to fear. That's just a story the grown-ups made up to try to keep us under control by fostering that fear in us that they call order. The natives are good, they're my friends and my father's, and yours too. (87)

Wenceslao becomes the agent who discredits the major fiction in the household. Once it is annulled, there is space for multiple substitutions within the power structure:

Si los antropófagos *no* existían, en cambio, si era todo nada más que una engañifa, bueno, entonces surgirían opiniones y posiciones contradictorias, una pluralidad de actitudes para afrontar lo que sucediera, cabecillas pasajeros que pretenderían arrebatarles el poder, herejías y disidencias incontrolables. (136)

If the cannibals did not exist, on the other hand—if it was all nothing but a hoax—well then, contradictory opinions would arise, a plurality of solutions to confront what was happening, uncontrollable heresies and revolts. (91)

The void left by Wenceslao's dismissal of the anthropophagi story propels the narrative of Donoso's novel:

Quitado el freno a pesar mío [el narrador]—el freno de no confundir lo literario con lo real—, se desencadena entonces el desmedido apetito de no ser sólo mi texto, sino más, mucho más que mi texto: ser todos los textos posibles. (492)

To let go the reins in spite of myself [the narrator]—the reins of not confusing the literary with the real—would be to unleash the immoderate appetite that this be not merely my text, but more, much more than my text: that it be all possible texts. (348)

Donoso's novel thus begins by setting down the "official story" based on the adult version of the story of the natives. When the authority maintaining that fiction is absent, there is an opportunity for its elaboration and displacement. Then, a less ordered game of substitutions ruled by chaos and dispersion takes over. Chapter 3, "Las Lanzas" [The Lances] (94–137; 61–92), marks this ramification into forking paths.[7]

The first of these alternative versions created by the children is "La Marquesa Salió A Las Cinco" [*La Marquise Est Sortie à Cinq Heures*], an ongoing theatrical performance controlled by Juvenal, the eldest. In this performance, children congregate and play out melodramatic roles that prepare them for a future in which they too will be able to exert some power, in place of the older generation:

90

Este cogollo de propietarios de la fábula administraba la fantasía, organizando sucesivos episodios de La Marquesa Salió A Las Cinco para tejer un sector de la vida de Marulanda que interponían entre sí y las leyes paternas, sin tener, de este modo, que verlas como autoritarias ni rebelarse. (95)

This core, the fable makers, directed the fantasy, organizing the successive episodes of *La Marquise Est Sortie à Cinq Heures,* weaving a pattern of life at Marulanda to interpose between themselves and the paternal laws, which by this token they were obliged neither to view as authoritarian nor to rebel against. (62)

This group functions very much like the adults—they "control" fantasy with a language that serves to distance them from reality in a conventional manner.[8] La Marquesa Salió A Las Cinco posits itself as "acción comunitaria destinada a mantener nuestros pensamientos alejados de peligrosas dudas" (97–98) [this communal action whose purpose is to keep our minds off dangerous doubts (63)]. Language aims to dazzle with the purpose of preventing the development of a critical consciousness. The children's theatrical game never purports to enact a rebellion even in the absence of the parents. On the contrary, Juvenal, "la Pérfida Marquesa" [the Perfidious Marquise], claims control over all the actors, assigning them roles to his liking: "Tú, Melania, serás la Amada Inmortal; y tú, Mauro no intentes huir, serás como siempre, el Joven Conde; y yo, la Pérfida Marquesa" (98) [You, Melania, will be the Beloved Immortal; and you, Mauro, don't try to sneak off, you're the Young Count, as usual; and I'm the Perfidious Marquise (64)]. Juvenal, himself an actor, merely mimics the gestures of parents and servants as he, and they, propose to mold the children's minds in a homogeneous way:

Así, durante los tres meses de encierro en el parque rodeado de lanzas, en las habitaciones fragantes de maderas nobles, en la infinita proliferación de salones, en el laberinto de bodegas que nadie había explorado, se consolidaría entre los primos una homogeneidad que los ataría con los vínculos del amor y del odio secretos, de la culpa y el gozo y el rencor compartidos. (59)

Thus, during their three months' confinement inside the lance-bound park, in the rooms fragant with noble woods, in the endless succession of salons and the labyrinth of unexplored cellars, a closeness was forged among the cousins which was to bind them with secret chains of love and hate, of shared guilt and pleasure and malice. (35)

This drive to homogeneity through the devices of a theatrical language, which veils meaning to maintain the status quo, points to the melodramatic enterprise.

As the oldest of the children in the mansion, Juvenal establishes order and refuses to admit that the parents will not return, even after nightfall of the first day. In the absence of the parents, he merely plays the role of the Majordomo who had always resorted to terror and violence to keep his subordinates in line. When Melania, "La Amada Inmortal" [The Beloved Immortal], loses her temper, Juvenal slaps her and assigns her a "proper" role:

> Tranquila, Melania: ahora tenemos que enfrentarnos con el estado llano, y si bien debemos calmarlo, podemos también cultivar su terror para así controlar por medio de él. A ver si eres mujer de veras, prima mía: ahora te toca actuar a ti. (137)

> Take hold of yourself, Melania: we must now face the rabble, and while it's our purpose to calm them down, we must also strike terror and seize control by its means. Let's see if you're really a woman, my cousin: it's your turn to act now. Go on! (92)]

Melania's role in the events to come is to neutralize Wenceslao's penchant for truth with fantasy:

> [Ella] se dio cuenta de que la historia, por decirlo de algún modo, la estaba arrastrando a desempeñar en ella, no sólo en la fantasía, un papel de estrella que iba a obligarla a abandonar la deliciosa indolencia que le era tan cara, para darse el trabajo de sustituir la historia por la fantasía, de modo que el lugar de ésta quedara acotado para siempre. (135)

> [S]he realized that History (if I may) and not Fantasy, as before, was thrusting her from the wings to star in its drama, which meant forsaking the delicious indolence so dear to her for the hard work of substituting Fantasy with History, the former to go back in the costume box forever. (91)

Juvenal and Melania prepare the stage so that when the parents do return a year later, all historical events (Adriano Gomara's rise to power, the establishment of a socialist regime within the mansion, the participation of Malvina, Arabela, and others in this new order) can be viewed as another episode of La Marquesa Salió A Las Cinco and therefore be annulled. Within the scope of La Marquesa Salió A Las Cinco, theater replaces history.

In *Casa de campo* as in *El obsceno pájaro de la noche,* several languages intersect and vie for attention to tell the story. Wenceslao's narrative purports to uphold the "truth" and follows the prescriptions of oral telling, with the storyteller present before an audience who can question him. The ideological context of his narrative is social change, or resistance to the parents who have imprisoned his father and lied to the children. The most rhetorically powerful language in the novel is the theatrical language of La Marquesa Salió A Las Cinco, a language that both separates the children from their parents and manages to maintain the status quo in the mansion. As Rilda L. Baker has so aptly put it:

> Las interacciones de los actores jóvenes en "La Marquesa" se destacan como una especie de melodrama o de *tableau vivant* (239) que no sólo emula las costumbres de sus padres, sino que también pone en alto relieve la fraseología folletinesca que emplea el narrador. (39)

> The interactions between the young actors in "La Marquesa" stand out like a melodrama or a tableau vivant (239) which not only emulate the parents' habits, but also emphasize the narrator's rhetoric as that of a serial story.

This melodramatic language, like that of the parents, is safely divorced from reality and is rigorously controlled by Juvenal. Both children and parents speak in long-winded sentences that call attention to the speaker's ability to use language well, but their words are void of meaning. In Juvenal's case, words have the expressed purpose of separating the speaker from his own emotions. In this respect, theatrical language in *Casa de campo* is at the service of repressive forces, both in psychological and ideological terms. With this novel, Donoso begins to illustrate that the melodramatic language used in La Marquesa Salió A Las Cinco can serve to censor knowledge. Because several languages coexist in the narrative field of this work, there is the opportunity of having one language, Wenceslao's in this case, expose the language of another, Juvenal's.[9]

Juvenal rules through terror because he himself lives in terror:

> Tengo terror . . . , terror de que se vayan para siempre . . . , terror de que se queden . . . , que noten mi terror . . . , que lo noten Melania y los demás . . . , y terror porque tengo que hacer algo para impedir que mi madre se vaya para siempre con mi padre. (157)

> I'm terrified . . . terrified they're going away forever . . . terrified they'll stay . . . that they'll see my terror . . . that Melania and the others will see it . . . and terrified because I have to do something to keep my mother from going away forever with my father. (107)

Juvenal's sense of ambivalence (he wants the parents to go and to stay) rises out of the fear that he is homosexual; he knows that a homosexual has no place in the Ventura's mansion. La Marquesa Salió A Las Cinco provides the stage for him to safely act out his role. Otherwise, he must represent his sexual fantasies behind closed doors and under the protection of the Majordomo and his military lackeys. While he feels abandoned by his parents, his position as the master of the house depends on their absence. Therefore, in order to exert his power, he must survive his fears that the parents will not return by denying the fact that night has fallen. His ability to maintain order and authority relies entirely on language's power of denial. To comply with Juvenal's mandate that night has not fallen, the Majordomo orders all windows painted black and lights turned on around the clock. For Juvenal and his repressive forces, time and history stop. In its place, the players substitute the fantasy that all things are normal, in yet another episode of La Marquesa Salió A Las Cinco.

The most important contribution of La Marquesa Salió A Las Cinco within the novel is that it points to the theatrical nature of events within the house:

—¿No te parece que toda esta despedida tuvo una apariencia ficticia de lo más sospechosa, como la escena final de una ópera?
—En nuestra vida aquí, todo parece una ópera. ¿De qué te extrañas, entonces? (15)

"Didn't you think this whole goodbye had a suspiciously fictional air about it, like the final scene of an opera?"
"Everything about our life here is like an opera. Why should this seem any stranger?" (4)

In opera, "music is charged with the burden of ineffable expression" (Brooks, *Melodramatic Imagination* 75). If at the beginning of the novel the children cannot express their anxiety about the parents' departure through words, then music must convey their repressed fears and apprehensions. Since music cannot be "heard" in the narrative form, Donoso resorts to duplicating the heightened beginnings and endings of opera, where the theatrical effects of massive crowd scenes and spectacular entrances and exits convey the weight of an event. If the parents tell the children that they will be gone for a one-day excursion, their grandiose exit communicates the fact that they will be gone for much longer: They leave in sumptuous carriages, manned by an army of servants who carry rugs and pillows for the parents' comfort, as well as enough provisions to last them the rest of the summer (14: 4). Like its beginning, the end of the novel is contaminated by the theatricality of the events, as the narrator declaims: "El telón tiene ahora que caer y las luces apagarse: mis personajes se quitarán las máscaras, desmontaré los escenarios, guardaré la utilería" (492) [The curtain must now fall and the lights come up: my characters will take off their masks, I will pull down the sets, put away the props (348)].[10]

The novel opens in an operatic mode with the parents' excursion and peaks in that genre with the entrance of Adriano Gomara and the natives, after Juvenal first commands that there be darkness, and then stage lights go on: "Pero las encendieron, y todo, entonces, comenzó a transcurrir como en un proscenio iluminado" (238) [But the candles were lit, and then everything began to unfold as if on a brilliant stage (165)]. And through the door, the regal figure of a young leader enters:

> El cortejo iba encabezado por un guerrero joven de estupendo porte, cubierto por un manto que caía dulcemente desde un bordado de alas granates en sus hombros, tocado por un yelmo con cresta de gramíneas azules. (240)

> The cortege was headed by a young warrior of stupendous bearing, clad in a mantle that fell gracefully from the wings of a garnet-studded collar about his shoulders, crowned by a helmet with a crest of blue grasses. (167)

This operatic march is intended to contrast with the "fake" garb of the cousins, and it points to their games as mere childrens' theater.[11] Moreover, the warrior's entrance enacts a historic past when the natives were not subjects but rulers. The encounter between the chieftain and Antonio Gomara represents in a theatrical manner the truths that Wenceslao had uttered: "Los nativos son buenos, amigos míos y de mi padre, y también de ustedes" (130) [The natives are good, they're my friends and my father's, and yours too (87)]. This majestic entrance portends a period of ideological and political transformations within the mansion: a period of hope and unity between socialist intellectual forces, Adriano Gomara, and the native forces. Through the language of opera, Donoso aims to disclose what has been hidden up to now: the relationship between Adriano Gomara and the natives, as well as the native's powerful and ritualistic history.

Events fall into melodrama when the Majordomo comes to power. Thus "el comienzo del melodrama" (269) [the unfolding melodrama (188)] ushers in a period when terror is the safeguard of morality:

> Allí, en el presbiterio, iluminados por la antorcha que Olegario mantenía en alto, eran figuras de una irrealidad despreciable: debían engañarse a sí mismos hasta creerse voceros de una ética inmaculada para justificar la violencia. (269)

> There in the chancel, by the glare of the torch Olegario was holding aloft, they cut contemptibly unreal figures: they had to talk themselves into believing they were spokesmen for some immaculate ethic in order to justify violence. (188–89)

The hope for historical progress is replaced by the stagnation of a government that rules by deceit and force. This historic flow of events is represented in the novel with a theatrical discourse that falls from the operatic to the melodramatic mode. Donoso's novel itself follows a melodramatic

95

agenda, vacillating between the veiling (by the parents, servants, and Juvenal through melodramatic language) and the unveiling (principally by Wenceslao and operatic gestures) of hidden truths and events in the family history.[12]

As in all melodrama, heroic characters represent a moral program. In its allegorical sense, *Casa de campo* plots the rise and fall of Salvador Allende (Adriano Gomara) and the subsequent establishment of political repression by Augusto Pinochet (the Majordomo). The inhabitants of the mansion, including parents, servants, children, and natives come to symbolize all the players in the historical drama that brought the country from constitutional democracy to military dictatorship.[13] The house undergoes a transformation from the place where historical continuity is ensured (59; 35) through slow disintegration (311; 219) and, partial renovation (313; 220), into a place of incarceration (364; 257). Finally, in ruins, the house becomes a space in which its inhabitants merely survive. In narrative terms, the house represents the stage where Wenceslao's oral history can be told, where Juvenal and his cousins mimic their parents' melodramatic agendas in La Marquesa Salió A Las Cinco, and where the natives' history can find its expression through operatic entrances and exits. These dramatically conceived languages will give way to more metaphorically defined codes as *Casa de campo* unfolds.

At the outset of the novel, the fence identifies the house as an enclosed, privileged space for the enjoyment of the bourgeoisie. The removal of the fence ensures the transformation of that space, and it is Mauro, "el Joven Conde," who initiates, or so he thinks, the secret removal of each of the lances that makes up the seigniorial fence. He starts by looking for the perfect lance, one that most resembles Melania, "la Amada Inmortal," a cousin he is allowed to love only within the context of La Marquesa Salió A Las Cinco. When he finds it, he decides to dig it up so that he can lie freely next to it in the gardens. This difficult task of digging alone consumes and defines him:

> Era el deleite de la mentira adolescente, necesaria para forjar la individualidad, el vértigo del secreto, de lo furtivo, que lo hacía único entre sus primos aunque ninguno de ellos conociera su superioridad. (109)

> It was this adolescent crime of lying, an essential step in forging individuality—the giddy thrill of secrecy, of furtiveness—that made him unique among his cousins, though none of them was aware of his superiority. (72)

This secret activity of removing and replacing lances allows him to be one of the first to rebel against Juvenal's authority:—Me niego a jugar—lo desafió Mauro.—Algo distinto tiene que suceder (98) ["I refuse to play," snapped Mauro. "Something new has to happen" (64)].

His project, begun in isolation, becomes a secret he shares with his three brothers: "Una cábala verdaderamente exclusiva" (116) [truly exclusive secret (77)]. Like Wenceslao, Mauro believes and wants to participate in the wave of change that overtakes the children when the parents leave. But unlike Wenceslao, Mauro's conception of change is gradual: "El, por su parte, debía esperar, saber, meditar hasta descubrir una respuesta a cuyo servicio pondría la totalidad de su fervor, que era mucho" (99) [He, however, would have to wait, study, meditate until he discovered an answer worthy to command the whole of his fervor, which was considerable (65)]. Mauro's character is defined by innocence, rational spirit, and erotic desire. Although enthusiastic about the changes taking place, Mauro would rather serve another's cause than formulate one. Compared to Juvenal, however, he represents one of the most dedicated leaders in the group (he will support Adriano Gomara's cause blindly).

Mauro's activity of removing lances at first excites him since it has no transcendental meaning: "La esencia misma de nuestro secreto es que carece de utilidad y significado" (101) [The very essence of our secret is that it lacks any purpose or meaning (66)]. Moreover, his removal of the initial lance is a purely individualistic task that responds to his own sexual desires. This act produces for him an unexpected result: the absence of the lance opens up a space that liberates first him and then his brothers to come and go as they please beyond the boundaries of the fence (117; 78). But rather than use the open space as a door to the outside, the four brothers just enjoy knowing that the opening exists. They take deep pleasure in having undone the family barrier and in sharing a secret unknown to the rest. Their pleasure is derived not from the result of their labor but from the process itself:

> Era sólo su existencia—la laboriosa tarea de soltarlas, extraerlas, reponerlas—lo que inflamaba sus imaginaciones: su belleza, su número, las características que diferenciaban a una de la otra. Cuando las hubieran liberado a todas de la argamasa—¿cómo? ¿cuándo?—y cada una volviera a ser unidad, elemento insustituible pero agrupable y reagrupable de mil maneras distintas y con mil fines distintos, no esclavizadas a la función alegórica que ahora las tenía presas en la forma de una reja, quizás entonces la metáfora comenzaría a revelarles infinitas significaciones ahora concentradas en esta apasionada actividad. (118)

Simply its existence and the laborious work of loosening, pulling, and replacing each piece inflamed their imaginations. The beauty, the number, the characteristics of the lances were invisible to all eyes but theirs, which alone could tell one from another. When all of them had been freed from the mortar (how? when?) and had become separate units, inexchangeable

97

elements that could nevertheless be grouped and regrouped in a thousand different ways and with a thousand fine distinctions, no longer slaves to the allegorical function that now held them prisoners in the form of a railing—maybe then the metaphor would begin to yield its infinite meanings, concentrated for the time being in this passionate toil. (78–79)

The detailed description of "this passionate toil" elucidates for the reader the writer's art of arranging words (lances) in new and unusual ways, grouping them in new metaphors so as to liberate them from society's imposed signifying chain. Before a new order can be established, language must be liberated from its stale and referential connotations and given new meaning. Unknowingly, Mauro's task is to remedy the damage done by both parents and the children involved in La Marquesa Salió A Las Cinco. They have all consistently created a fictitious reality through the use of a stultifying language. Radical transformations occur as the result of Mauro's activity.

But Mauro releases the powers of language in an unconscious, fatalistic manner. After removing thirty-three lances, equivalent to the number of cousins in the house, the four brothers realize that the rest have already been loosened and that the labor they considered their secret task, their cabala, had been predestined all along:

> ¡Qué desilusionante su empeño, qué lejos de señalarlo como individuo en busca de un idioma único para su rebelión, se identificaba con las generaciones precedentes haciendo sólo lo que estaba destinado a hacer! (124)

> How disillusioning his cause, which, far from marking him as an individual in search of some unique idiom for his rebellion, would merely identify him with the preceding generations, doing only what he was destined to do! (83)

Mauro is disillusioned by his role as a small link in a chain of events. He has yet to understand the significance of his now diminished gesture. But his individual effort becomes a collective one when the remaining children join in to tumble down the whole fence. His secret *cabala* becomes a game, and what is more humiliating, it constitutes another episode of La Marquesa Salió A Las Cinco: "Esto de arrancar lanzas, todos estaban de acuerdo, era el capítulo más fascinante e imprevisto de La Marquesa Salió A Las Cinco" (127) [This lance pulling, everyone agreed, was the most fascinating and unexpected chapter of La Marquise Est Sortie à Cinq Heures (85)]. Chaos and chance have entered into the game. As with all language, once it is created it slips from the hands of its maker, taking on its own life and producing its own effects. The children thoroughly enjoy downing the lances, yet, when the fence disappears, Amadeo, the youngest of them, cries: "—¿Quién va a volvel a ponel las lanzas?" (127) ["Who'th going to put back the lanthes?" (85)]. The protective barrier, now gone, gives rise to the ancient fears regarding the natives (the cannibals). With all the cousins participating in the event, Mauro has lost control of his creation and given birth to an open space that threatens anarchy and fear.

Mauro's way of dealing with the new enigma (who loosened the rest of the lances?) is to avoid all explanations: "—Nadie te ha pedido explicaciones—gritó Mauro.—En cuanto se intenta explicar algo se plantean las dudas y comienza el miedo" (123) ["Nobody asked you for explanations!" shouted Mauro. "As soon as you try to explain something you make room for doubt and that's when fear begins!" (82)]. Once Mauro loses control, there is room for another authoritative figure, Wenceslao. Now that Mauro has discredited the language of the parents (a language whose words have fixed meanings and stand closely related to each other in an enclosed signifying chain), Wenceslao is free to offer the substitute of legend: Several generations ago, the lances had been forged by the natives as weapons. When they were defeated by the Venturas, those same lances became the fence that was built to isolate the family from the population that performed the labor. Years back, the natives (agents of change) had released the lances, leaving only thirty-three in place, thus anticipating the solidarity between children and the natives against the parents. According to Wenceslao's story, the natives were friends, not cannibals (130; 87).

In a society where the official version of events cancels out all others, oral tradition (because of its unofficial status and its capacity to proliferate quickly) supplies the alternative interpretation of events. Moreover, Wenceslao's legend gains credibility because of the vacuum of authority left by the parents, and with no one to protect them from the "fierce" natives, it is more soothing for the cousins to accept Wenceslao's legend. Mauro, now understanding his place in a greater context, concludes:

> Sí: la explicación de Wenceslao sobre el origen de las lanzas era satisfactoria y tenía más que el aire, la estampa clarísima de la verdad. ¿Cómo sabía tantas cosas Wenceslao? El orgullo de Mauro, ahora disuelto, se transformó en una anhelante necesidad de llevar más allá el misterio de las lanzas que ya no era misterio, ponerlo al servicio de algo, o de alguien que le diera toda su categoría. (131–32)

> Yes: Wenceslao's explanation of the origin of the lances made sense, and had not just the ring but the clear stamp of truth. How did Wenceslao know so much? Mauro's wounded pride was becoming an urgent need to delve deeper into this mystery of the lances that was no longer a mystery, to put it to work for something or someone who could restore his prestige. (88)

At this critical moment in the novel, two stories (Mauro's and Wenceslao's) converge with the purpose of giving meaning to the puzzle of the loosened fence. Also at this time, Wenceslao brings together two threads that seemed unlikely to coincide. After explaining the origin of the fence, he proceeds to make clear to the children that the originator of the idea for the parents' excursion is none other than his father, Adriano Gomara. Like a detective story by Borges, chapter three ties all the threads together through the agency of Wenceslao. Adriano, with the help of Wenceslao and Arabela, implanted the idea of an idyllic spot that the parents should visit. In their absence, he and the natives would build a new order in the house: liberalism would replace the Ventura's conservatism.

Thus far, the three leaders among the children have each established a language: Juvenal imposes the language of theatrical illusion based on fear; Mauro, the literalist, stumbles upon metaphoric language that releases the children from bondage; and finally, Wenceslao emerges with the language of legend, which prepares the way for revolutionary action. Chapter three, appropriately called "Las Lanzas," which symbolize the building blocks of all languages (lances are singular objects that can be organized to forge change), serves as a grounding chapter, a place from which three factions can diverge and multiply. The end of the chapter signifies that opening of potential possibilities with an architectural metaphor: "Y Juvenal abrió de par en par las ventanas" (137) [And Juvenal flung wide the windows (92)].

Not unlike other novels written by Donoso, *Casa de campo* uses the house as a microcosm of the universe the children inhabit (Chile) and as a metaphor for the novel as a house of fiction. Within that house of fiction, an array of languages weaves through the material of the text, as each seeks to gain supremacy.[14] But as we have seen thus far, each language is superseded by another in a struggle to found new origins, reshape historical and political trends, or establish a mode of expression that gives ample space for multiple interpretations. In contrast to the multiform nature of language, the characters within the novel, inhabiting an allegorical as well as a theatrical stage, play a rather fixed role; there is little room for individual transformation as each child vies for space in the limelight of Donoso's representation.

Wenceslao is by far the most dangerous of all the children because he can think for himself (295; 207), a characteristic he inherited from his father. For years he plotted with Arabela, the near-blind librarian, so that on the day the elders left the mansion he could liberate his confined and sedated father. Wenceslao's most outstanding personality trait is that he is an optimist, he is able to hope: "Si uno no siente esperanza, Arabela, uno se queda frío y solo durante toda la vida, y cuando llega la edad de entregarse a alguien o a una causa, uno no puede hacerlo" (28) [If you

100

don't feel hope, Arabela, you'll be cold and alone your whole life, and when you're old enough to give yourself to someone or some cause, you won't be able to (14)]. With the help of Arabela, he strikes a deal with his father's guards, and it is Arabela who finds secret maps and transforms them, conjuring up the spot for the summer outing (30; 15) that lures the parents away from the house.

Tiny Arabela only exists for the parents as long as she provides a service for them. Otherwise, she prefers to disappear within the confines of the library to work on her own peculiar projects. Arabela's wisdom is derived from sources that baffle Wenceslao; after all, the library is filled with "empty" volumes (32; 17). And once her mission of creating a utopia for the parents is accomplished, she recoils from further participation in Wenceslao's "collective action" (31; 16). Much later, when the repressive forces of the servants take over, Arabela proves to be the most courageous. She steps forward and becomes the advocate of children who "disappear":

> Cuando digo "desaparecer"—recalcó Arabela, calándose por fin las gafas y escudriñando toda la altura del Mayordomo sin encontrar nada allí salvo cantidad pura—quiero decir, específicamente, que ustedes lo [Cosme, el ajedrecista] han tomado prisionero y se lo han llevado. (345)

> When I say *disappear* stressed Arabela, replacing her spectacles at last and scrutinizing the Mayordomo's full length without finding anything there but solid mass, I mean specifically, that you and your men have arrested him and taken him away. (242)

Her crime is to have redefined this word "disappear" as its meaning shifts. In the adults' conservative linguistic code, there is no room for shifts of meaning. Like Wenceslao, who insists on speaking a historically referential language, Arabela wages a battle against a violent linguistic convention that insists that children do not disappear, but are eaten by the cannibals.

Soon after her confrontation with the Majordomo, Arabela herself disappears (345–46; 243–44), survives torture, and yet dies as the result of the Ventura's denial of her weakened condition (452; 319). She dies in the arms of one of the foreign woman, who clearly sees that the girl is suffering from the effects of a prolonged torture. Because Arabela represents those who are detained, tortured, and made to "disappear," she symbolizes the collective pain of all those whose fate becomes "unknown." Her principal task in the repressive society is to give new meaning to the word *disappear* and literally pay for that meaning with her life.

Wenceslao's ability to survive depends heavily on his gifts of discrimination, criticism, and clear thinking, all of which enable him to recognize the truth, to remember the past, and to create new forms of being. He has endured his mother's insistence on dressing him up like a girl and on keeping his hair long merely because she wanted a girl. Among his peers, however, he constantly insists that he is indeed male (16; 5). And soon as the parents leave, he moves to action by cutting his hair and dressing in male garb (26; 12). After presenting himself as a male before the mirror, he frees his father from a straitjacket, and his father recognizes him as his son (51; 30). Wenceslao's birth into consciousness depends on his father's recognition and approval through linguistic means. The child is very aware that Adriano once almost sacrificed his son's life (as Abraham would have done) to gain the solidarity of the natives: "[L]os nativos congregados le pidieron este sacrificio como prueba de que era capaz de todo por ellos" (359) [(T)he natives asked that sacrifice of him as proof that he would do anything for them (255)]. Because of the biblical parallel, Donoso brings up Wenceslao to the stature of a hero, a founder of a nation. His life is projected as a metaphorical resurrection: "[C]reí, de hecho, haber muerto" (360) [I thought I really died (254)]. Therefore, Wenceslao is alive in spite of both mother and father; the first wanting to annul his gender, the second his very right to existence. Yet, he is still his father's son, and early in the novel he recognizes that he is too young to be a leader: "Yo soy muy chico para tener otro programa que el de mi padre" (29) [I'm too young to have any scheme but my father's (14)]. At the peak of his father's power, however, he becomes disenchanted when Adriano fails to anticipate the multiple obstacles that will ultimately cause his demise (234–36; 162–64). Mauro, on the other hand, who is disciplined and faithful to the cause, supports his uncle unconditionally. After the coup topples Adriano, Mauro falls alongside his uncle, while Wenceslao survives by hiding underground in the basement where his two sisters died and where Adriano Gomara had first taught his children and wife the true history of the house and natives. Wenceslao moves from Adriano's sphere of influence to the childrens', to the natives', and even to the servants'. Metaphorically, he ascends the tower where his father was trapped for many summers, inhabits the main level with his cousins, and finally survives in the labyrinthine paths of the salt mines that lie beyond the basement of the mansion. There, he patiently cares for the wounded Agapito, the servant who made it possible for him to escape (355; 250). Because he has occupied all levels of the house at different times, he is its true master.[15]

It is Malvina, with her illegitimate status and existence on the margins of the Ventura fortune, who transcends the boundaries of tradition. She outdoes Hermógenes, the manager of the gold, in the game of capitalism. In the elders' moral code, Malvina's success is "despicable" for three reasons: she gains control of the gold by betraying Casilda, the bookkeeper of the family accounts; she establishes an alliance with the natives, teaches them the value of money, and gives them the knowledge of their exploitation; and finally, she enriches herself by gaining the confidence of foreigners. Malvina is the only cousin who makes a complete break from the clan; she begins to command her destiny in a space far beyond the confines of Marulanda.[16] At the narrative level, however, Malvina, like Wenceslao (who represents a narrative device to tie stories and communities together), has been nothing but another pretext for the narrator to advance the events of his intrigue:

> Mis lectores recordarán que en la primera parte de esta novela Malvina tuvo una figuración fugazmente protagónica al proporcionar a Casilda y Fabio lo que necesitaban para huir. Figuración que no fue gratuita, puesto que no sólo me serví de ella como *deus ex machina* para precipitar los acontecimientos narrados en ese momento, sino que la introduje con el fin de que actuara más tarde como una especie de vehículo para lo que ahora me propongo narrar. (457)

> My reader will recall that in the first part of this novel Malvina won a brief moment of stardom for providing Casilda and Fabio with their means of escape. This role was far from gratuitous: I not only used her as deus ex machina to advance the action at that point, but I also introduced her with the idea of having her serve me later as a kind of vehicle for what I now propose to narrate. (323)

From this point on, the narrator no longer uses characters to weave the stories together, but himself comes in, and, in a very self-conscious manner, begins to tie all the loose threads together so that the narrative can come to a close.[17] Heroes and protagonists lose importance, the weaving together of theatrical and metaphorical languages within the novel make up the texture of the story as it comes to a close.

Upon the return of the parents after a year of absence, time is defined by a new pattern that will mark out the rhythm of life for the children and the natives:

> Oyeron el triángulo premioso, tañido por la figura cubierta por un manto a rayas que desde la tribuna ofrecía los ritmos apropiados para sobrevivir. Obedecieron porque no encontraron alternativas, y además les pareció lógico, apto. (498)

> They heard the stern triangle from the stage, rung by the old man in the striped blanket, providing the basic rhythm of survival. They obeyed. There was no other choice, and besides it seemed logical, proper (352)

The parents have returned only to die in the thistle storm predicted in the nightmare at the beginning of the novel. This thistle storm marks the beginning of the prolonged military rule, and the inhabitants of the house will have to fashion new communal rules for survival. It also marks the

103

beginning of a period of silence imposed by the governing powers as well as the ultimate silence of the end of the novel. Under this repressive order, there is no room for rebellions or forking paths. History has ceased, and the collective will takes precedence over individual self-definition.

After perceiving the flaws that will lead to the demise of his father, Wenceslao voices his own concerns about the destructive effects of time: "¿Y el tiempo . . . , el desesperante problema del tiempo que podía, con su ambigüedad, disolverlo todo, destruir personajes y programas, transformándolos en mostruosidades?" (236) [And what about time . . . ? the desperate problem of time which, in its ambiguity, could undo everything, destroy people and plans, making monstrosities of them all? (163)]. Just as the dual levels of theatrical representation (operatic and melodramatic) place emphasis on a rhetorical veiling and unveiling of events, the temporal split between real and fictional time raises questions of chronological and narrative reality. At the heart of the childrens' theatrical games lies the assumption that fictional time compresses the real:

Lo que sucede—explicó Bernice a los demás—y yo lo sé porque soy moderna y mis hijos me lo cuentan todo como a una amiga, es que en La Marquesa Salió A Las Cinco suelen computar cada hora como si fuera un año, para que de este modo el entretenido tiempo ficticio pase más rápido que el tedioso tiempo real. (254)

"What this is all about," Bernice explained to the others, "and I know because I'm so modern and my children tell me everything friend to friend, is that in La Marquise Est Sortie à Cinq Heures they always count each hour as if it were a year so that fictitious play time will go faster than the tedious real time." (178)

Bernice's qualification of real time as boring and fictional time as entertaining is quite useful to the adults: it supports their contention that they were only out for one day. In order to negate reality, therefore, what is real is interpreted in the fictional terms of the childrens' games. By perpetuating a fiction, La Marquesa Salió A Las Cinco, the parents erase the state of abandonment in which they have left their children, but more importantly, they negate the results of the passage of time in their absence.

The adults' conservative conception of time is cyclic; generations come and go, but the safe space that they have created inside the summer estate ensures that each set of Ventura replacements bears the imprint of the previous one. Yet Casilda has managed to violate that safe, controlled passage of traditions:

—Si aceptas que hemos estado afuera un año significaría que en realidad hubo tiempo para que naciera un niño. Y eso es imposible, porque

Casilda es casta y pura como todas nuestras hijas y como lo fuimos nosotras a su edad. (265)

"To accept that we've been away a year would mean that there really was
time for a child to be born. And that is impossible, because Casilda is as
chaste and pure as all our daughters and as we were ourselves at their
age!" (185)

The parents cannot accept change in their children, because it would not
only violate their sense of propriety but also transform the mansion that
was once in perfect bourgeois order into a commune that houses a revolution (256; 179). Having bought into a utopian excursion that was not of
their own fabrication, the Venturas have inadvertently allowed change.
What used to be fiction (the rapid change of time and events in La Marquesa Salió A Las Cinco) is now reality.

The refusal of chronological time had even preceded the return of the
parents. To erase the passage of days, the Majordomo, in conjunction with
Juan Pérez and the Chef, creates an environment within the house that
does not permit the children to view the passing of day and night nor to
experience the ritual bodily changes such as hunger and sleep in a system-
atic way. The Majordomo orders Juan Pérez to destroy all watches, clocks,
and calendars—in short, all objects that mark the passage of time. All
windows are painted black, all crevices plugged so that natural light may
not touch the children. Finally, the Chef must provide rich banquets at all
hours of the day so that human rituals such as dining at certain hours will
be relegated to the animal response of relieving hunger. These actions
grant the Majordomo power over the flow of history until the parents
return:

[D]e modo que quede anulada la diferencia entre día y noche y todo
transcurra en el remanso de lo que permanece afuera de la historia,
porque la historia no se reanudará hasta el regreso de los amos. (330)

[T]he difference between day and night shall be canceled. All will hence-
forth take place in the doldrums of History, for History shall not resume
until the masters come home. (232)

In the absence of chronological time and history, the children are
reduced to the basic rhythms of survival in what now appears to be a
prolonged present:

Sumergidos en la tenue penumbra de los candiles, los niños parecían flo-
tar como peces moribundos, absortos, sin embargo, en la silenciosa tarea
de sobrevivir, ya que la sobrevivencia en las actuales condiciones, era una
arriesgada forma de rebeldía. (334)

Submerged in the lamplight's tenuous bloom, the children seemed to float like dying fish, absorbed, nevertheless, in the silent task of survival, which under present conditions was a daring expression of rebellion. (235)

The control of time becomes a source of power for the Majordomo so that he not only defines reality for the children but also for adults:

[L]a meta no era atrapar a los niños dentro de esa realidad que él estaba inventando, sino a los Ventura mismos cuando regresaran. Tarea por cierto más difícil. Pero como al fin y al cabo son las leyes las que crean la realidad, y no a la inversa, y quien tiene el poder crea las leyes, era sólo cuestión de conservarlo. (331)

[T]he goal was not to trap the *children* inside this reality he was inventing, but rather, when they returned, the Venturas themselves. A more ticklish job, to be sure. But since after all it is the laws that create reality, and not the other way around—and since whoever wields power creates the laws—it was simply a matter of preserving authority. (233)

Power over the conception of time and history becomes power over basic human rights. Under the guise of servitude to the Ventura's moral principles, the Majordomo redefines history by controlling quotidian reality.

The only way to rebel lies in reinstating and/or maintaining the daily rituals that mark the passage of time.[18] Wenceslao, who now inhabits the darkness of the underground passages, counts the days with the number of loaves of bread that Amadeo is able to secure for him and Agapito. Living on the ground floor, Amadeo has found a cracked window through which daylight shines; when night falls, he goes down to the basement and delivers the bag of four loaves that constitute the next day's ration for the two internal exiles (355; 251). Unable to measure the passage of time by clocks, Amadeo and Wenceslao invent their own convention, their alternative to the fiction offered by the Majordomo:

Yo [Wenceslao] acudo a su llamado: me entrega una bolsa de pan—panes contados, que, ya que nos servirán para regularizar el hambre, será una manera de instaurar una cronología inventada, de pan en pan, una ficción, o mejor decir un "acuerdo," que es lo esencial en toda ficción. (356)

I [Wenceslao] answer his call, he gives me a bag of biscuits . . . biscuits which, since they regulate our hunger, are a means of establishing an invented chronology, biscuit by numbered biscuit: a fiction, or better yet an "agreement"—the essential element in all fiction. (251)

A true offspring of a "liberal" upbringing, Wenceslao equates time with a progressive definition of history, a history clearly tied to equally progressive linguistic conventions. For Wenceslao, then, this fictional link between bread and time via Amadeo's witnessing of light changes, consti-

106

tutes a reason for hope. Through Amadeo, he is aware that somewhere outside his self-imposed exile there is a sense of history: "[P]or medio de Amadeo, de ese pelito, se reestablece mi relación con el exterior poblado por la historia a la que tengo derecho" (356) [*(T)hrough Amadeo, through that little crack, I reestablish contact with the outside world peopled by the History that is rightfully mine* (251)]. In effect, when it is time to escape, the two children communicate in "bread" language: "Pero antes de apagarla veo que en el papel hay un mensaje: DENTRO DE DOCE PANES EN EL CASERIO. Sin firma. Es él. Y me lanzo a correr por el pasadizo gritando: Agapito . . . Agapito" (362) [*But before blowing it out I glimpse a message on the paper: IN TWELVE BISCUITS AT THE SETTLEMENT. Unsigned. It's him! And I start running down the tunnel yelling, Agapito . . . Agapito . . . !* (255)]. Freedom from political captivity requires the freedom to create alternative linguistic codes, a practice that Donoso puts to full use in *Casa de campo*.[19]

Caught in the thistle storm at the end of the novel, even that most hopeful of children, Wenceslao, is reduced to counting time, no longer with bread, but with nothing more than his breath. Along with all others who have chosen to stay in the house and survive the cyclical storm, he can only cling to the model stoic persistence suggested by the characters of the trompe l'oeil waiting for the moment when history will again move forward:

> Pronto, en el salón de baile, quedaron tumbadas las figuras de grandes y niños y nativos confundidas, apoyadas unas en otras, en los almohadones, cubiertas por las mantas a rayas tejidas por las mujeres de los nativos, respirando apenas, con los ojos cerrados, con los labios juntos, viviendo apenas, y para que no murieran ahogados en la atmósfera de vilanos, los atendían, elegantes y eficaces, los personajes del fresco *trompe l'oeil.* (498)

> Soon, in the ballroom, the bodies of grown-ups and children and natives alike lay mingled, resting in each other's laps, on the pillows, muffled in striped blankets woven by native women, scarcely breathing, eyes shut, lips sealed, barely alive. And hovering around them to make sure they didn't die under the choking cloud of thistles, were the discreet, the elegant figures in the trompe l'oeil. (352)

The novel ends with a tableau vivant, a group of silent figures whose collective gesture of survival projects the novel's significant message.[20]

In its final page, the novel emphasizes the stillness of the figures: their inability to witness the passage of time, their incapacity to do anything but wait out the storm. But with a telltale gesture, the master of the fiction we read freezes real historical time (Chile between 1973 and 1978), so as to represent Pinochet's dictatorial mandate. Able to control only fictional time, José Donoso—living in external exile—closes with the hopeful vision that the characters who have inhabited his house of fiction, *Casa de campo,* may help those living in internal exile in Chile to survive.

Unlike the Majordomo, who restricts time to a hopeless present ("—¡Silencio! ¡Aquí no ha pasado nada!" (301) ["Silence! Nothing has happened here!" (212)]), Donoso, through the linguistic resourcefulness of his many characters, offers the possibility of always being able to create another fictional space and time in which to survive, and live. The narrator, who in a sense is the last character that the novel will displace, talks about the novel's narrative life and how it is inextricably tied to his own: "*[E]sta* historia que, de alguna manera que no acabaré nunca de entender, es, sin duda, la mía" (492) [*(T)his* story which, in some way I will never understand, is undoubtedly mine (348)]. Like Yu Tsun in Borges's story, the narrator manages to both define himself and lay out the paths for the characters that inhabit his written text. A writer's existence endures as long as his characters persist in inventing languages that transcend the limited spaces to which they are confined. Limited to the act of breathing, these characters are forced to abandon any grandiose representations (opera or melodrama).

The closing scene of the novel, however, gives way to a new theatrical form: tragedy. The spotlights of opera and melodrama have now been replaced by the static scene of a national tragedy—a classic genre in which historical events are compressed into the unity of one day.[21] This stillness brings back the Majordomo's "Silence! Nothing has happened here!" (212), recalling the words spoken by Bernarda Alba at the close of Federico García Lorca's play. Both Donoso and Lorca posit the closed house as a symbol of the oppressive atmosphere created by military forces. Both impregnate the silence within with a multiplicity of voices that speak out against it. In this novel Donoso presents the first panel of a Chilean national triptych which begins with a tragic look at a stifling present and ends with a hopeful transition into the future with *La desesperanza.* Like Borges's "El jardín de senderos que se bifurcan," Donoso's novel focuses on the contradictory and dismal uses of language in history and fiction. When those in political power detain the singular projection of history, those who write must reinstate it by providing multiple, alternative forking paths.

4

THE ANDROGYNOUS NARRATOR
IN *EL JARDÍN DE AL LADO*

Like *Casa de campo, El jardín de al lado* (1981) [*The Garden Next Door*] speaks through many voices. In the first five chapters, we hear the story of Julio, a Chilean exiled in Spain, as he tells it. The sixth and final chapter, however, reveals Gloria, a translator and Julio's wife, as the "real" narrator. To create distance as she tells her story, Gloria had assumed her husband's voice for the first five chapters of her novel. Gloria's own literary voice in the final chapter includes a dialogue between herself and her literary agent, also a woman. In Donoso's novel, the male and female narrators appear to speak in two distinct manners; Julio from an aesthetic and political distance, and Gloria by overt dialogue in a melodramatic tone. The interaction between the male and female voices and their modes of expression produce the androgynous dialogue that forms Donoso's novel. Their composite voices constitute the writer's "sanctioned Babel" (Barthes 4).

The female narrator writes in order to see herself and so that others may also see themselves: "Era necesario que yo construyera algo fuera de mí misma, pero que me contuviera, para 'verme': un espejo en el cual también se pudieran 'ver' otros" (253) [I would have to create something outside myself that would, however, also include me so that I could "see" myself: a mirror where others could also "see" themselves (231)]. Gloria's mirror reflects her own image as well as that of the male narrator she impersonates. The male narrator, Julio, shuts himself in a Madrid apartment to rewrite his novel and views the events that transpire in the garden next door separated by the double glass of a third-floor window. The male narrator "sees" through the window, which reflects back his past and his unresolved commitment to his country. Unseen, yet lurking behind both narrators, stands Donoso's persona. In this novel, Donoso's "seeing" through the glass of a double narrator ("doble cristal en la ventana" (114) [double glass windows [99]) becomes his metaphor for literary production. "Seeing" in Donoso's terms means projecting a character's interiority onto an exterior image or scene. As soon as Julio and Gloria arrive at the Madrid apartment where they will spend the summer, Gloria leaves the interior safety for the exterior world of militant exiled groups in Madrid. Julio, however, feels he must write, and prepares to do so at a table next to two windows in the living room; two windows separated by a painting of a set of curtains.

In the first three sections of the novel, Julio alternately sees the beautiful garden next door, where a young duchess plays with her children, and the childhood garden in his mind's eye:

> Abro las cortinas de mi dormitorio. Entre las hojas que la brisa conmueve, el sol, un segundo, brilla directo y me enceguece: bajo el palto del jardín de al lado mi padre ya inválido chasquea sus dedos para convencer al perro que venga a echarse a sus pies, o quizás sea un esfuerzo para llamarme a mí, porque desde su tumba me ve escondido aquí entre las cortinas. (71)

> I draw the curtains. For a split second the sun shining through the leaves stirring in the wind blinds me: under the avocado tree in the garden next door my father, an invalid now, snaps his fingers to make the dog come and lie at his feet, or maybe he's trying to call me, because from his grave he can see me hiding here behind the curtains. (58)

In this passage, where Julio stands in front of a window to project his interior struggles onto a scene beyond, the reader sees the Chilean writer's indebtedness to the "Preface" of *The Portrait of a Lady* by Henry James:

> The house of fiction has in short not one window, but a million—a number of possible windows not to be reckoned, rather; every one of which has been pierced, or is still pierceable, in its vast front, by the need of the individual vision and by the pressure of the individual will. . . . They are but windows at best, mere holes in a dead wall, disconnected, perched aloft; they are not hinged doors opening straight onto life. But they have this mark of their own that at each of them stands a figure with a pair of eyes, or at least with a field-glass, which forms, again and again, for observation, a unique instrument, insuring to the person making use of it an impression distinct from every other. (46)

If we further compare James's quotation to the following text by Donoso, we see the recurrence of windows as symbolic of the multiplicity of views possible within the novelistic genre:

110

Voy examinando las ventanas del departamento: "piso", me corrijo. Permanezco unos minutos frente a cada una, considerando lo que desde cada una veo: rechazo las que no se abren sobre el verdor de la casa del vecino. También rechazo la que da sobre los arriates, y también la ventana desde la que apenas se divisa una casa más pequeña al fondo del parque. Rechazo hasta las dos ventanas simétricamente espectaculares del *living* con la cortina simulada entre ambas. Regreso a la ventana de nuestro dormitorio porque es la que prefiero. (70)

I . . . go around inspecting the windows of the apartment—the "flat," I correct myself. I pause a few minutes at each window, studying what I can see from each. I pass up those without a view of the neighbor's garden. I also pass up the one facing the clusters of flowers alongside the wall, and the one from which I can barely make out a smaller house in the back part of the park. I even give up the two spectacular symmetrical living-room windows with the false curtains between them. I go back to our bedroom window, because it's my favorite. (54)

The apartment in Madrid, like many of the houses in Donoso's works, represents the writer's house of fiction. Its multiple windows serve to distance the narrator from what he sees outside and force him to define a unique vision by choosing a specific window, an artistic impression distinct from every other. But, as we shall see in close textual analysis, Julio's distinct vision is readily counteracted by other ways of seeing in the novel. Julio's bedroom window is only one of many found in *El jardín de al lado.*

Donoso's vision reflects back to James's emphasis on the visual, the histrionic, or what the American writer called the "dramatic scene."[1] James repeatedly emphasized that characters and situations had to be placed under the guise of an observer who shed a specific light on the subject to create the effect of a stage play: "We bear in mind at the same time that the picture of Nanda Brookenham's situation, though perhaps seeming to a careless eye so to wander and sprawl, yet presents itself on absolutely scenic lines, and that each of these scenes is itself, and each as related to each and to all of its companions, abides without a moment's deflexion by the principle of the stage-play" ("Preface" to *Awkward Age,* in *The Art of the Novel,* 115). It is important to underline James's emphasis on the relationship between scenes as one follows the next. Donoso will exploit "the principle of the stage-play" to the fullest in *El jardín de al lado:* narrators and scenes upstage one another and produce the effect of a "play" in the text.

Julio's "seeing" is a conscious exercise in creating an artificially dramatic scene to displace his poor present: "El sortilegio radiante del exterior avasalla y suplanta mi pobre realidad" (103) [(T)he radiant magic spell of the world outside subdues and replaces my poor reality (88)]. As the narrator, he assumes the mask of voyeur who sees yet is not seen. Such a distance gives him the power to set the scene in motion so that the exterior reflects his nostalgia for Chile:

> El sueño del regreso se refiere a cierta ventana que da a cierto jardín, a un tapiz de verdes entretejidos de historias privadas que iluminan relaciones de seres y lugares: éstos configuran el cosmos que hice nacer en el jardín al que ahora me asomo, hace ya más de medio siglo. (66)

> [T]he dream of returning involves a particular window opening on a garden, a tapestry of greens crisscrossed by private histories that illuminate our ties to people and places. (53) [these make up the world that I engendered in the garden that I now observe, more than half a century ago. (my translation)][2]

Julio's unwritten text appears before the reader as a dreamlike vision, uniting past and present in the image of a static garden. The enclosed, paradisiacal garden constitutes the place of gestation for the novel. The male narrator, brooding over his past and his exiled present, plants the seed that, in the final chapter, will germinate in the female narrator.

With the window closed so that he does not hear the music or the conversation from the outside, Julio sees the garden as a stage set, "como de escenografía" (103) [as stage scenery (89)]. The figures outside resemble a frieze brought to life by the observer's gaze: "Ante mi vista este friso se va componiendo por medio de pequeños gestos que los une al pasarse un vaso, al acariciar un cuello" (104) [Before my eyes this frieze is in the process of being composed; little gestures join the figures together: someone handing someone else a glass, or stroking the back of a neck (89–90)]. At the center of the frieze stands the object of the narrator's desire, the blond woman that recalls Gloria's past physical attributes:

> Ella está ahí: la campana de oro, la más Brancusi y dorada y pulida de todas, con sus gestos largos que nada tienen de indolente y la jaula de sus costillas y la escueta suavidad de la pelvis revelada por el brevísimo bikini, transfigurada en un esmirilado [sic] objeto de lujo que parece no tener relación alguna con la *hausfrau* que esta mañana examinó el atado de puerros. (104–5)

> She's there: the gold bell, the most Brancusiesque, the most golden and polished of all of them, with long movements that have nothing indolent about them, with her rib cage and the natural softness of her pelvis revealed by the skimpy bikini, transformed into an immaculate object of luxury that seems to have no connection with the *Hausfrau* who examined the bundle of leeks this morning. (90)

The woman outside becomes a polished object, a static figure, who, unlike Gloria in the present, does not berate him for not writing. At the center

112

of the scene the Brancusi figure, elongated and sexless, suggests the androgynous narrator who silently projects his/her story. The fantasy created beyond the double window is a metaphor for Julio's stilted vision of his Chilean past. Through the narrator's distanced gaze, seeing equals creating a sculpted scene.

While the window is shut, Julio thinks of Debussy's "L'après-midi d'un faune," a ballet where figures are set in motion by the magic of music. But Julio loses power over his production as soon as he opens the window and lets in the sounds of laughter and jazz. Under the narrator's control, the scene is impressionistic and highly stylized, but as he reaches out to touch it, it changes in tonality to reveal its opposite:

> Abro la ventana buscando fragancias y melodías: entonces, como a causa de mi interferencia, las figuras de la euritmia indescifrables pero conmovedoras, de *L'après-midi d'un faune* en su versión contemporánea, de pronto cambian, se tornan caricaturescas, cómicas, de actitudes y gestos exagerados que no pretenden otra cosa que la risa, no la armonía ni el contacto, en cualquiera de sus avatares. (107)

> I open the window to look for fragrances and melodies: then, as if I had burst in on them, the undecipherable but moving eurhythmic figures in *L'Après-midi d'un faune* in its modern version suddenly change; they turn into caricatures, comic poses, and movements exaggerated to draw laughter, not harmony and body contact in any of its forms. (92)

The scene is not, nor can it be, orchestrated by one director or narrator. The figures are still exaggerated caricatures of the narrator's experience, but now they are dancing to their own tune, beyond his control. With the motion of a wrist, the silent, static language of Julio's observations becomes motion, sound, and caricature. Donoso's novelistic discourse emphasizes the move from one language to another and creates the critical space with the sound of laughter.

Throughout *El jardín de la lado,* and particularly in Julio's sculpted scene, Donoso experiments with a literary discourse that employs visual, plastic, or theatrical modes of expression, each emphasizing its difference yet entering into dialogue with the others. By opening the window, Julio sets in motion a metonymic displacement that ushers in Gloria's carnivalesque scene. When we see Julio's narration through Gloria's eyes, we gain an even greater ironic perspective. Knowing that the first five chapters of *El jardín de al lado* are actually the beginning chapters of an unfinished novel by Gloria, the reader is compelled to reconceive the novel. Julio's lingering nostalgia becomes a litany of self-serving, self-indulgent complaints and his stylized scenes become melodrama now that his emotions appear highly sentimentalized. Moreover, the switch from the male to the female point of view serves to underscore a change in literary style. If opening the window on Julio's scene had the effect of laughing at, or parodying, a highly contrived mode of expression, the introduction of a female narrator tends to dismiss the power of an all-knowing male authority.

The function of the writer as creator of the garden scene points to the gesture of the male god who brings life through the power of his gaze. Because chapter six later reveals that the narrator/writer is Gloria and not Julio, the male engendering gesture of giving life through sight gets replaced by the powers of the female narrator/writer who gives life through the word as spoken voice. If traditionally it is the female who speaks through silence, in Donoso's novel, it is the male narrator who creates a silent, visual scene, while Gloria ushers in voice through conversation with another. The narrative becomes conversational as the previously "hated" agent, Núria Monclús, befriends Gloria over a business luncheon to discuss the publication of Gloria's, not Julio's, novel. This dialogue, rather than being implicit as in Julio's interweaving of several artistic languages, adopts a direct, explicit mode of communication, bluntly divulging the character's interior struggles regarding exile and creativity instead of projecting them onto exterior scenes. No interpretations are necessary regarding the character's motivations: the narrator tells it all.

It is as if Gloria, now turned Sherlock Holmes, adopts a plainspoken tone to summarize the intrigue between husband (first narrator) and wife (second narrator) so as to ensure that Núria (her editor and reader) fully understands what has transpired. Donoso's novel has seemingly dared to condescend to his Boom readers by appealing to the whodunit technique of explaining the case. But Donoso's narrative case is not that elementary. Gloria has undermined the male narrative scene and gained power by using the language of the powerless: woman-talk.[3] As Gloria speaks to Núria, the voice of a noncanonical genre is heard— a conversational tone that recalls two women gossiping and brings to mind scenes from a romance novel:

> Y presa del furor de mi deseo que así fuera, lancé el libro a la otra cama. Que se fuera a la mierda. Que se perdiera para siempre. Que se suicidara. Que me dejara tranquila con sus mentiras sobre el entusiasmo de Núria Monclús y su repentina riqueza. (253)

> And overcome by my furious wish that this would come true, I hurled my book at the other bed. Let him go to hell. Let him get lost for good. Let him kill himself. Let him leave me in peace with his lies about Núria Monclús's enthusiasm and his sudden windfall. (231)

Far from belittling the feminine genre, this passage signals the entrance of yet another language into the fabric of the text. This time it is the reader

114

who laughs, joining in the knowledge that this new linguistic addition serves to displace one narrator and usher in another.[4] The last chapter achieves an ironic distance from Gloria's narration; her feminine discourse, traditionally denigrated as a popular genre, now undermines Julio's narration and is established as the ultimate (because final) authority in the text. The novel diffuses the differences between "male" and "female" discourse when it becomes clear that there has been only one female narrator all along. Feminine (metonymic) discursive strategies are valued as much as masculine (metaphoric), stylized, many layered scenes. Donoso's dialogic discourse emphasizes the interweaving of the voices rather than their separation. What must be considered, however, is the new dimension that is added to the narrative voice under the feminine guise.

Why would a female writer wish to impersonate a male voice in order to see herself? Before adopting her assumed persona as a successful writer, Gloria saw herself as her father saw her, and later as her husband saw her, a beautiful stylized figure to be observed and flaunted. Julio constantly describes Gloria in ironic or pejorative terms, thinking of her as a beautiful woman who has lost the elasticity of her youthful years:

> Le aseguré [a Pancho], de paso, que Gloria, pese a sus cincuenta y más años, a veces podía encarnar conmovedoramente—como en este mismo instante, por ejemplo, con el dolor de su rostro inscrito en la penumbra del polvo de oro y de los ojos pintados en las alas de las falenas—una fantasía prerrafaelista. (21)

> I also assured him that for all her fifty-plus years, there were times—such as this very moment, with the pain inscribed on her face in the shadow of the gold dust and the crumbled wings of moths in the bottom of the lamp overhead—when Gloria was the living picture of a Pre-Raphaelite fantasy. (12–13)

Gloria, a woman who was raised to marry well, has dedicated herself to translating and writing feminist articles, instead of producing a work that would reflect a healed image of herself. In her first novel, she chooses to relate her experience through a male voice because it is through men's eyes that she has seen herself up to the present. Only after undergoing a deep depression, when she separates herself from her husband by not speaking to him, does she begin to "see" herself as a person capable of dialogue.

Before writing the novel, Gloria's greatest failure consists in not having the courage to "see" and to define herself beyond the role conveniently prescribed for her: "No es fácil verse obligada a enfrentar toda una nueva manera de vivir, una mujer sola que no sabe muy bien qué ni quién es" (262) [It's not easy to find yourself forced to face a whole new way of living, when you're a woman who's alone and isn't quite sure what or who

115

she is (239)]. The process of redefinition begins with her silence; it is from here that she perceives that the image she has adopted is male determined and not truly her own. In her analysis of Donoso's novel in "Authority and Play," Lucille Kerr defines Gloria's silence as "a form of resistance" and "an assertion of power" (49). In regard to women's roles, Shoshana Felman states: "From her initial family upbringing throughout her subsequent development, the social role assigned to the woman is that of serving an image, authoritative and central, of man" (2). The rejection of the role that serves as mirror to man is often defined by society as madness. A woman loses her femininity (the Brancusi figure) and becomes something else, a parody of herself. After forsaking the fantasy of the Brancusi figure, Gloria faces the void (the depression) out of which she must fashion a new speaking self. Yet madness, and in the case of Donoso's novel, depression, are a form of protest that is harmless to the social order, for it leaves the woman impotent and unable to effect any significant change in her life: "Madness is the impasse confronting those whom cultural conditioning has deprived of the very means of protest or self-affirmation. Far from being a form of contestation, 'mental illness' is a request for help, a manifestation both of cultural impotence and political castration" (Felman 2). By falling into depression Gloria does ask for help in a traditional manner: Julio begins to care for her and her psychiatrist flies in from Barcelona to get her through the crisis. But Gloria transcends impotence to write and to define herself as a woman writer, one who sees herself in a position of power. Furthermore, within the narrative domain, Gloria usurps the role of narrator from Julio and is empowered to speak, not by a man, but by another woman, her literary agent.

Toward the end of the novel, Gloria speaks from outside the parameters of male authority, clearly working to attain self-definition through concentration on work and the enjoyment of simple pleasures:

Sí, [Gloria] estaba disfrutando, algo que yo no podía tolerar porque hacía tanto tiempo que yo no sentía placer con nada, y menos que nada con mi trabajo. Gloria, que jamás tuvo la pretensión de ser una "creadora," sabía hundirse en la concentración: aunque lo negara, aunque fuera tan neurótica que situaciones de esta clase se producían con escasa frecuencia, sentía placer al hacerlo, y más de una vez le dije que ésa era su cualidad salvadora, su medio de sobrevivir a todo, saber hundirse en la pasión del trabajo. Yo, en cambio, mediocre, perezoso, era un creador de verdad. (36–37)

[Y]es, she was enjoying herself, something I couldn't stand, because it had been ages since I'd found pleasure in anything, much less my work. Gloria, who had never pretended to be 'creative,' knew how to sink deep in concentration: she might deny it, she might be so neurotic that it hardly ever took place, but she was happy doing it, and I would often tell her that it was her saving grace, her means of surviving everything. I, mediocre and lazy, was the real creator. (27)

During her depression, Gloria speaks to no one but her therapist who comes to see her once a week. Pets are her only other contact; when she begins to speak again, it is to them that she addresses her first words. The pleasure of touching them triggers communication, just as it is pleasure that drives her to continue working on her manuscript. Neither Gloria's observations of her past through the scenes created in the garden nor her political or feminist activities produce the necessary cure to her damaged self. It is ultimately writing, a silent communication with another, the reader, that heals Gloria as a woman.

But even in writing, she starts out on the socially accepted path of the authoritative voice: she speaks through a male narrator. In her article on madness, Felman presents the difference between speaking for women and speaking as a woman. One who speaks for women speaks from an authoritative, male perspective, and thus necessarily places women in a subservient role. In the first five chapters, written by Gloria but narrated by Julio, the character Gloria is in fact subservient to the narrator's point of view and is depicted as a sculptured figure, static, and unable to act on her own. A woman's voice must speak from a place that does not recognize its opposite: "The challenge facing the woman today is nothing less that to 're-invent' language, to re-learn how to speak: to speak not only against, but outside of the specular phallogocentric structure, to establish a discourse the status of which would no longer be defined by the phallacy of masculine meaning" (Felman 10). By ironically subverting Julio's voice through the appearance of the female voice at the end of the novel, Gloria begins to define her own stance as a writer. Gloria finally creates her own voice by writing in a manner that is truly her own: in dialogue with another woman.

In Donoso's novel, the reader sees two narrators, each in front of a window looking out to review the past before going on to assume a revised role in life. In order to see himself, Julio narrates, projecting a multilayered scene using the languages of music, architecture, sculpture, and dance. Gloria, on the other hand, impersonates Julio in the first five chapters, finally revealing herself through gossip and female conversation. In their article on sexual linguistics, Gilbert and Gubar distinguish between male and female literary fantasies, maintaining that the male fantasies constitute a distancing from the mother tongue, while female literary fantasies return to the primacy of the mother tongue: "By now it should be clear that women's imaginary languages arise out of a desire for linguistic primacy and are often founded on a celebration of the primacy of the mother tongue. For men, however, the case is different. 'Sexism in language,' as Christiane Olivier has pointed out '[may be] the result of man's fear of using the same words as women, his fear of finding himself in the same place as the mother'" (535). Julio looks back to the garden in Chile and sees a dying mother, which might well represent Chile dying under Pinochet's rule. Because Julio's (and Donoso's) novel speaks of exile and political commitment to a country under military rule, one must raise the question as to whether there is not a lack of authorial responsibility in a work that utilizes a multiplicity of languages so as to "remain as it were neutral with regard to language" (Bakhtin, "Discourse" 314). *El jardín de al lado* posits the question of what kind of language a text must use when within the realm of politics, but it does not answer it explicitly.[5] As a son and a writer, Julio turns his back on his political responsibility and creates a fantasy using a language that emphasizes several other forms of art. His fantasy, a conceptual and formalistic distancing between the two gardens, rejects the enunciation of the mother tongue, the Chilean word. In the last chapter, on the other hand, Gloria speaks with a voice linked to the popular genre of the romance novel, a genre that tends to be more faithful to "lower" linguistic modes, those related to the vernacular, and therefore closer to the mother tongue. If we read *El jardín de al lado* as an autobiographical novel (see Luciano Pérez-Blanco), the switch from the male to the female language would mark a conscious transformation in Donoso's expression toward a return to, rather than a distancing from, the mother tongue.[6]

The feminine voice opens chapter six by dispelling the image of the literary agent, Núria Monclús, as castrating female. That image had been established by Julio:

> Se murmuraba que esta diosa tiránica era capaz de hacer y deshacer reputaciones, de fundir y fundar editoriales y colecciones, de levantar fortunas y hacer quebrar empresas, y sobre todo de romperle para siempre los nervios y los *collons* a escritores o a editores demasiado sensibles para resistir su omnipotencia. (44)

> The rumor was going around that this arbitrary goddess was capable of making and breaking reputations, merging and founding publishing houses and literary collections, of building fortunes and breaking companies, and, worse, of shattering forever the nerves and the balls of writers or editors who were too sensitive to resist her power. (33)

Chapter six substitutes for that image the open, trusting conversation between the two women, now writer and agent, regarding Gloria's literary future. By listening to the male and female voices in respect to their careers, the reader realizes that rather than there being gender determined

118

languages (the male creating a visual palimpsest, the female an open dialogue), there are writers' relationships to writing that might be termed feminine or masculine.[7]

In *El jardín de al lado,* the male relationship to language and writing is conflictive. Julio envies the successful Latin American writer because he enjoys a Hollywood-like notoriety. His own image as an unpublished writer is forever contrasted with that of Marcelo Chiriboga, a successful writer from Ecuador. The male author writes to compete: any failure is considered a castrating defeat. Gloria's female relationship to writing, however, engages language as a tool of discovery to "see" herself. Furthermore, the last chapter of her novel is the result of a collaboration between Gloria and Núria. After Gloria expresses her frustration with trying to find an ending to her novel, Núria suggests that she make their conversation the last chapter; Gloria follows her advice. Unlike Julio, she envisions writing not as conflict or competition, but rather as collaboration in playful dialogue. Gloria also finds pleasure in her work; the novel closes with the sound of Núria's laughter: "Núria rió, casi a carcajadas diría yo si no hubiera sido algo tan controlado, pero ciertamente un equivalente a la carcajada" (264) [Núria laughed, I'd say it was almost a horselaugh if it hadn't been so controlled; it was certainly her equivalent of a horselaugh (241)]. The controlled sound of laughter, the sound of a language that consistently parodies itself in its multiple manifestations, best describes Donoso's novel.[8]

Separation of masculine and feminine voices establishes differences between their forms of expression. The act of interpretation, however, demands that we reinstate those voices to their positions in the text, where, rather than being in opposition, they are superimposed. Male and female voices coexist: Donoso's narrator is the androgynous figure that effects an inversion of values. If in *El lugar sin límites* Donoso's protagonist rises above his hell through transvestism, in *El jardín de al lado* the narrator (Julio/Gloria) creates a polyphonic dialogue that frees him/her from preconceived notions of the Latin American literary persona as the strong, male, politically committed figure. Speaking about the new public role of the Latin American writer, Mario Vargas Llosa states: "El novelista se ha convertido en un personaje popular, al que se retrata en los periódicos y se le piden autógrafos en la calle" (123) [The novelist has become a popular character whose snapshots appear in the news and who must sign autographs on the streets]. Donoso parodies that role in the flashiness of Marcelo Chiriboga, a writer of bestsellers pursued by admirers as if he were a movie star (133–38; 116–23).

Even though the novel clearly favors the androgynous role of the narrator, the first five chapters still link the male voice with the problematics of a politically committed language. While Julio is perpetually concerned

119

with the issue, he utilizes a language that establishes a distance between linguistic sign and its referent (Pinochet's Chile), and places a curtain (Salvatierra's painting) between the two. Julio's novel, the one we never read, would establish a dialogic tension between the historic and the aesthetic. When speaking on the subject, Oscar Montero states:

> La novela que Julio quiere hacer sería el lenguaje privilegiado que resolvería ambigüedades estéticas y políticas, entregando al buen lector no sólo la verdad histórica, sino la presencia de un valor que Julio considera fuera de la historia y que califica de belleza, deseo o placer, y que es, en fin, el valor de la escritura misma. La novela establecería un diálogo eficaz, privilegiado porque se inscribiría en la historia y a la vez la trascendería como discurso. (452)

> The novel that Julio wants to write would contain that privileged language that resolves aesthetic and political ambiguities, bringing to the good reader not only historic truth, but the presence of a value that Julio considers to be outside of history and that he qualifies as beauty, desire or pleasure, and that is, in the final analysis, the value of writing itself. The novel would establish an accomplished dialogue, privileged, because it would be inscribed in history while it would go beyond its discursive strategies.

Donoso does in fact accomplish in his novel the dialogue that Julio never realized in his unpublished novel. The reader, however, is more aware of Julio's response to exile than to the actual political oppression that endures in his country. While Julio as male narrator constantly postpones a decision on his political commitment by not rewriting his manuscript, Gloria speaks to it openly:

> Te quiero explicar que yo, como persona, no es que no siga exaltada, políticamente, y sobre todo en relación a Chile. Haría cualquier cosa para que la situación cambiara en mi país. Pero sé que eso es ajeno a la literatura, quiero decir, ajeno por lo menos a mi literatura. (262)

> It's not that I'm no longer politically restless, especially about Chile. I'd do anything to change the situation in my country. But I know this has nothing to do with literature, at least with my literature. (240)

Like *Casa de campo,* where Donoso allegorizes Allende's fall and Pinochet's rise to power, this novel about exile endorses a veiled form of political expression. Moreover, the novel airs Donoso's own musings about his imminent return to Chile. In an interview in the Chilean press before writing the novel, Donoso answers the question Why return?:

> Porque ansío sentir, aquí adentro, las motivaciones primarias que han hecho de mí un escritor. Porque Chile es mi país y volver es poder tomar

parte en el proceso. . . . Si vuelvo pondré una distancia entre mi vida en el extranjero y mi presente y así voy a poder cumplir mi próxima meta: escribir sobre el desarraigo, sobre mis 17 años fuera de Chile y lo que fueron para mí, cómo han conformado mis palabras, mi lenguaje, mis vivencias. (Jurado 4)

Because I want to feel, here inside, the primary motivations that have made me a writer. Because Chile is my country and returning is the only way to take part in that process. . . . If I return I will place a distance between my life in exile and my present and only then will I be able to accomplish my goal: to write about exile, about my seventeen years outside of Chile, and what they represented for me, how they have shaped my words, my language, my experiences.

In *El jardín de al lado,* Donoso "sees" his own literary biography and although in a coded manner, through it, he projects his concerns about the political reality in his country. Like Julio, Donoso postpones "seeing" Chilean reality to concentrate on the process of returning to a (mother) country that beckons him.

If masked behind the windows in *El jardín de al lado* lurks the figure of José Donoso, the writer, we must look to see what image is reflected back to us. The first visual image is the jacket of the book, a painting of a couple whose faces are each covered by a white cloth (Magritte's *The Lovers*).[9] The image represents the veiled images of the male and female narrators, intertwined in their frontal stance, yet silent and impersonal. We know their gender only by the clothes they wear. They stand separated by their sex yet united by the anonymity the thick veils provide. As narrators, Julio and Gloria show their differences by the languages they use to project, encode, and "clothe" their inner fantasies. Gloria has been the more disguised. Her coming out from behind the veil attracts the reader's attention precisely because her voice appears for the first time at the end of the novel, itself a privileged position in the text. Ironically, she who was veiled throughout most of the narrative speaks in the least veiled manner in the novel. With the exception of the multiple voices belonging to the witches in *El obsceno pájaro de la noche,* this is the first time in Donoso's works that the narrator is feminine.[10] The superimposition of the feminine voice on the masculine privileges the first, yet on a second reading, and in conclusion, the narrators are seen to be inextricably bound, one to the other. They are the double glass in the window, through which the reader views one scene after another. The figure of Donoso as writer has disappeared discreetly behind the curtain of the narrators' composite voices.

The displacement of one narrator by another and of one language by another marks Donoso's discourse as metonymic rather than metaphoric. Even as feminist criticism struggles to define the feminine voice in literature written by women, it is often concluded that the underlining of difference is in itself "part of the phallocentric design" (Stanton 177). Language defined as a limitless (metonymic) field where the processes of exploration of the feminine take place is the best theoretical approach to literature that feminist critics have to offer. As Stanton lucidly demonstrates in her article on difference, the idea is not new, yet it opens up the field rather than confining it to the limitations of conventional metaphors of the masculine and feminine. In the final analysis, languages and gender traits fuse: it is the female narrator who has spoken from the beginning; the metaphoric traits attributed to Julio's language belong to Gloria's as well. Ultimately, the novel closes with the voice of the androgyne as symbolic of Donoso's narrative vision, uniting both male and female fantasies in an interweaving of values and languages.[11]

5

POLITICAL AND PERSONAL
TRANSFORMATIONS IN *LA DESESPERANZA*

After having published two novels (*Casa de campo,* 1978, and *El jardín de al lado,* 1981) that follow the trajectory of Chile's history during the Pinochet years, José Donoso wrote *La desesperanza* (1986) [*Curfew*], a novel of political transformations—both of the country as it rises out of the hopelessness of more than a decade of military dictatorship and of the Chilean intelligentsia as it evaluates its role in the political opposition to Pinochet. Donoso ruthlessly scrutinizes Chilean political factions by following the lives of three characters: Mañungo Vera, once an exponent of protest songs who has returned to Chile after years of apolitical exile in Paris; Judit Torre, a radical activist who yearns to serve populist causes in spite of her bourgeois upbringing; and Pedro López (Lopito), a poet who once held some promise but now hides inside his drunkenness to assuage his failures.

The novel is divided into three temporal segments—evening, night, and morning. The evening corresponds to a wake for Matilde Urrutia, the poet Pablo Neruda's wife, when members of the right, the left, and moderate parties reevaluate the years of the Popular Unity Party (headed by Salvador Allende) as they remember and honor Neruda. His wife's death closes a chapter in Chilean politics: "Hasta aquí llegaba la historia" (69) [The story ended right here (62)].[1] From the panoramic view of a bygone era in the first section, the novel plunges into the nightly curfew, when Mañungo and Judit review their individual pasts and question their bourgeois lives. This second part of the novel takes place in the streets of Santiago, where the reader comes into contact with the radical underground forces as well as the secret military police. Morning brings together Matilde Urrutia's burial and the chronological present, as the cemetery becomes the site for political renewal: for Lopito, who foolishly "offends" the police and becomes a victim of the repression, and for Mañungo Vera, who turns his temporary visit back to Chile into a permanent commitment to stay and participate in his country's future.

Even though it bears the name *La desesperanza,* the novel persists under the sign of hopeful transformation as it moves through night to morning, with the destiny of Chile being closely tied to the fate of its protagonist Mañungo Vera:

> ¿Era simplemente la desdichada historia contemporánea, y en ella, inseparable, el capítulo de su propia historia, lo que había llegado a ensombrecer para Mañungo la imagen gentilicia del Caleuche de arboladura de oro, transformándolo en otro? Ca: otro. Calén: ser otro. Caleún: transformarse en otro ser o en otra cosa. (122)

> Was this simply another chapter in the wretched history of our times? His own personal history, which had managed to darken for him the familiar image of the *Caleuche* with its golden masts, and transform it into something else? *Ca:* other; *calén:* to be other; *caleún:* to transform oneself into another being or another thing. (114)

Throughout the novel, Donoso reiterates the theme of transformation under the guise of the southern Chiloé myth of the Caleuche vessel, the ship of art that can lead its crew to either destruction or to a promised beautiful city of the future. Mañungo has grown up believing in that myth, always expecting to become the artist capable of effecting aesthetic transformation. But after leaving Chiloé and becoming involved in political work, he has lost contact with that hopeful mission—except for the voice of the old woman who brought him up and who insistently called Mañungo's name and reminded him of his hopeful fate:

> Nadja [la mujer de Mañungo] le confirmó que sí, ella también oía lo que él llamaba la voz de la vieja, un grito de esperanza asegurándoles desde el otro hemisferio que en su pobre país pronto sobrevendría el cambio por el que todos los de esta orilla luchaban. (18)

> Nadja [Mañungo's wife] agreed that yes, she too heard what he called the voice of the old woman, and it was like a shot of hope, reassuring them from the other hemisphere that in his poor country the change for which everyone on this side was fighting would soon take place. (12)

But for Mañungo the artist, Chile's current events overshadow the golden sheen that he had previously associated with artistic pursuits. His idealistic vision of art's power to transform has to be redefined. Under repressive political conditions, art (the vessel) and history are so intertwined as to threaten the ship's crew with disaster: "En estos tiempos que corren el

Caleuche sólo lleva a sus pasajeros al exterminio" (123) [(T)hese days, when the *Caleuche* is out, it only carries its passengers to death (114)]. Through the musings of his character, Donoso reevaluates the nature of art and the position that the artist must assume in the context of a despairing historic period. Art as a ship must chart a course that does not evade political involvement (if only because it can no longer do so), and yet it must also navigate in an evasive enough manner so as not to lead its crew (artists) into oblivion (through censorship, exile, "disappearance," and other equally controlling means of repression). Mañungo Vera, who has been exiled in Paris for thirteen years, will now transform himself to continue steering what he still considers his most adept expression of dissent: song.[2] If, upon arrival in Santiago, Mañungo only perceives the blackness looming in the horizon, close analysis of his lack of commitment will help him recapture the brilliant—even if not completely effective—powers of language to realize change.

When outlining the characters of Mañungo Vera and Judit Torre, Donoso places under scrutiny the function of the intelligentsia within the context of a populist struggle. Both characters are initially presented as neurotic and highly individualistic. They are incapable of either empathizing with the masses, who truly risk their lives in pursuit of actual change, or of acting in any effective way that would not be immediately neutralized by the military forces. The conflict at the heart of the bourgeoisie's commitment, or lack of it, lies in its incapacity to fuse the spheres of the private and the public, in its incapacity to forsake individual pursuits for the sake of collective interests.

In the case of Mañungo, hysteria manifested itself in the loss of his voice in the midst of a well-attended European concert when it became evident to the singer that his fervor for the cause was no longer what it should be:

> [L]os temas de protesta política y experiencia colectiva. Tengo esos temas metidos muy adentro, pero ya no creo en ellos como única forma. No puedo librarme de ellos y sin embargo los detesto, valga mi ambivalencia. (128)

> [P]olitical protest and collective experience. Those things are burned into me, but they're not the only ones. I can't get rid of them, but I hate them. I'm ambivalent. (119)]

Mañungo and his public began to question his political fervor after ten years of singing the same songs and after it became evident that his name no longer appeared on the list of those who could not return. The singer faced accusations of having used politics to his own advantage: "Mañungo Vera utilizó al partido para hacerse carrera" (63) [Mañungo Vera used the Party to make his own career (57)]. Several years after his nervous breakdown, he began to question his own individualistic motives, but assumed them nonetheless:

Quiero ser dueño de mis dudas para solucionarlas desde adentro, porque para mí, por ahora por lo menos, ser artista significa rechazar todos los rótulos. Tengo que conocer, que conocerme, que viajar, que leer y conocer gente distinta y estudiar antes de elegir y definirme. ¿Individualismo pequeño burgués? Puede ser. Lo asumo con dolor aunque también con deseo de redimirme. (63)

For now, all I want is to be the owner of my own doubts so I can work them out for myself. Besides, for the time being at least, I can only be an artist if I reject all labels. I have to get to know things—myself especially—travel, read, meet new people, and study before I declare my loyalty and choose. Is that petit-bourgeois individualism? Maybe. I'm sorry I have to go that route, but it's the only way I can work things out for myself. (56)

His desire to make amends now that he has returned to Chile marks a consciousness of ambivalence that he did not have at the time of his nervous breakdown in Europe. By losing his voice, the public figure, the symbol, suddenly became a private person who had to be psychoanalyzed for three years. Personal doubt as to his function in the radical movement (Mañungo had supposedly belonged to the Movimiento de Izquierda Revolucionario [MIR]) did not have a place in the vision of the masses; for them, the power of political song should have been sufficient to compel the singer toward a sustained commitment:

Ser serio, para ellos, era cantar de revolución, vivir de revolución y política, pensar de revolución y política, hundidos en la tragedia colectiva, desterrando y maldiciendo cualquier atisbo de modesto problema individual. El, Mañungo, ya no podía más. Quería ser persona privada. (126)

To be serious for them meant singing about revolution and politics, to romanticize revolution and politics, to live on revolution and politics, to think about revolution and politics, immersed in the collective tragedy, banishing and cursing any hint of modest personal problems. He, Mañungo, just couldn't take any more. He wanted to be a private person. (117)

With these musings regarding artistic commitment (124–28; 116–19), the omniscient narrator questions the bourgeois nature of the artist who breaks down psychologically in order to return to the private sphere and thus disentangle himself from the pressures of the masses, holding him up as a public symbol of populist struggle. Further, the last sentence in

126

the quotation defines the nature of *La desesperanza,* a novel in which neither the language games of *El obsceno pájaro de la noche* nor the use of
pleasure as catalyst, as in the creation of a text in *El jardín de al lado,*
finds expression.[3]

La desesperanza defines the dilemma of any artist working under Pinochet's Chile:

> He estado en mi país unas cuantas horas. No sólo me metí en un beren-
> jenal ideológico por cantar y después por no cantar *Santiago ensangren-
> tado,* sino que no hemos logrado salir del eterno discurso que nos escla-
> viza. ¿No dices que aquí no se puede hablar de otra cosa? Ya ves. (128)

> I've only been back for a few hours. First I walk into an ideological hor-
> nets' nest for singing and then for *not* singing "Santiago Bathed in Blood."
> Now I see we still haven't managed to free ourselves from the slavery of
> this eternal discussion. Didn't you say no one can talk about anything
> else? Now you see what I mean. (119)

Like its characters, the novel itself cannot talk about anything but the
political situation in the country. In fact, much of the first part of the novel
is devoted to describing the voices of differing sectors of the left that attend
Matilde's wake. Mañungo Vera returns to his country after years of absence (much like Donoso) principally to visit an aging father and to introduce his child to his country of origin. He is immediately faced with making decisions that will be criticized by all sides of the political spectrum.
Mañungo soon realizes that the artist in Chile cannot be apolitical and
that conscious and responsible choices must be made continuously. Because the artist was abroad at the time of the coup, he now wants to recu-
perate the historical time lost and to be present and involved in the next
moment of transition from military rule to constitutional restoration:

> Por eso, creo, me vine, para ver si puedo recuperar esas partes mutiladas,
> y regenerarlas como la cola de una lagartija. Quisiera reincorporarme a
> la historia de mi generación para volver a cantar, pero no como un
> muñeco de marca prestigiosa. Regresar a Chile en estado de sitio es incor-
> porarme a la locura de este segundo golpe de Estado, ya que no viví el
> primero. (127)

> I think that's why I came back, to see if I can find those mutilated pieces
> or regenerate them like a lizard regenerating its tail. I'd like to reenter the
> history of my generation so I can sing again, but not sing like a high-
> priced doll. Coming back to a Chile under state of siege is to take part in
> the madness of this second coup d'état, since I didn't live through the
> first. (118–19)

Mañungo is clearly unable to make an immediate transition from the private to the public sphere upon his return to Chilean life. The process of

transformation follows the trajectory of the whole novel from the beginning to the end, where Mañungo is finally able to define his role as an artist in a country ruled by repressive forces.

Although the figure of Mañungo may be interpreted as a composite of several Chilean singers (Angel Parra and Patricio Manns, for example), the novel intends to confuse the figure of singer and novelist: Donoso, too, was absent at the time of the coup and returned when Pinochet was still in power. As the novel utters its first words, it reveals Donoso's search for a new voice.[4] Unlike prior novels keyed under the sign of disguises and trompe l'oeil, *La desesperanza* purports to hide behind no veils: "se trataba de no actuar sino de ser" (15) [(I)t wouldn't involve acting, but being (9)].[5] The search for such a frank voice sets up a chain of associations beginning with the protagonist.

Mañungo Vera arrives in the neighborhood of Neruda's house and hears the growling of the old lion Carlitos in the San Cristóbal zoo. Mañungo makes an immediate connection with Neruda's voice, who chose the neighborhood in order to be able to hear Carlitos. But in the absence of the poet, the lion's voice is nothing but a "saldo de cuerdas vocales estropeadas" (9) [frayed vocal cords (4)]. Mañungo, however, is obsessed with the ailing lion as the symbol of the artist grown decrepit and impotent:

> Decían las malas lenguas que al compañero Carlitos le faltaban casi todos los dientes, que sufría de mal aliento y de *spleen,* y que sus achaques lo incapacitaban hasta para asustar a los niños que con la boca untada de algodón de dulce se burlaban de él porque no rugía más que en la noche y de miedo: un león de porquería, en suma. Pero era nuestro león y el país no disponía de medios para comprar uno mejor. (9)

> People said comrade Carlitos had barely a tooth in his head, that he had bad breath, that he suffered from melancholy, and that his chronic indispositions made him incapable of scaring even the children, who, their mouths filled with cotton candy, would make fun of him because he only roared at night or when he was afraid—in sum, a cowardly old lion. But he was *our* lion, and the nation didn't have the money to buy another. (3)

While standing next to Matilde's coffin, Mañungo infuses the call of the lion with the power of his childhood myths from Chiloé so that now the lion's voice is that of his nursemaid who taught him how to sing. Soon after, the voice becomes the roar of the Pacific Ocean as it breaks near Neruda's seaside house in Isla Negra (68; 61). By the end of his long meditation, Mañungo has transformed the sad voice of the lion into the roar of the Pacific Ocean and appropriated that power for his own voice: "El conservaba su garganta viva, con capacidad para rugir como el león o como la voluta del océano en que se había cristalizado el vuelo de Matilde" (70) [(H)e kept on singing, roaring like a lion or like that ocean wave in which Matilde's image was frozen (63)]. During the funeral, when the burial of Neruda's widow has already become a public affair, in spite of efforts made to keep it private, Mañungo retreats to the sphere of personal isolation. It is not until much later that the protagonist realizes that the boundaries of the private and the public, neatly established and preserved by the middle classes, are no longer functioning in his country and that new norms of behavior must be adopted.[6]

Mañungo's new voice has been touched by the genius of Neruda, whose poetry empowered a message with a linguistic surface understood by all. Safely hidden behind the protagonist who returns and must reconsider his role within the Chilean intelligentsia stands the figure of Donoso. At the beginning of the novel, the author, in his customarily ironic fashion, offers us his self-portrait in the image of Carlitos, the aging lion, as he prepares to effect a transformation of both the self-image of Mañungo Vera, the singer, and of his own persona as a writer.

If the character of Mañungo Vera serves to bring forth questions of artistic voice and social commitment in the face of impending historical change, the character of Judit Torre confronts the problematics of political action for the bourgeoisie. Once a radical university student and member of the MIR (148; 136), Judit Torre is first described as "una muchacha rubia de deslumbrante belleza equina, parecida a Virginia Woolf" (28) [(A) blonde of astounding equine beauty—she looked a little like the young Virginia Woolf (21)]. Hers is the stereotype of a well-bred member of the Chilean high bourgeoisie, complete with feminist overtones. The novel traces her rebellion against her family during her university years, when she becomes involved with the MIR (141–43; 132–34), as well as her total break from her patrimony and the right to be buried in the family mausoleum (284; 268). After having severed all family ties, her political involvement becomes the center of her life. Because of her clandestine work against the Pinochet regime during the seventies (140; 133), she is detained and tortured for eight days. Her "disappearance" puts her in contact with a group of women who will work together in the underground. Having been detained integrates her into what she calls "mi red de mujeres" (149) [my women's group (140)]; yet she cannot fully participate in their collective being because her torturer did not rape her: "No participé en la fiesta de esa majestuosa forma colectiva" (130) [I didn't take part in the feast of that majestic collective form (121)]. She was singled out and spared sexual violation because of her white skin and her unmistakable social class: "Dicen que me muevo como un caballo de raza, que vuelco mi pesado pelo rubio como un galgo afgano: todos los lugares comunes que describen la abstracción de mi origen" (131) [They say I move like a thoroughbred horse, that I toss my heavy blond hair around like an Afghan hound: all the commonplaces that describe the abstraction of my origin (122)]. Judit became "[L]a intocable. La intocada" (129) [(T)he untouchable. The untouched (120)]. Because of her class, a woman like Judit Torre enjoys a privilege that women of the working class do not share. Knowing that even at the moment of torture she receives deferential treatment sets her apart, keeps her from participating in the "collective feast" that would fully integrate her into the class struggle.

Judit Torre's participation in the underground movement is marked by a series of privileges accorded to those of her class. She survives the rigors of clandestine life by finding refuge for short periods with friends like Fausta and Celedonio who allow her to stay with them, eat well, listen to music, and enjoy the luxury of private spaces (148–51; 139–41). But those interludes bring on guilty feelings and diminish the hate and desire to avenge the disappearance and death of others less fortunate than she. Eight days after having "disappeared," her name appears on the front page of the papers: *"Dama de sociedad transformada en delincuente común"* (140) [*Debutante Turns Criminal* (132)]. Her classification as "debutante" saves her from oblivion: "En la cárcel pública yo estaba un poco a salvo porque de ahí no se desaparece" (141) [In the public jail I was a little better off because you don't disappear from there (132)]. Fausta and Celedonio are able to rescue her from detention as soon as they know where she is. In the final analysis, it is Celedonio's gift of gab and Fausta's fame as a second-rate writer that save Judit. The couple's linguistic virtuosity overwhelms a judge who is, in any case, more interested in establishing a literary relationship with the well-known Fausta Manquileo than with adding another name to the rank of the disappeared (161–64; 149–53).

Because Judit cannot see herself as a victim of the political system by virtue of not having been raped by her torturer, she fashions herself as a victim of her own social class. She plays the role of the hysteric and assumes the trauma of a scene that did not take place. Because she cannot admit to the other women that she did not share their experience, she is forced to live a lie in order to preserve her place in the community of the victimized. She fervently desires to become one with the other women, yet knows that her ancestry and guilt separate her from their reality. Her phantasmagoric search for a role that never was (that of belonging to the working class) makes her fall into the victim's role vis-à-vis Mañungo: the two had been lovers in the sixties and they resume their relationship upon his return. He now derives pleasure from thinking of her as a rape victim: "Porque Mañungo, yacente bajo los acantos, no se sintió canalla al experimentar un estremecimiento de placer con la idea de que Judit fuera violada" (140) [Because Mañungo, lying under the acanthus, didn't think he

130

was a bastard when he felt a shudder of pleasure at the idea of Judit's being raped (131)]. Judit herself had felt a complicitous desire when her torturer made her scream as if she were being raped: "Y yo me desgañito aullando como una perra porque estoy alcanzando un placer culpable que nunca antes había alcanzado" (130) [I shout my lungs out howling like a bitch because I'm reaching a shameful pleasure I'd never felt before (121)].[7] Hence, part of Judit's torture consisted in playing an enforced complicit role with the torturer that isolated her from the other women:

> Grito de terror ante mí misma, porque en esta situación totalmente dese-rotizada grito de vergüenza ante mi placer mientras en las otras celdas mis compañeras aúllan como yo, pero por torturas distintas a la tortura del perdón. (130)

> I shout with terror at myself, because in this totally unerotic situtation I shout my shame at my pleasure while in the other cells my friends are howling like me, but because of tortures different from the torture of being exempted from torture. (121)

She must take revenge against her torturer, because by not performing his role of raping her, he isolated her from the community of the women who were raped. For Judit and Mañungo who never experience the full weight of the political system's violence, the threat of such violence becomes a sensual game:

> Mañungo tuvo la sensación de que su amiga concebía el peligro como la materia prima de lo lúdico, y temió por Judit, más que nada porque este desequilibrio lo tocó, y por primera vez se sintió atraído por Judit. (121)

> Mañungo felt that Judit took danger as the raw material for play. He feared for her, particularly since this imbalance afflicted him as well, and for the first time that night he felt . . . wanting Judit. (112)

Because Judit and Mañungo enjoy the privilege of their class and therefore escape real violence, they turn that gap in their experience into an erotic playfulness with death, in a ludic interlude that fills the entire middle section of the novel.

Judit's project to find and kill her torturer constitutes her present clandestine work. Her "political action" is indistinguishable from her personal agenda of eliminating the cause for the guilt she feels in relation to the other women. Ada Luz and Auristela help her in her search and Judit's vengeance becomes a communal project:

> —¿Te lo confirmaron?
> —Todo confirmado.
> —¿Quién lo confirmó?

131

—Se cuenta el milagro, pero no el santo. Pero puedes estar tranquila. En
ese Mercedes vendrá tu hombre.
—Nuestro hombre.
—Nuestro hombre. (92–93)

"Was that confirmed?"
"All confirmed."
"Who confirmed it?"
"We talk about miracles, dearie, but we don't mention the saints who
work them. But you can rest easy. Your man will be in that Mercedes."
"Our man."
"Our man." (87)

When searching for her torturer, Judit literally dresses to kill, abandoning
her usual garb of jeans and olive green shirts for a silk dress and a small
purse that conceals her weapon. Particularly in the case of Judit as a representative of the bourgeoisie, there is a tendency in the novel to reduce her
character to a cliché about class and sex. In the beginning of the novel she
is compared to a racehorse and a pedigreed Afghan. Later she is denigrated as a bitch by her torturer (130; 121). During the curfew hours,
accompanied by Mañungo, she endangers her life to protect a small female dog in heat from the onslaught of a pack of hounds. The little white
dog becomes for her the symbol of the female victim that she now has to
save: "Necesitaba salvar a la perrita blanca de los violadores" (192) [She
had to save the white bitch from the rapists (180)]. When the small bitch
is attacked, Judit projects her as the victim that she should have been. By
objectifying the role of the female recipient of male violence, Judit is able
to assume an active role and rescue the white dog, and herself, from the
passive stereotypic female role. Unable to save the animal from her despicable situation by warding off the dogs, Judit opts to kill the white bitch
and thus liberate her from her fate. By killing her, Judit objectively kills
her own desire to be the victim. Although she destroys that aspect of herself that confuses desire with violence, she does not forget about it. She
insists on holding on to the dog's carcass through the night and actually
cradles it in her sleep. Her gesture signifies a sort of mourning as she
separates herself from the effects of the psychological victimization that
she was subjected to while detained. Because she symbolically plays out
the scene of violation with the dogs (193; 181), she expiates the guilt for
the desire she felt while her torturer made her scream as if she were being
raped. She is an active participant rather than a victim, and thus frees
herself from the guilt she carried. She no longer has to seek out her elusive torturer.

Having been exposed to torture and sexual abuse when she was detained, Judit Torre has already suffered a violent, externally imposed vio-

lation of her private space. That which belongs to the private sphere has been abused at the public, political level. Moreover, she has been made to think that because her violation was not physical, it did not actually take place. Judit's preoccupation with the white dog signifies for Mañungo an unnecessary risk taken for exclusively private, psychological concerns:

> Detrás del arbusto, Mañungo se lanzó a toda carrera. ¿Qué hacía, le gritaba? ¿Estaba empeñada en que la detuvieran? ¿No se daba cuenta del peligro que corría con la patrulla probablemente sobre aviso, las sirenas listas, los *walkie-talkies,* los silbatos? Judit le gritó que se fuera, él no entendía nada, no le quería hablar nunca más, ni verlo nunca más porque no podía entender nada. (192)

> Mañungo ran out from behind the bush. What was she doing? he shouted. Was she trying to get caught? Didn't she realize the danger she was in with the patrol probably on the alert, sirens ready, walkie-talkies, whistles? Judit shouted at him to go away, that he understood nothing, that she never wanted to speak to him again, that she never wanted to see him again, because he was incapable of understanding anything. (180)

Although Mañungo is capable of having a nervous breakdown during a live concert and thus exposing private concerns to the public eye, Judit's playing out of a symbolic scene so as to liberate her psyche of the torture and sexual abuse imposed on her constitutes, for him, an irresponsible action.[8] When shooing the dogs away from the white bitch Judit yells: "Váyanse, déjenla, perdónenla" (192) [(S)cat, leave her alone, pardon her (181)].[9] By this gesture, she not only asks others to forgive the animal, but she also forgives herself. Given the fact that the neat dividing line between private and public in the sexual sphere has already been violently obliterated, her daring rescue and killing of the white dog affirm that her political work (the seeking and killing of her torturer) must be an act of integration in which all of the characteristics of being female participate in their full measure. In Judit's life, the dangers of political underground work include the risks involved in making love in public spaces during the hours of curfew (138–39; 130–31), as well as externalizing through symbolic scenes the horrors of the torture suffered.

When Judit leaves the secret police's house, she realizes that her desire for vengeance will never be satisfied. When she confronts Ricardo Farías, the man who may have been her torturer, she is uncertain that his voice is the nasal voice of the individual who refused to rape her (170–83; 159–71). She has the opportunity to kill him, but does not, perhaps realizing that such an act might be futile given the limited amount of information regarding "nuestro hombre" [our man]. Because of lack of information, she will never find the torturer—the secret nature of political police work makes it impossible to investigate and punish its deeds. Furthermore, killing Ricardo Farías would lead to another "disappearance," one from which she would not emerge. The resolution regarding her violation has to come from within herself. By killing the white dog she literally puts to rest the unresolved feelings of her wounded female self and she ceases to be a victim. Once Judit externalizes the violence that was imposed on her from the outside, she becomes free of it. Because she has gone "public" with her pain, she has given desire a political signification: "Fundamentally, it is the same with women as with representations: both are deceitful so long as they remain private, but become legitimate as soon as they become public and produce a political effect" (Canto 351). By refusing to keep her emotions secret, Judit legitimizes them in the public sphere and places them in the political forum where they belong.

Lopito is the third character in the novel presented as a victim of the system by virtue of blurred lines between the public and the private. Although he is a mestizo, he rises to the intellectual elite during his university years when he publishes a book of poetry that is widely read by youth in the sixties. Unlike Mañungo, who rose out of the poor working class to fame and fortune in the bourgeoisie, Lopito has fallen from the intellectual elite during the Pinochet regime to the marginalized poor, surviving only because of the generosity of old friends (mainly Judit). He imagines himself a *poète maudit;* his life has been filled with ridicule and humiliation, and his grotesque face is a reflection of his life:

> El humo del cigarrillo se escapaba entre los escasos dientes verdosos de la sonrisa de Lopito, fija y arcaica como la de un huaco. La piel del desollado que le ocultaba el rostro verdadero parecía quedarle estrecha, revelando el rojo crudo de sus encías y del borde de sus párpados. Como para desechar las intolerables verdades de Judit, se pasó una mano desde su frente calzada hasta su mentón prognático y fue como si con ese gesto bajara una cortina que transformó su mueca sonriente en una máscara de tortura. (38)

> Cigarette smoke filtered through the few remaining greenish teeth that punctuated Lopito's smile, as fixed and archaic as the face on a pre-Columbian idol. His face was covered over by skin that seemed peeled off someone else's, but it was a tight fit, and left the crude red of his gums and the edges of his eyelids exposed. (32)

His face reveals the violence of a body—of a race—turned inside out. The mask he wears barely covers the burning complexion of a drinker; it also betrays the suffering inflicted by years of political repression. He constantly plays the role of the old court jester, whose jokes constitute a biting yet harmless commentary on the powers that be. Yet no one listens to Lopito because he complains without end: "Hace años que Lopito no dice

134

nada que valga la pena oír" (105) [He hasn't said anything worth hearing for years (98)]. It is precisely because of his drinking binges and his constant whining that he becomes the perfect vessel for all the "truths" in the novel. Lopito constantly reminds his friends of his humble origins:

> Me estoy muriendo y a nadie le importa . . . Me duele el estómago . . . , enfermo . . . , úlcera gástrica, de las de roto, las que dan cáncer, no úlcera duodenal de persona decente y neurótica y sensible como debía ser. (105–6)

> I'm dying and no one cares . . . my stomach hurts . . . sick . . . gastric ulcer, the kind bums get, the ones that turn into cancer, not a duodenal ulcer like a decent person, someone neurotic and sensitive, the way it should be. (98)

Lopito's countenance, which betrays his mestizo origins; the common name that reveals a lack of aristocratic ancestry ("Pedro López, Lopito— 'si me hubieran bautizado con un nombre como Celedonio, por ejemplo, nadie me diría Lopito'" [39] [Juan López, the popular Lopito—"If I'd been born with a name like Celedonio, no one would dare call me 'Lopito'" (33)]); and his alcohol dependency because of which he loses all control of his actions make Lopito a prime target for victimization.

In direct contrast to the cynicism and cowardice revealed by Lopito's grotesque countenance is the hopefulness and strength of his daughter's conventionally unattractive face:

> Pero cuando la Lopita sonrió, explicando la película cortesana que daban en la tele, brilló la luz de los significados prisioneros en las apariencias, y la inteligencia transformó su cara de niña fea en una gloriosa máscara grotesca relacionada con toda una sensibilidad del arte y de la cultura. (256–57)

> But when Lopita smiled, explaining the movie about kings and queens they'd been watching on TV, the light of meanings hidden in appearances shone through, and intelligence transformed her ugly little girl's face into a glorious grotesque mask. (242)

The contrast between father and daughter is established to underline the dismal and joyful faces of Chilean reality at the moment of Matilde's death. Mañungo and his son, unable to identify with any but the highly fortunate such as themselves, see her misfortune in aesthetic terms: she is ugly. The girl is representative of the oppressed, working class mestizo: "la ambigüedad asiática de su cara larga y oscura" (256) [The Asiatic antiquity of her face, as long and dark as her father's (242)]. In regard to his daughter, Lopito distinguishes two kinds of laughter: "Si se reían con ella o si se reían de ella" (256) [whether people were laughing with her or at her (241)]. As a father, he can immediately recognize that Juan Pablo, Mañungo's son, is laughing with rather than at her, and this recognition brings the two fathers closer together (as characters and as symbolic representations of artists and intellectuals who sympathize with populist causes). In Donoso's novel, the children express joyfulness over participating in their first historical event: "—Y va a caer . . . , y va a caer . . . —se puso a cantar y a palmotear la Lopita—. ¿Vamos a la revolución, Jean-Paul?" (257) ["And it will fall . . . and it will fall," Lopita began to sing and clap. "Shall we be on our way to the revolution, Jean-Paul?" (243)]. The children's laughter and political naivete turn a moment of sorrow into a carnival of hope and freedom.[10] They alone can participate in such blatant celebration of the historical period that is being buried at the funeral.

In *La desesperanza,* the cemetery scene becomes a circumscribed space within which a currently forbidden form of expression (a political rally) can take place. The police have set up a gray ring of special police cars. Inside them sit "rígidos torsos de maniquí sin cabeza que con sus musculosos brazos cruzados encima del pecho esperaban el momento de actuar sobre la muchedumbre" (258) [the passengers, revealing their headless, mannequin bodies sitting with their muscular arms folded over their chests, waiting for the signal to do something to the crowds (244)]. These cars are greatly feared by the population because of their mysterious inhabitants and their state-of-the-art equipment. People have already become accustomed, on the other hand, to the green trucks filled with uniformed police: "grandes camiones verdes apostados en las cuadras cercanas al camposanto, erizados de siluetas con casco y metralleta" (258) [big green trucks standing on the streets near the cemetery, bristling with helmeted silhouettes carrying automatic weapons (244)]. But within the gray ring inside the cemetery and next to the green trucks, vendors sell ice cream, balloons, popcorn, juices, and other native delicacies: "pregonando a gritos, mirando sin pestañear a los agentes temidos" (258) [all being hawked—and stare unblinkingly at the feared agents (244)]. And in this space, in this festive atmosphere, abrupt and unexpected transformations take place. Young people recognize Mañungo Vera and surround him, requesting his autograph, but fan enthusiam turns to mob violence and the idol is pushed to the floor. Soon recovered, Mañungo lifts Lopita on his shoulders and in an instant she becomes "una trapecista de circo que agradece las ovaciones después de una actuación maestra" (268) [calm as a trapeze artist acknowledging the audience's ovations after executing a masterful trick (254)].

The festive gaiety is interrupted when the funeral procession arrives. The presence of Matilde's coffin turns the festival into a political rally. The coffin is carried in by the communist youth wearing red T-shirts. Everything is silent for a moment. Then one group begins to chant and others follow, until a contrapuntal rhythm is set up and, finally, the Internationale is sung. The cemetery becomes a free zone: "Este [el cementerio] era tierra franca donde el pueblo por primera vez podía reunirse sin sanciones y gritar lo que quisiera, un espacio de libertad, tal vez el último antes de la asfixia definitiva" (270–71) [It had become a free zone where, for the first time, the people could gather without sanctions and shout whatever they wanted; a space of liberty, perhaps the last until the definitive asphyxia (256)]. Formal speeches follow, but the people have had their say. The jovial description of the funeral scene recalls Bakhtin's definition of the marketplace feast: "The face of the people of the marketplace looked into the future and laughed, attending the funeral of the past and present. The marketplace feast opposed the protective, timeless stability, the unchanging established order and ideology, and stressed the element of change and renewal" (*Rabelais* 81). By depicting the scene as a moment when both the weight of death and the hope of protest songs find expression, the novel gives credence to hope for the future, even though a definitive asphyxia would immediately follow.[11]

True to the utopian character of medieval laughter, Lopita's joyfulness in revolutionary ideals as she chants "—Y va a caer . . . , y va a caer" (257) ["and it will fall . . . and it will fall" (243)] gets thwarted by the reality of the military oppression. At the end of the funeral, Lopita begins to perform a dance for Mañungo in front of the police, who are waiting for everyone to depart. Lopito intuits the ridiculousness of the scene as he recognizes the laughter of the men: "El policía desmoronado de risa sobre la capota del auto, se estaba *riendo de ella, no con ella,* y el corazón de Lopito se inflamó con la afrenta" (291, my emphasis) [The policeman, doubled up with laughter on the hood of the car, *was laughing at her, not with her,* and Lopito's heart became inflamed at the insult (275, my emphasis)]. Having drunk too much, Lopito starts insulting the men and cannot restrain himself from going beyond the boundaries set by authorities: "[A]sesinos de mierda . . . , torturadores . . . , vendidos . . . , pacos culiados . . . , ustedes mataron a la Matilde. . . , ustedes los matan a todos. . . , vendidos. . . , torturadores." (292) [Fucking murderers . . . torturers . . . thieves . . . stinking cops . . . it was you who killed Matilde . . . you killed all of them . . . crooks . . . torturers (276)]. Lopito is arrested. His friends try to save him by claiming he is just a drunk, but it is too late. He is taken to police headquarters and sentenced to perform forced labor in the back of the police headquarters, but his ailing heart cannot withstand the strain, and he falls dead. The clownish figures of father and daughter become tragic puppets in the hands of the police, once they have dared express themselves with the freedom permitted only during carnival time.

The clown has been reduced to doing an animal's labor, and not even

Mañungo's notoriety can save Lopito from police violence. In the final analysis, Lopito dies because a private gesture such as the defense of his daughter from public ridicule acquires grave political overtones in his country: "tuvo [Mañungo] que aceptar como se acepta el golpe definitivo de un vencedor: no existía la vida privada entonces, porque si no era más que eso, era una frivolidad" (302) [(Mañungo) had to accept it the way one accepts the winner's knock-out punch: private life ceased to exist (285)].

Lopito is the sacrificial offering who reawakens Mañungo Vera's consciousness. Rather than return to the comfort of his Parisian life, Mañungo stays in Chile to help fight the commonplace yet persistent battles that will slowly help foster a working definition of a viable future for his country. With Lopito's death, previous words regarding hope and despair reverberate in the novel's title:

> Estábamos todos con el dedo índice corto, decía Lopito, como los republicanos españoles que golpeándolo contra la mesa repitieron durante cuarenta años de exilio: *Este año cae Franco . . . , este año cae Franco. . . ,* y el desgaste de ese inútil énfasis les fue acortando el índice de tanto golpear, y Franco no cayó y se quedaron los pobres rojillos con las esperanzas pudriéndoseles adentro mientras sus prohombres morían y mutaban las pasiones y las ideas se avejentaban . . . , idéntico a lo que les estaba pasando a los chilenos empecinados en no perder la esperanza, que era lo único que era necesario perder para comenzar otra vez desde cero, y asumir la desesperanza ahora manifestada en esporádicos brotes de violencia sin sentido a que la intolerable represión del régimen los empujaba. (261)

> We all have shorter index fingers now, Lopito was saying, like those Spanish Republicans who pounded their fingers against the table for forty years saying "This year Franco's going to fall . . . this year Franco's going to fall," and the useless wear they caused by banging on the table made their index fingers shorter. And Franco didn't fall, and the poor pinkos were left with their hopes rotting inside them while their leaders died or changed passions and ideas. Which is just what was happening to the Chileans who stubbornly refused to lose hope, the very thing they *had* to lose to begin over from zero, to bear the burden of despair that manifested itself in sporadic outbursts of senseless violence which the regime's repression pushed them to. (247)

Like Bakhtin in his study of Rabelais's work, Donoso in his novel reevaluates the functions of laughter, carnival, and hope within the parameters of an authoritarian society. Carnivals have consistently been used by oppressive regimes to vent the tensions that could ultimately accumulate and be released in revolutionary movements. Rather than hope for renewed utopias that failed with Allende's Popular Unity in the early seventies, the

Chilean novelist adopts, at least in the guise of Lopito, a revised mask of "desesperanza" [despair], a mask that would represent the actual burden of despair born by all Chileans; but it also contains within it a strong dose of "esperanza" [hope]. Lopito's eloquent speech stresses that if one starts from zero a truly new sense of freedom will emerge in Chile. An underprivileged citizen, "un roto" [a bum], who unlike Mañungo and Judit cannot save himself, Lopito serves as a foil to the bourgeois couple and becomes the scapegoat who bears their guilt and failed political commitments. By virtue of being the town drunk in Bellavista, Lopito assumes the guise of the clown in the public demonstration, uttering truths others fear to pronounce.

For Mañungo Vera, having to witness and accept his friend's violent death brings Judit's past experience with torture into a new light:

> Y todo él, en ese breve instante, amó por lo menos, ese fragmento de Judit que eran sus probables llagas, completando su amor de antes con un amor como el de la Lopita, y el amor por su amigo conducido al oprobio. (307–8)

> And all of him, in that brief instant, loved at least that fragment of Judit, her probable scars, completing his love of before with a love like that of Lopita, and his love for his friend being led to infamy. (289)

After one significant day with his friend and lover, Mañungo gains a sense of his country's transformation during his absence, and with that consciousness he realizes his own impotence: "Esta, entonces, es la tortura, se dijo Mañungo, y yo soy testigo de ella y no puedo hacer nada, que es otra forma de tortura" (307) [This is torture and I'm witnessing it and I can't do a thing, which is another kind of torture (289)]. With the realization that he could not prevent the violence against others, Mañungo comes to terms with the necessity of remaining in Chile to bear witness: "Después de veinte horas en mi país puedo asegurarles que nunca he tenido nada tan claro como que me vengo a quedar" (323) [In any case, after twenty hours in my country, I can assure you that I have never been clearer on any subject than I am on this matter of staying (303)]. The first and most necessary step in Mañungo's transformation has already taken place: he has become conscious of Chile's reality in its moment of despair, of *desesperanza*. Beyond that, he, like many Chileans, must find the strength to derive hope from hopelessness, "esperanza" [hope] from "desesperanza" [despair], in the reconstruction of a new country from zero. Toward the end of the novel, Fausta Manquileo, the novelist, returns to the myth of the magical art vessel that obsessed Mañungo upon his arrival. But rather than sail to ruin, with Mañungo's transformation, the vessel regains its golden promise: "y allí se levanta una ciudad de oro que refulge como el velamen del buque, quien se atreve a embarcarse en el buque de arte vivirá para siempre, y no conocerá el insulto de la muerte" (328) [and there's a golden city there that glitters like the sails on the ship, and anyone who dares embark on the ship of art lives forever, and will never know the insult of death (309)].

The novel ends with the image of the children playing in "Chile en miniatura" [Chile in miniature], an amusement park where the writer can hope for a better future for the next generation. But Fausta's moment of mythical rapture is tempered by Mañungo's arrival with the news that Lopita's father has died. Donoso ends with a note of hope tainted by the presence of violence and death. Mañungo's transformation on his return to Chile is grounded on a new sense of desire (as defined for him by Judit), a new sense of death (marked by the violence inflicted on Lopito), and a new vision of life in a country undergoing catastrophic changes (as outlined by Jean-Paul and Lopita). The next generation possesses a new sense of reality and history because it bears a different kind of violence than that experienced by Mañungo in childhood whose mother was swept away by southern storms. Standing next to Matilde's coffin, Mañungo defines love in a mythical sense, with the memory of Matilde as a powerful, sensual force rising from the waves of the Pacific. After spending a night of curfew with Judit and seeing his friend Lopito die unnecessarily, he comes to terms with a sober rather than mythical definition of life and love. If at the beginning of the novel Mañungo maintains that "la violencia por la violencia es señal de desesperanza" (72) [violence for violence's sake is a symptom of despair (65)], by its completion he declares: "No justifico las bombas. Pero las comprendo" (323) [I am not justifying bombs, but I do understand them (304)]. After refusing to sing a political song at Matilde's wake and remaining anonymous at the cemetery, Mañungo, because of Lopito's death, abstains from his silence and makes a political statement to the press. But as a singer he plays a limited role in a country where the effectiveness of censorship erases his pronouncements to the press before he even leaves the police station.

After having written two novels that deal with Pinochet's regime in a veiled manner, Donoso chose to scrutinize the political left—and specifically those proponents from the bourgeoisie like himself—in order to jolt them (and himself) from their exclusively private concerns into the realm of the public and the political.[12] Donoso's voice, unlike Mañungo's, reaches beyond geographic limitations and echoes the hopeful voice of the nursemaid who persistently calls the artist back to his homeland to take part in forging a new future. Taking the cue from Neruda's populist voice under the guise of Carlitos, the aging lion, Donoso reevaluates his own novelistic voice and produces a much less veiled novel than in the past. (One must recall the jacket of *El jardín de al lado,* which portrays two

140

veiled faces from Magritte's *The Lovers.*) In *Casa de campo,* the writer (Arabela) plays the role of the near-blind librarian (Borges), the keeper of thousands of leather-bound volumes that are empty, and contain no pages, no context of any kind. In *El jardín de al lado,* the writer (Gloria) wears the mask of the authoritarian, male voice in order to find her own form of expression. But in *La desesperanza,* the singer (Mañungo) charts a new course in his Caleuche vessel, so that his song bears witness to a current, political reality.[13] By wearing the mask of a singer, the author is capable of uttering a more accessible message. The three novels dedicated to Pinochet's repression mark a formalistic trajectory: from the first, which favors allegory, to the last, which proclaims a politically committed role for its author. Specifically with the character of Judit, the novelist offers a heroic transformation from private to public concerns so that the victimized can rise above a passive role and become an activist in spite of obvious personal and political limitations. Change is both necessary and ambiguous—a cause for both hope and fear. Mañungo and Judit undergo transformations that help them integrate the private and public spheres, that help them find ways of moving from one to the other without violent and destructive consequences. But Lopito, unable to effect such a heroic feat, pays with his life. Survival under the violence of a military regime depends on the artist's ability to be transformed by the power of committed song, of words that speak of violent, harsh realities, of myths that insist on rescuing the word *esperanza* within *desesperanza.* In *La desesperanza,* Donoso has done just that.

6

Donoso's Triptych:
Backdrop for a National Tragedy

Let us return to the image of the triptych to establish relationships among the three politically committed novels. If *El obsceno pájaro de la noche* projects the fantasies of a purported deaf-mute as he recreates his internal life, *Casa de campo* allegorizes the transition from institutional democracy under Salvador Allende to military dictatorship under Augusto Pinochet. Although there is an obvious move from reflective to political concerns, both novels deal with the proliferation of languages in basically the same manner: one language institutes itself at the center of the text only to be displaced by another. While in *El obsceno pájaro de la noche,* the displacement of languages represents a struggle to secure a space for defining the creative self, in *Casa de campo* the shift of linguistic codes empowers and disfranchises whole populations. In the latter novel, with the progression from the relative vacuity of pronouncements by the children in La Marquesa Salió A Las Cinco to the language of survival invented by Amadeo and Wenceslao, the novelist proposes that in Chile's oppressive reality there is a hegemonic effect in every use and misuse of language. Thus, the language of children's theatricality, which was conceived with the explicit purpose of entertaining and keeping the children in line, is appropriated by the servants and the parents to restore a conservative definition of order. In this first novel about the institution of military dictatorship in Chile, the writer begins his triptych by depicting language within the constraints of strict censorship.

To signify the rigidity as well as the liberating possibilities of language, the writer deploys the metaphor of a fence built with individual lances. Words may be extracted from their fixed context, as lances may be extracted from a fence, and made to accommodate multiple meanings. Displacing words from their assigned structure opens up an infinite array of rhetorical possibilities, and, within a system in which there is the possibility of alternation and substitution of meaning, there is always the risk of losing control. The dismantling of the fence by the children is an action rooted in rebellion. In poetic terms, the felling of the fence may be equated to the disintegration of language at the end of Huidobro's *Altazor.* Whether it be in poetic or political terms, the effect of dismantling any preestablished order results initially in chaos. In Donoso's *Casa de campo,* the children's unknowing act of liberation gives way to the creation of several linguistic codes. These codes range from the return to a rigid structure imposed by the military, to a reinstatement of a phantasmagoric language by the La Marquesa group, to the creation of language as a vehicle of historical renovation, and to the minimalist use of language as a tool of survival, as with Wenceslao and Amadeo. In every case, in *Casa de campo* language carries a political charge, whether it be repressive or liberating.

For a novelist who always resorted to theatricality as a representational mode in order to drive a wedge between reality and fiction, this marks a pivotal point after which Donoso will increasingly question an insistence on the language of artifice. With *Casa de campo,* his work takes a tentative step toward a narrative voice clearly conscious of historical transformations. This novel is not so much about particular political events in Chile as it is about the catastrophic transformation of language in the private and public spheres of a repressive society. This having been said, I must reiterate that Donoso's incursion into the political sphere in his novels takes place within the prescribed stage of a dramatic scene. Thus, the children speak the language of escapism while engaging in La Marquesa Salió A Las Cinco and revolutionary rhetoric makes its entrance under the lights of the operatic mode. Finally, military declarations such as "Nothing has happened here," uttered by the Majordomo, recall García Lorca's tragic ending in *La casa de Bernarda Alba.* Each linguistic code corresponds to a theatrical mode, and, this theatricality is constantly self-conscious of its artifices. However, still under the guise of allegory and theatricality, in *Casa de campo* Donoso begins to fashion his own linguistic revolution, taking an initial step away from the absurdist and decontextualized games of *El obsceno pájaro de la noche.*

Having outlined the differing voices in Chile's political arena in *Casa de campo,* Donoso goes beyond the silence of an asphyxiating thistle storm to reconsider a transformation of the writer's voice, a voice that is closer to gossip than to allegory. This transformation gets played out in *El jardín de al lado* as a tension between two writers: Julio, the failed male narrator, and his wife Gloria, translator and political activist. With this composite image of the writer, the novel progresses from an emphasis on a dramatically conceived narrative, which affords Julio a comfortable distance between past and present, to an adoption of melodramatic scenarios and the straightforward dialogue between Gloria and her agent. In *El jardín de al lado,* an individual's dilemma regarding the process of writing gets acted out through two distinct voices, neither of which gains complete authority over the text. Both are validated as they express ambivalence toward the prospect of returning to Chile and participating in personal and political transformations. Ultimately, the novel addresses, in a composite voice of concern, questions of exile and creativity and reshapes Julio's stylized discourse into a much more accessible oral interchange. Donoso's resulting product marks a transition from a written language modeled after the convention of written text as palimpsest (not unlike the allegory in *Casa de campo*) to favor a more vernacular image of the spoken language through emphasis on melodramatic overtones.

El jardín de al lado prepares the way for *La desesperanza,* a novel in which the artist is no longer a writer but a singer. With this last of three novels on Chile's history, Donoso abandons the stage set for the political arena. If there is theatricality being played out here, it is in open spaces and with a cast of thousands (the political demonstration at Matilde Urrutia's burial). The artist's mission is redefined within an ironic awareness of the necessary use of personae. Under the guise of Mañungo Vera, the figure of the writer leaves the international limelight of pop stardom to return to a political arena and utter a cry of dissent. Rather than hide behind the disguises fashioned for the singer by his promoters, the artist lashes out publicly against military oppression.

It is quite fitting to juxtapose *Casa de campo* with *La desesperanza.* In fact, one could imagine the character of Arabela, who was tortured and then died in the first novel, becoming Judit Torre, who was tortured and attempts to kill in the second. Likewise, Mañungo Vera may be considered a reincarnation of Francisco de Assis, the singer who represented Víctor Jarra in *Casa de campo.* In effect, the same cast of characters surfaces in the first part of the last novel. Moreover, both works transpire in the space of one day, and both envision a revisionary rather than a revolutionary political process.

In these three novels, by depicting political and personal transformations, Donoso's narrative has shifted from personal to collective concerns. Each novel is mindful of the fact that in times of severe oppression and censorship, art becomes the vessel for historical memory. It is as if the characters of La Marquesa Salió A Las Cinco had abandoned the stage of their tableaux vivants and moved into the arena of political theater— Arabela, now turned Judit, "dresses to kill" to be effective in clandestine work; Francisco, now turned Mañungo, gets another chance to interpret the New Song; and Agapito, now turned Lopito, dresses as the drunk

144

clown in political demonstrations. No longer finding the allegorical garb comfortable, Donoso bares the clandestine work of radical dissidents for his audience.

Casa de campo ends with the image of the trompe l'oeil, with its fixed characters ready to surface and alleviate the suffering of the inhabitants of the mansion. *El jardín de al lado* moves from the static sculpted scene controlled by Julio to a dynamic, extemporaneous performance ushered in by Gloria's intervention. Finally, *La desesperanza* closes with the children looking for the Caleuche vessel, the model ship in the museum, that will transport them to the promised land of Chile's future. In each case, Donoso employs a static image that is capable of magical transformations at the wave of the wand of creative artifice.

Because of the great emphasis in these three novels on plastic and dramatic forms of expression, they must be viewed as a national triptych; each panel marking a progression from the stillness of asphyxia to tentative gestures of transformation. If the triptych first depicts children who must act out prescribed roles within an increasingly stifling atmosphere, it ends with a handful of young people eager again to face the future with idealistic slogans: "Shall we join the revolution Jean-Paul?"

If left and right panels mirror each other as they allegorize and reinterpret a long period of crisis in Chile, the center panel concerns the artist's musings on his creative process: Julio stands as the withdrawn creator of the allegorical tale, while Gloria reaches out with a more realistic, less mediated discourse. Like the trompe l'oeil in *Casa de campo,* the panel positioned here provides a static metaphor ripe with vital possibilities.

In this triptych, the novels establish a tension between the moments of contemplation and balance found in the plastic arts and the transformative action of dialogic confrontation. In Donoso's creations, theatricality, history, and legend are the forces that bring characters into motion as they step out of the tableaux vivants. They stand ready to leave the comforts of a summer mansion and inhabit the empty streets of Santiago on a night of curfew. Donoso, the principal player in this drama, closes the triptych, hoping that his services as master painter will no longer be required to reinstate the flow of history.

7

MASKING HISTORY IN "TARATUTA"

In the novella "Taratuta" (1990) ["Taratuta"], Donoso as narrator begins by making us aware of the need to question official versions of history:

> Como tantas cosas relacionadas con el legado Schmidt, este párrafo está lleno de datos que parecen contradecir los que aportaban otros tratadistas. ¿De dónde sacó Walter la autoridad para afirmar que era Lodzinski el apellido de este personaje, y no Taratuta, ni Moskovsky, como aseguran otros, ni Kammerer, que fue el apellido que adoptó al retirarse finalmente a San Remo? Krupskaya, en sus MEMORIAS, afirma que Nicolás Schmidt murió en la prisión zarista víctima de las torturas de sus carceleros. Pero Walter favorece la hipótesis de la mala salud del joven industrial, probablemente tísico como varios miembros de su familia. Otro cronista habla de suicidio. Aseguran, también, que la herencia de Nicolás Schmidt se dividió en tres partes. ¿Cuál es la verdad? (11)

> As with so many things relating to the Schmidt legacy, this paragraph is full of facts that seem to contradict those brought out by other writers. By what authority does Walter state that Lodzinski was the person's surname and not Taratuta or Moskovsky as others assert, or Kammerer, which was the name he adopted when he finally retired to San Remo? Krupskaya, in her *Memoirs,* states that Nicholas Schmidt died in the tsarist prison the victim of his jailers' tortures. But Walter favors the hypothesis of the young industrialist's frail health, probably tubercular like several members of his family. Another chronicler speaks of suicide. They also assert that Nicholas Schmidt's inheritance was divided three ways. What is the truth? (14–15)

146

As made explicit by this quotation, history purports to arrive at a truth, yet falls into ambiguity and contradiction. While in *Casa de campo* Donoso exposes the role that language plays in the hands of the military regime in Chile, in "Taratuta" he focuses on the nature of historical discourse itself with its inconsistency and lack of resolution.

"Taratuta" attempts to retrace the trajectory of the disappearance from Soviet historical records of a marginal character in Lenin's entourage with the pseudonym of Taratuta.[1] In order to effect this disappearing act, the novella erases the traditional concepts of genealogy, textual authority, beginnings, and endings; it substitutes for them a randomly determined, collectively forged fictional account of history. All of these textual strategies highlight the uses and abuses of historical and fictional conventions in order to challenge the cultural and political contexts of those discourses.

In narrative terms, Donoso's novella imitates the historical character's disappearance by making historical discourse disappear at the same time that alternative fictional languages appear. For example, the descendant of the Soviet Viktor Taratuta, Horacio Carlos Taratuta—a red-haired Argentinian—disappears from the narrator's life at the end of section two. Narrative voice shifts from the historical to the personal at the beginning of section three and suddenly Horacio Carlos reappears again as if by magic. The reappearance of the "lost" character coincides with a shift from historical to literary discourse. Thus, within the fabric of the text there are two parallel discourses that are juxtaposed so as to parody each other. On one hand there is fiction; on the other, historical discourse surfaces in quoted texts from three verifiable sources. The first and most extensive of the three is Gerard Walter's biography of Lenin as published in translation by Grijalbo. The quoted passage does not deal with Lenin, but with Nicolás Schmidt, a Russian millionaire who died in prison and left a large part of his estate to the Bolshevik Revolution. Second is a fragment from the memoirs of Krupskaya, Lenin's wife, which describes the social life of the Russian emigrés in Paris. Third are three fragments of letters by Lenin that speak of Taratuta, the Russian playboy who managed the Schmidt inheritance for the party; Charlie Chaplin, whose irony the Russian leader finds interesting; and the enigmatic smile of the Gioconda, whose meaning seems to escape Lenin. All three sources serve as comic relief in Lenin's letters which deal mainly with the makings of "la plus grande des révolutions que le monde ait connues" [The greatest revolution that the world has known] (Walter, "Note Préliminaire" 7).

The presence of historical sources within a fictional narrative questions the fictionality of that text. Further, since the narrator of the novella is José Donoso himself, we are led to question whether we are reading a memoir of his intellectual curiosity. The narrator clearly distinguishes between this novella and an article he has supposedly published in Spanish and Latin American newspapers entitled "Lenin: Nota a pie de página" (12) ["Lenin: A Footnote" (16)]—my bibliographical search of the article uncovered the short piece "Lenin" in *El Mercurio* published by Donoso April 7, 1985 in Chile. "Taratuta," in short, makes a collage of historical and journalistic discursive practices and so points to the fluidity of the fictional process. Conversely, by quoting passages that introduce Lenin's interest in extravagant figures like Taratuta and in forms of art that play with sarcasm and irony, Donoso exposes the ironic side of historical discourse and obscures the neat margins between history and fiction.

In addition to the actual quotations that appear in the novella, there are two reworkings of Walter's biography in sections 6–8 (39–61; 37–63) and in section 11 (77–81; 78–82). Compilation and summary of the existing data has been consciously transformed into a story because of the contradictory nature of the available record:

> Después de años de ir recogiendo en ecos de textos las astillas dispersas y las versiones trizadas de la historia del legado Schmidt, resulta tan nebulosa, nunca referida de una manera completa por una sola autoridad sino por distintos exégetas y de maneras tan *contradictorias* y llenas de *lagunas,* que no puedo imaginarme cómo logré sintetizar las variantes ni a qué versión de los hechos recurrió mi memoria para improvisar, esa noche en El Viso, algo que puede haber sido más o menos semejante a esta narración. (39, my emphasis)

> After years of going along gathering the scattered splinters and the shredded versions of the story of the Schmidt legacy in the echoes of texts, everything has turned out so hazy, with nothing referred to in a thoroughgoing way by a single authority, but by different scholars and in such *contradictory* ways, and so *full of gaps* that I can't image how I managed to synthesize the variants or to which version of the facts my memory had recourse in order to improvise on that night in El Viso something that might have been more or less similar to this narrative. (41, emphasis mine)

The narrative that we read is thus a creative improvisation on a faulty, contradictory record. "Taratuta" includes a written transposition of a dialogue between the narrator "José Donoso" and the Argentinian descendant of the Bolshevik Taratuta. Moreover, whenever the narrator assumes the historical tone, which is markedly more serious than the rest of the novella, he always starts with the premise that he will be relating the Schmidt case, when in fact, the main concern of these particular sections is with the characters of Taratuta, the Bolshevik, and Taratuta, the redhaired Argentinian. There is always a movement from Lenin, to Schmidt, to Taratuta the Bolshevik, to Taratuta the Argentinian Jew.

The narrator assumes a critical tone whenever he exposes the shortcomings of the historical record. However, he, too, sins through the same absentmindedness when he quickly digresses from Schmidt to Taratuta. Furthermore, Donoso is in essence repeating Walter's gesture, who in his introduction to the biography confesses to having failed to fill all the gaps left open by twenty years of faulty investigation on the Bolshevik leader:

> Tâche immense, et qui dépasse de beaucoup les moyens dont dispose l'auteur du présent ouvrage. C'est pourquoi le lecteur ne sera pas surpris d'y constater maintes lacunes. . . . [C]e livre est insuffisant sous bien des rapports. Mais, aussi, on n'a nul scrupule à déclarer qu'il est, en tout état de cause, moins mauvais que ceux qui, avant lui, avaient traité ce sujet. Et puis, et surtout, on tient à dire hautement que, de la première ligne à la dernière, il n'a eu qu'un seul, un constant, un obsédant souci: celui d'écouter la voix de la vérité historique. (Note Préliminaire)

> [A huge task, which goes far beyond the many means that this author possesses. That's why the reader will not be surprised to find many a gap. . . . This book is insufficient in many respects. But also, one can declare without any scruples that it is, in any case, better than those that have dealt with the subject before it. And then, above all, one wishes to say forcefully that from the first to the last line there is but one, constant, obsessive goal: that of listening to the voice of historical truth.]

But, whereas Walter's concern is to arrive at the historical truth, Donoso's novelistic interest compels him to digress:

> Confieso que no fueron las grandes marejadas de la historia ni el desfile de personajes señeros los que atraparon mi fantasía, sino hechos triviales, personajes secundarios, a veces no más que una alusión al pasar, una sombra, una nota a pie de página relacionada sólo tenuemente con los acontecimientos fundamentales. (9–10)

> I must confess that it wasn't the great groundswells of history or the parade of singular personages that caught my fancy, but rather trivial events, secondary characters, sometimes no more than a passing allusion, a shadow, a footnote only vaguely connected to the fundamental happenings. (13)

If the purpose of history is to arrive at the truth, and that of fiction is to digress, they nevertheless share the obsessive drive to fill in the gaps left by earlier texts. Moreover, both types of discourses function because of contradiction.

The quotation regarding the contradictory nature of the historical record brings us directly to the literary discourse that underlies the novella and its dialogues with history. This literary discourse is historical in nature as well, for it serves to reevaluate the ironic discourse of the Argentinian masters Borges, Cortázar, and Bioy Casares. Although the novella actually refers to "Autopista del Sur" ["The Southern Thruway"] by Cortázar and *Fotógrafo en La Plata* [*The Adventures of a Photographer in La Plata*] by Bioy Casares, it is with Borges, who is never mentioned in the text, that the novella truly dialogues. From the outset, "Taratuta" sets up a very Borgesian set of relations between historical and fictional texts, the main difference being that in Borges's stories, historical references are in themselves fictional. In Borges's intertextual games, the ironic tone privileges fictional over historical discourse (e.g., "Pierre Menard, autor del Quijote" [Pierre Menard, Author of the Quijote]), whereas Donoso at least starts with "true" historical sources embedded in his text. Which leads to the question: Is Donoso simply revisiting Borgesian postmodernist games, or is he juxtaposing them against the historical to redefine Latin American literature vis-à-vis contemporary social and political contexts?

Everything about the character of Taratuta rings of Borges. First of all, the narrator secures knowledge of Lenin's biography through an acquaintance in Moscow. Having read Walter's biography, he corresponds with his friend, referring to specific paragraphs in the text that deal with Taratuta. As expected, the copy that the Russian friend holds does not include the paragraph in question (e.g., "Tlön, Uqbar, Orbis Tertius"): "Quedé estupefacto con su respuesta: no sólo jamás había oído hablar del legado Schmidt, y para qué decir de Taratuta, sino que no encontró el párrafo de mi cita en su edición del Walter" (11) [I was dumbfounded by his answer: not only had he never heard of the Schmidt legacy, but what was that talk about Taratuta, since he couldn't find the paragraph I'd cited in his edition of the Walter book (15)]. While Borges's games with a disappearing imaginary planet lead to a discussion of the nature of language, Donoso's gesture at the disappearance of a historical character serves to point to the presence of censorship in the Soviet Union:

> Quedé descontento con mi versión del asunto del legado Schmidt, como si me hubiera aventurado a un ámbito extrañísimo cuya totalidad desconocía y que, por quedar bajo la tutela de guardianes con derecho a arrancar páginas y eliminar párrafos, nunca llegaría a conocer. (12)

> I was still unhappy with my version of the Schmidt legacy matter, as though I'd ventured into a very strange environment whose totality was unknown to me and which, being under the tutelage of guardians with the right to tear out pages and eliminate paragraphs, I would never get to know. (16)

The reference to censors in this circular way, as "guardians with the right to tear out pages and eliminate paragraphs," underlines the rhetorical devices to which writers must resort in order to evade them. Furthermore, the mention of censorship in the Soviet Union serves as a reminder that matters are not that much better in the Southern Cone (Argentina, Chile, and Uruguay). When the narrator travels to Buenos Aires for a book fair, he comments on the situation in Chile:

> El distanciamiento por corto tiempo, pone en perspectiva tanto mis problemas personales, como las urgencias políticas y sociales de mi país, y constituye un respiro de la agobiante "coyuntura" que tiende a ocupar todo nuestro horizonte. (71–72)

> Getting away for a short time put both my personal problems and the urgent political and social needs of my country into perspective and it provides a breathing spell from the overwhelming "bind" that tends to occupy our whole outlook. (73)

The word "coyuntura" [bind], already set apart by quotation marks, refers to a censored situation that is very much on the mind of his readers.

Like many of Borges's characters (i.e., the Asian spy in "El jardín de senderos que se bifurcan" ["The Garden of Forking Paths"], the Russian Taratuta stands out because of his marginal aspect:

> No lo dije en mi artículo para la Agencia Efe porque entonces no lo sabía, que Taratuta, además de su profesión de terrorista y de su nombre espectacular, poseía una melena y una barba colorada que lo debían hacer blanco fácil para las balas de la policía, que siempre logró evitar. (12)

> Since I didn't know it at the time, I didn't mention in my article for Agencia Efe that Taratuta, in addition to his profession of terrorist and his spectacular name, had a red beard and mane that must have made him an easy target for police bullets, which he always managed to dodge. (16)

At the beginning of the novella, both Donoso and the Argentinian Taratuta (who is searching for his ancestors while at the same time hiding from the military in Argentina) are in the dark as to the "true" character of the Russian ancestor. Moreover, both Horacio Carlos Taratuta (by wearing a wig to hide his red hair) and the narrator (by not including the information about the red hair in the article) practice the art of self-censorship in order to appear in the public eye.

It is the redness of the ancestor Taratuta that is being hidden, meaning that he was a Bolshevik, and that he was Jewish (in Latin American countries, light, curly hair is often associated with being Jewish). In fact, there is a question as to the Jewish ancestry of the young Taratuta (Horacio Carlos) who is himself unsure of what he is:

> Es discutible el origen judío de la familia: la ausencia de circuncisión en el caso del Taratuta porteño lo prueba, porque, ¿qué padre puede ser tan atolondrado como para privar a su hijo de un simple rito de iniciación y así hacerlo miembro de su tribu? (26)

151

The Jewish origins of the family are debatable: the absence of circumcision in the case of the Buenos Aires Taratuta proves it, because what father would be so rash as to deprive his son of that simple rite of initiation that made him a member of his tribe? (29–30)

The young Taratuta, who was raised by his father alone and was therefore bereft of his Jewish matrilineage, was not circumcised, precisely to protect him. Taratuta's father is known to have disappeared in Buenos Aires during the period of the Dirty War. The young Taratuta, however, does not know on which side of the war his father fought (18; 21). This complete lack of knowledge leaves Horacio Carlos with an insatiable desire to search for his lost origins. When living in Spain, he reads Donoso's article about the Soviet Taratuta, and his voyage to self-identification begins.

Even though Horacio Carlos Taratuta grew up with the ambivalence of an invented name, he chose to define himself as Jewish. Yet, the fact that he was not circumcised robbed him of full connection with that identification. When he was of school age, his classmates stripped him naked and performed a symbolic circumcision that left him covered with red ink. The red hair and the red ink entitled him to the "privilege" of discrimination:

> Tiraron sus pantalones al canal, empolvaron su cara con tiza blanca del pizarrón, y derramaron un frasco de tinta roja sobre su sexo. Lo despacharon chorreando sangre apócrifa de una circuncisión apócrifa, al patio de los grandes, que cayeron en manada sobre él. (17)

> They threw his pants into the canal, covered his face with chalk dust, and poured a bottle of red ink over his sex. They sent him off dripping the apocryphal blood of an apocryphal circumcision into the courtyard of the older boys, who fell on him in a pack. (20)

For Horacio Carlos, self-definition is tied to the writing process: chalk and ink initiate the young man into membership in the desired community. Moreover, it is due to Donoso's published mention of the name "Taratuta" that the Argentinian first becomes aware of his famous ancestor. Placed within a literary frame, the story of the Argentinian Jew follows a melodramatic agenda where a fledgling discovers his aristocratic ancestry and his fight for identity and recognition come to an end. In melodrama, there is an explicit movement from disguise to revelation.[2] The Soviet Taratuta had chosen to assume an alias to define himself as a terrorist and protect his Jewish ancestry. Scholars disagree on his original name:

> ¿De dónde sacó Walter la autoridad para afirmar que era Lodzinski el apellido de este personaje, y no Taratuta, ni Moskovsky, como aseguran otros, ni Kammerer, que fue el apellido que adoptó al retirarse finalmente a San Remo? (11)

By what authority does Walter state that Lodzinski was the person's surname and not Taratuta or Moskovsky as others assert, or Kammerer, which was the name he adopted when he finally retired to San Remo? (15)

The assumption of the name Taratuta, a name that cannot be associated with any particular nationality, even in a melting pot such as Argentina, becomes for Horacio Carlos's father a mask that should have ensured survival, but did not. The orphan, eager to be related to a clan of some kind, identifies himself with those who, like him, historically bear the sign of the outcast. Like all well-kept family secrets, that sign is carried in the unconscious of all its members, but is as visible as red hair to all those outside the family. If Jewishness is handed down matrilineally, and Horacio Carlos did not know his mother, the alias or the capacity to invent one's origins is transmitted patrilineally. Even before he knew of the existence of other Taratutas in the world, Horacio Carlos had already invented a name for himself: Tahoca (Taratuta, Horacio Carlos). For those who lack origins, self-definition is a function of naming oneself, a writing function.

When Donoso, the "true" writer, meets Horacio Carlos, who is functionally illiterate, the act of self-definition becomes a joint venture:

El papel de mago, de pronto, me apeteció: la arrogancia de un escritor puede hacerlo desafiar dragones y obrar prodigios, y la desorientación de este muchacho condenado a vivir *una historia sin comienzo* me conmovía.

No sólo me conmovía. Desde las páginas expurgadas de la biografía de Lenin de Gerard Walter, una figura había venido postulándose como héroe, yo no sabía héroe de qué, pero esa figura avanzaba hacia nosotros desde antes que yo supiera de las ansiedades de Horacio Carlos. Ahora, sin embargo, con un destello de barbas y melena coloradas, la función de Viktor Taratuta se me aclaró: esta función, lo supe al fin, era la de acoger a Horacio Carlos y decirle: ¡ven! (38, my emphasis)

The role of magician suddenly caught my fancy: a writer's arrogance can make him challenge dragons and work miracles, and the disorientation of that boy condemned to live *a story without any beginning* moved me.

It didn't only move me. From the expurgated pages of Gerard Walter's biography of Lenin a figure had risen claiming to be a hero, I didn't know hero of what, but that figure was coming toward us from a time before I knew about Horacio Carlos's anxieties. Now, however, with a flash of red beard and mane, Viktor Taratuta's function became clear to me: that function, I finally learned, was to welcome Horacio Carlos and tell him: come! (40, my emphasis)

An arrogant narrator in search of a hero and a nameless outcast in search of an identity meet on the common ground of narrating origins.[3] The implication that narrative life is very much like the real life of the Taratuta ancestry, a life without origins, brings us back to another very Borgesian concern that erases the boundaries between life and literature ("Borges y yo" ["Borges and I"]).[4] From the very beginning of the novella, Donoso is concerned with the fact that Taratuta is more like a character than a person, and that therefore, it will be difficult to write about him: "¿Cómo moverse entre esta gente y manejar estos seres con su aire de haber nacido calzados y barbados y con sus papeles ya asignados, de la mente de otro escritor?" (13) [How could I move about among those people and manipulate those creatures with that air of theirs of having been born with shoes on and a beard, their roles already assigned by the mind of another writer? (17)]. Is Donoso expressing a kind of anxiety of influence because many of Borges's characters in *Ficciones* [*Labyrinths*] are battling with their Jewish origins during the height of the Nazi persecution?[5] More than an anxiety that Borges has said it all and much better, there is a desire on Donoso's part to make the Borgesian connection so that his reader does not forget that the issue here is one of prejudice against and extermination of dissidents, at this time in reference to Argentina during the Dirty War.

Just as Horacio Carlos could not forgive his father for having failed to circumcise him, Donoso, in this novella, berates his literary father for not having spoken against the military junta in the seventies. Even though Borges in his short stories and essays certainly did attack Nazi fascism in Europe and Argentina during the thirties and forties, he remained silent when faced with a similar situation in his later years.[6] By establishing a literary dialogue with the deceased writer, Donoso corrects Borges's omission and offers a distinctly Borgesian piece in which he attacks the dismissal of historical contexts as a complete lack of literary responsibility.

Like the history that it is contesting, Donoso's "Taratuta" functions under the sign of contradiction.[7] Borges's intertextual discourse is inscribed within the novella in order to dismantle it and offer an alternative use to metafiction. Although like Borges, Donoso is ultimately talking about the uses and misuses of literary language, the Chilean novelist consciously plays games of magical substitutions in order to inscribe them in a contemporary historical and social context. Up until the time of the arrival of Horacio Carlos in the text, the reader readily recognizes the parodic dialogue that is being established with Borges. On a first reading, Donoso's novella seems to be taking a step backward and rehashing old metafictional concerns regarding the loss of power of the narrator and the primacy of fiction over history. After a careful analysis of the role that historical and fictional discourses play in "Taratuta," however, it becomes evident that they are made to stand side by side in order to underline the limitations of both. Moreover, with the unexpected arrival of Taratuta's descendant on the scene, the novella rejects a purely bidimensional discourse (fiction versus history) and welcomes a multiplicity of marginal languages into the fabric of the text.

> La segunda circunstancia que después de un tiempo me llevó a involucrarme en la historia del legado Schmidt fue recibir una carta firmada por cierto Horacio Carlos Taratuta Roserman, con remitente en ESTUDIO PARAPSICOLOGICO TAHOCA, calle de la Escalinata 26, sobreático, Madrid (España). La carta casi se me cayó de las manos al leer el apellido del firmante. (15)

> The second circumstance that got me involved in the history of the Schmidt legacy some time later was the receipt of a letter signed by a certain Horacio Carlos Taratuta Roserman with the return address of Tahoca Parapsychology Studio, Calle de la Escalinata 26, Upper, Madrid (Spain). I almost dropped the letter when I read the name of the person who'd signed it. (18)

With this poorly handwritten letter enter two marginal discourses, the epistolary and the parapsychological. It most be noted that because the young Taratuta is barely literate, his letter does not fall into the nineteenth-century tradition of epistolary literature. Rather, it is reminiscent of other contemporary Latin American writers' use of popular genres (i.e., Manuel Puig) to valorize vernacular language and undermine an elitist definition of the artistic. As a consequence of the unexpected letter in Donoso's text, the narrator loses his historian's aplomb. From this moment on, his narrative authority will cease to be singular in nature and will become contaminated with other unexpected voices.

With Horacio Carlos, the thrust of the narrative becomes a drive for self-definition often propelled by melodramatic impulses: "the indulgence of strong emotionalism; . . . inflated and extravagant expression; dark plottings, suspense, breathtaking peripety" (Brooks, *Melodramatic Imagination* 11–12). Up to his contact with Donoso's article in *Diario ABC,* the young Taratuta had turned to the stars in search of his origins. Sections 4–10 of the novella constitute Donoso's narration to Horacio Carlos regarding his investigations of Viktor Taratuta, which could inscribe the protagonist within a pseudoaristocratic lineage. The narrator advises his reader, however, that the story was interrupted by the arrival of Zonga, Horacio Carlos's lover and practitioner of occult arts:

> Quiero aclarar que esa noche en El Viso mi narración quedó trunca, no sólo porque es en su esencia fragmentaria, sin más comienzo que el sitio por donde parece posible abordarla, y sin otro final que una serie de conjeturas, sino porque Horacio Carlos desapareció a consecuencia del incidente con la Zonga. Así, jamás he tenido la ocasión para contar el cuento completo. (39–40)

155

I want to make clear that on that night in El Viso my narrative was cut off, not only because it is essentially fragmentary, with no beginning other than the place where it seems best to start, and with no other ending than a series of conjectures, but because Horacio Carlos disappeared as a consequence of the incident with La Zonga. Therefore, I have never had a chance to tell the complete story. (42)

Besides being an exposition on the nature of fiction à la Borges, the novella that we read results from Donoso's inability to complete an oral narration. Whenever a Taratuta intervenes in history or in a story, a melodramatic tone imposes itself:

Mi olfato de novelista percibió al leer el párrafo de Walter, que esta historia—la fortuna fabulosa, el terrorista de nombre espectacular, Lenin y la prosaica Krupskaya buscando un marido "de tout repos" para la ingenua Elizaveta que a la manera de las farsas de Labiche ya tenía amante—era la maqueta de un folletín portentoso que yo apenas alcanzaba a entrever. (11)

When I read that paragraph in Walter, my novelist's sense of smell picked up on the tale—the fabulous fortune, the terrorist with a spectacular name, Lenin and the prosaic Krupskaya looking for a husband *de tout repos* for the innocent Elizabeta who, as in a farce by Labiche, already had a lover—and I saw the basis for a tremendous serial novel, even if I only had a glimmer of it. (15)

Although the expectations of the melodramatic plot are not realized for Horacio Carlos—he never achieves an aristocratic standing—the narrator succeeds in subverting the interest of the reader so that the subject Lenin becomes secondary to the destiny of a marginal character. At the heart of the melodramatic agenda lies an interest in the quotidian rather than the heroic (Brooks, *Melodramatic Imagination* 15).

"Taratuta" vacillates between the historically determined discourse of the narrator and the parapsychological interruptions of the character. Soon after Donoso's oral narration begins, Horacio Carlos cuts in so that he may become participant in the making of his own past:

—¿Lo nombran en muchos libros?
—Sí . . . , tuvo un papel un poco . . .
—¿En qué mes nació?
—No tengo idea.
—Seguro que en julio.
—¿Por qué?
—Debe haber sido Leo.
—¿Por qué?

—Por su don de mando. Los Leo son autoritarios y escalan posiciones de influencia. Por eso Viktor Taratuta llegó a ser un protagonista de la historia, como decía mi profesora. (42–43)

> "Do they mention him in a lot of books?"
> "Yes . . . , he had a role that was a little . . ."
> "What month was he born in?"
> "I have no idea."
> "It had to be July."
> "Why?"
> "He must have been a Leo."
> "Why?"
> "Because of his gift of command. Leos are authoritarian and reach positions of influence. That's why Viktor Taratuta got to be a protagonist of history, as my teacher used to say." (44–45)

Viktor Taratuta was indeed a protagonist of history. According to Donoso, however, he was no more than a Don Juan, but according to Horacio Carlos he was "el financista de los bolcheviques" (45) [the financier of those Bolsheviks (47)]. Horacio Carlos's "purely accidental" participation has the effect of stealing the show from Lenin and Viktor Taratuta so that they are marginalized in Donoso's narration. Horacio Carlos not only becomes the protagonist but the creative participant as well:

> Callé para no contestarle que me parecía embrollado además de poco probable su razonamiento para atribuirse el apellido, la tribu, y el origen. Tampoco quise discutirle las cualidades con que su fantasía adornaba a sus supuestos antepasados. (46)

> I remained silent in order not to reply that I thought his reasoning, attributing to himself the name, the tribe, and the origins, was a little farfetched and also not very probable. Nor did I wish to dispute the qualities with which his fantasy adorned his putative forebears. (48)

Donoso's silence allows for a much more entertaining and less historical narration. If we recall that the first circumstance for the engendering of the novella was an obsession with "la sonrisa de gato oriental de Lenin" (9) [Lenin's Oriental cat smile (13)], we can surmise that Horacio Carlos not only stole the stage from his spectacular predecessor, but also from Donoso himself, who as narrator projects his ironic tone onto the face of Lenin.

Horacio Carlos's intrusion is the result of a fortuitous meeting between character and narrator. It is true that the narrator Donoso writes an article and his character responds with a letter of inquiry. But when Donoso, in spite of his doubts, answers the letter to establish an encounter in Madrid, where Horacio Carlos now lives, the letter is returned, "addressee unknown." When Donoso goes to Madrid in order to meet his literary agent, he accidentally ends up in the coffee shop where Horacio Carlos works. This "accidental" encounter, however, is not quite so accidental. It is tied to the narrator's professional and personal life. He returns to the neighborhood, which is coincidentally Horacio Carlos's, in order to savor a pastry that had been both his and his wife's predilection during their exile in Spain:

> Cuando viví en aquel vecindario hace cerca de un cuarto de siglo, sobre todo en invierno antes de ponerme a trabajar, ˙yo hacía rápidas excursiones matinales a comprar esas pastas tiernas para nuestro desayuno porque a mi mujer le encantaban. Cuando vuelvo a Madrid me las arreglo para pasar por esa calle con el propósito de probar una ensaimada perfecta. (21)

> When I lived in that neighborhood a quarter of a century ago, especially in winter before settling down to work, I would make a quick morning trip to buy some soft pastries for breakfast because my wife was in love with them. Whenever I get back to Madrid I always manage to take a walk along that street with an aim to tasting one of those perfect buns. (23)

Because the taste for pastries is conveniently tied to his personal and professional life, it cues the reader to the connection with Proust, a writer to whom Donoso has confessed a great indebtedness.[8] If Proust uses the famous madeleine to trigger the rescue of a lost memory, Donoso uses the search for his "ensaimada" [pastry] to usher in a collaborative type of narration.

The second meeting with Horacio Carlos likewise is tied to literary pursuits. Two years after the Madrid encounter, Donoso goes to Buenos Aires for a book fair, takes a walk through Palermo with an old friend "Pepita," Josefina Delgado, and subsequently they end up in a coffee shop owned by Horacio Carlos and Zonga. The novella concludes in dialogue between Donoso and Pepita, the latter constantly challenging Donoso's narrative authority regarding the Taratuta story. This succession of café scenes that underlines the collaborative nature of "Taratuta" also establishes a link between the fictional and the historical. Krupskaya's quoted passage concerns Taratuta's love for the political gatherings at Parisian coffeehouses: "*Nuestra gente se pasaba el tiempo sentada en los cafés hasta muy tarde por la noche. Taratuta era un gran aficionado a la vida de café y poco a poco los demás rusos que iban llegando fueron adquiriendo sus mismos hábitos*" (49) [*Our people spent their time sitting in cafés until quite late at night. Taratuta was a great lover of café life and little by little the other Russians who were arriving began taking on the same habits as he* (51)]. The gathering of political circles in cafés is of course not much different from that of literary circles. The narrator's insistence on that fact erases the boundaries between historical and fictional discourses.

Donoso's narrative, begun by attempting to rescue history from its insufficiency at arriving at the truth, ends with a dialogue that discovers the forgotten characters of that history—characters that appear incognito because of the historical persistence of censorship and oppression in Latin American countries. Because of this political reality, Horacio Carlos's discovery of his origins has resulted in the scarring of his face and in the wearing of a wig in order to conceal the nature of his identity. Having returned to Argentina to reassume his marginal nationality, the immigrant Jew resides in a country that is marginal to the European center where his ancestors helped forge a revolution. Horacio Carlos and his friend Zonga end up as owners of a coffee shop in a lost neighborhood in Buenos Aires. The wigs they wear make it difficult to be recognized. When Donoso and Pepita, who sit to have a drink at the end of their walk, suggest to the waiter that he might be Horacio Carlos Taratuta, he recoils and joins Zonga, the center of his life until the writer's arrival: "La Zonga era la única persona que conocía con la que realmente tuvo una relación y por esto constituía para él un centro" (88) [because La Zonga was the only person he knew with whom he had a real relationship and that's why she was a center for him (88)].

Horacio Carlos's center is in itself a caricature of a television character. In fact, when the narrator first meets Zonga, he sees her through a window (65; 66), and watches her transformations of dress (from Morticia to a small-town schoolteacher) as if on a silent television screen:

> Una imagen olvidada de la "trivia" de mi adolescencia se interpuso para hacerme entender cual era la matriz, tal vez inconsciente, que la subyugaba: La Zonga se creía Morticia, de Charles Addams, imagen de lo cómicamente sepulcral. (66)

> A forgotten image of the "trivia" of my adolescence interposed itself to make me understand what the basis, unconscious perhaps, of what dominated her was: La Zonga thought she was Charles Addams's Morticia, an image of the comically sepulchral. (67)

After losing track of both characters, Donoso confesses that the transforming Zonga was another version of a recurring character in his works: "reconozco en este personaje residuos de otros personajes míos" (71) [I can recognize in that character the residue from other characters of mine (72)].

More importantly, Zonga, a symbol of the humorously sepulchral, appears as if on a silent screen and functions very much like Charlie

Chaplin, whose humorous black-and-white silent figure served to bring to millions a whimsical yet mordant criticism of the fascist figures Hitler and Mussolini in *The Great Dictator*. Horacio Carlos's disoriented character makes him the butt of jokes (i.e., the scene in the Madrid coffee shop where someone trips him when he's holding a tray full of dishes), and mirrors the countless abused outsiders that Charlie Chaplin played throughout his career. Donoso quotes one of Lenin's letters regarding Chaplin:

> —*Expresa una actitud escéptica o satírica hacia lo convencional, e intenta dar vuelta al revés todo lo que comunmente* [sic] *es aceptado, desfigurándolo con el fin de demostrar la ausencia de lógica en nuestros hábitos diarios. ¡Complicado pero interesante!* (53)

> *He displays a skeptical or satirical attitude toward the conventional, and he attempts to turn everything that is commonly accepted upside down, disfiguring it with an aim to showing the absence of logic in our daily habits. Complicated, but interesting!* (54–55)

Lenin's description of Chaplin's aesthetics is indeed a description of Donoso's own novelistic enterprise. The distancing effect that he practices with the interposing silent screen, the use of historical quotation to describe his own creative process, the transformation of character as symbolized by the assumption of a particular dress, and a prevailing interest in the grotesque are but a few of the novelistic effects that Donoso has practiced throughout his career. These techniques have the explicit purpose of showing an absence of logic in human behavior, and, in this novella, specifically of political oppression in Argentina. In "Taratuta," this appeal to the humorously grotesque so commonly found in mass media serves to honor a creative genius such as Chaplin, who risked his career to convey a political message to the masses. As a novelist, Donoso is keenly aware of the limitations of his scope, and, in effect, is afraid that his intervention may have done little to change his character's destiny. His friend Pepita tells him: "—Estás partiendo del supuesto de que tus palabras, esa tarde en El Viso, lo conmovieron tan a fondo, que le cambiaron el destino" (89) ["You're starting with the supposition that your words that afternoon in El Viso moved him so deeply that they changed his fate" (89)]. Donoso is clearly conscious that his extemporaneous contact with Horacio Carlos may have done little to rescue the character from his nameless existence, but his novella does rescue a historic period that was forgotten by Borges. With "Taratuta," the Chilean novelist performs an ironic inversion of a Borgesian form to expose the historical context left silent in the mastery of the Argentinian writer.

The collaborative effort between Donoso and his friend Pepita functions to deflate the image of the omniscient narrator. Throughout the novella, the interventions of Horacio Carlos and those of Donoso's critical female interlocutor confront the authorial figure and point to the provisionality of his enterprise: "Claro que lo que te conté no es verdad. ¿No te das cuenta que lo que acabo de contar no es más que un borrador . . . ?" (89–90) [What I told you of course isn't true. Do you realize that what I've just narrated is only a rough draft . . . ? (89–90)]. The essence of Borges's fiction, as described and parodied by Donoso, is its metalinguistic, self-referential nature. "Taratuta" constantly returns to the narrator's preoccupation with his task, and this preoccupation is repeatedly subverted by the interventions of Horacio Carlos, Zonga, and finally Pepita (representing the critic), who, with their direct interpretation of the historical events at hand, bring the narrator's exaggerated self-importance down to earth. Donoso has in effect masterfully replicated Borges's ironic tone, but he has managed to subvert it by contaminating the text with the language of the so-called extraliterary: parapsychology, television, and film.

Donoso drives home his efforts to surpass Borges by habitually postponing the novella's end. "Taratuta" tries to end on page 69; 71, but, after several attempts, does not succeed until page 91; 91. In effect, it approaches a game with Pepita repeatedly assuming that her friend's narration is complete and Donoso replying with a new possible conclusion. This game pokes fun at Borges's implicit postponement of the end in stories such as "La muerte y la brújula" ["Death and the Compass"], "El milagro secreto" ["The Secret Miracle"], and "El jardín de senderos que se bifurcan" ["The Garden of Forking Paths"]. In all of these, the protagonist's death is postponed so that his dramatic story can be told; the death of the character neatly coincides with narrative death. In Donoso's "Taratuta," this is not the case. Horacio Carlos not only survives but his life story lacks any dramatic interest and resides in the quotidian horror of silent repression. The essential element of Donoso's novella surfaces at the end. Pepita and the narrator are about to leave after concluding that the couple they suspect to be Horacio Carlos and Zonga cannot possibly be them. Then, they notice the name of the coffee shop, Yelisavetgrad, the place of origin for all the Taratutas:

> Corrimos a tomar un taxi que pasó por la otra esquina. Le di la dirección de Pepita para pasar a dejarla. Cuando partimos en dirección contraria a la dirección hacia donde se fue la Citroneta, Pepita me preguntó:
> —¿Tú crees que importan . . . ?
> —¿Qué?
> —Los nombres. Yelisavetgrad, por ejemplo.
> —Sí. Mucho. En muchos sentidos. (91)

161

We ran to catch a taxi that was passing by the other corner. I gave Pepita's address so I could drop her off on the way. When we took off in the opposite direction from where the Citroneta had gone, Pepita asked me:
"Do you think they're important?"
"What?"
"Names. Yelisavetgrad, for example."
"Yes. A lot. In a lot of ways." (91)

What is in a name? It was originally the outlandish name *Taratuta* that propelled Donoso to pursue the story: "[D]ebo confesar que para mí, llamar esta historia LODZINSKI O MOSKOVSKY, no TARATUTA, le quitaría gran parte de su encanto. Incluso dudo si hubiera emprendido la tarea de escribirla" (39) [I must confess that for me, calling this story *Lodzinski* or *Moskovsky,* not *Taratuta,* would take away a great deal of its charm. I even doubt that I would have undertaken the task of writing it (42)]. In this novella, the narrator bears the name José Donoso, a gesture that both repeats and subverts Borges's own definition as a writer in "Borges y yo" ["Borges and I"]. The name *Yelisavetgrad,* which at first Donoso could not find in a map because it was changed under the Stalinist regime, supplies the protagonist with the grounding which he has sought all his life. For both Horacio Carlos and Donoso, the novella confronts issues of genealogy in and out of literature. In Donoso's narrative, the name Yelisavetgrad, which was conveniently erased for political reasons, recalls censorship, that hegemonic activity of eradicating names and paragraphs from the face of the earth and from history. The reinstatement of those names, however forgotten, has become the essential element in Donoso's fiction since *Casa de campo.* With this novella, he consciously outlines a poetics of contemporary Latin American literature in an effort to go beyond gratuitous metalinguistic games. Furthermore, its surprisingly serious ending reminds the reader that words do indeed have significant meanings, and that literature—specifically Latin American literature since the seventies—is firmly grounded in a political and historical context that cannot be ignored.[9] Donoso, like his contemporaries, forges a literature that communicates human concerns in the face of censorship.

To counteract the seriousness of the historical context, "Taratuta" refers to Charlie Chaplin's humor, to Zonga's "sepulchral smile," and to "La Gioconda." The fact that Donoso portrays Lenin as not understanding Gioconda's meaning, presumably that of her smile (53; 55), juxtaposes the seriousness of history with that of the multiple enigmatic faces of literature. The perplexing nature of that smile points to a literary tradition of irony in Latin America that hovers above the unresolved contradiction between the discourses of fiction and history. Much contemporary Latin American fiction continues to express that contradiction between truth and deceit, and also expands its scope to encompass the voice of the marginalized. Marginal figures such as Horacio Carlos and Zonga may lack the "literacy" to pursue all the hermeneutic leads in "Taratuta," but they are capable of tapping into the language of mass culture to forge their destinies. Donoso's audience for a novella such as "Taratuta" is clearly the literary sophisticate; his message addresses the present state of Latin American literary history. He points to a canon that has transcended itself to go beyond the Borgesian poetics of literary self-consciousness to encompass the languages of melodrama, oral tradition, and mass communication. Donoso supersedes metafiction by contextualizing it in history: in social, political, and in literary terms.

CONCLUSION:
CAST OUT OF DONOSO'S HOUSE OF FICTION

If eyes are the windows of the soul, Donoso envisions windows as the opening to artistic consciousness. If behind every window in Donoso's many houses stands a figure focusing on an object through the artificial lenses of field glasses, it stands to reason that an observer, a reader such as I, could stand in the same place as the object being observed and return the figure's gaze. In his interpretation of *Las Meninas* by Velásquez, Michel Foucault places the observer of the painting in the same place as the object of the painter's gaze: the King and Queen. They stand outside and their images are being painted on a canvas unseen by the viewer. The ensuing visual dialogue highlights the subject's position *and* the perspective of the creative figure. Since the painter of *Las Meninas* that we see is "really" outside himself, all the characters in this scene stand together; with Velásquez, the royal couple, and the observer all occupying the invisible spot outside the painting. Likewise, Donoso's oeuvre, from *Coronación* to "Taratuta," effects a fictional dialogue between creator and observer, a dialogue that follows the creative and observing gazes in their deflecting and confronting modes.

Leaving the implied dialogue between novelist and reader, let us return to the window and the field glasses. It has been my contention that Donoso's field glasses refract through the prismatic lense of the melodramatic imagination. Under multicolored lights, ordinary subjects are heightened and made grotesque, hyperbolic, and comical, and are raised above their anonymous existence. Thus, the arteriosclerotic nonagenarian Misiá Elisa is crowned like a queen and depicted as a saint in her moment of death; the deaf-mute servant of decrepit old ladies wears the papier-mâché mask of a Giant's head and becomes the progenitor of a redeeming fiction; the demented figure of Adriano Gomara walks to the rhythm of grand opera and ushers in a new social order; and a nameless Jewish immigrant in Buenos Aires assumes the pseudonym of his illustrious ancestor and uncovers the overwhelming forces of political censorship and military repression.

But characters are not necessarily the subjects of Donoso's critical gaze. At center stage stands the motion of displacement, which calls attention to a fictional language at the precise moment that it is being substituted by another. This allows for a linguistic dialogue that privileges visual narratives, be they in the pictorial, theatrical, cinematographic, or televised mode. Thus, the emphasis is on tableaux vivants, which recall the eighteenth-century melodramatic genre and are always charged with emotional signification (*Coronación*); on trompe l'oeil, which plays with classical pictorial tenets that deceive the observer (*Casa de campo*); and on grotesque situation comedy characters that point to the duplicity and fragmentation of any persona ("Tartatuta").

Besides the displacement of languages, Donoso also focuses on the ambiguous nature of his expression as it concerns gender. From the very inception of his novelistic career, there is a marked ambivalence regarding gender that is resolved through the language spoken by La Manuela of *El lugar sin límites*. The feminine and the masculine fluctuate as each takes its turn on the stage of the novel. Manuela's transvestite experience ends in disaster, and it is not really until *El jardín de al lado* that there is an explicit consideration of the gender of the creative voice, as the female narrator upstages the male's voice. Through the female voice, the author interjects vernacular forms, a practice that he employed early on in his career through the voices of the maids in *Coronación*. Ultimately, we see the garden through the double glass of the androgynous narrator. Finally, in "Taratuta," narrative voice is postulated in dialogue between José Donoso and Josefina Delgado, two friends talking in the pleasant atmosphere of a Buenos Aires café. The latter, Pepita, is the female version of José "Pepe" Donoso, whose timbre is now refracted into its feminine and masculine overtones.[1] It is impossible to overlook, however, that the feminine version of the name is in the diminutive. If Donoso consciously projects a dialogue between the genders, he stills betrays the hegemony of the male voice. It is easy to detect the ambivalent formulation of many female characters, such as the grandmothers in the first two novels, Peta Ponce in *El obsceno pájaro de la noche,* and the female dog/Judit in *La desesperanza.* Ultimately, however, there is a concerted effort to give credence to a discursive practice that incorporates both feminine as well as masculine perspectives.

Having reviewed the tenor of Donoso's voice, we are left to consider the problematics of Donoso's language when confronted with a social or political crisis in his native Chile. In *Casa de campo,* the author uses an allegorical language to mimic his characters' outmoded dialect in La marquesa salió a las cinco. In *El jardín de al lado,* Donoso's male narrator offers a politically committed language that is rejected in favor of a more aesthetic idiom in the voice of Gloria, the ultimate narrator of the novel. Here, the novelist presents the ongoing tension between the exclusively propagandistic message and the purely self-reflexive art in the guise of two different painters, and he ends by favoring a dialogue between the two. The last novel of the triptych, *La desesperanza,* abandons the visual metaphor of the creative observer and adopts the tonality of song whereby poetic voice, and Neruda's voice in particular, is resurrected as an unfettered voice against political oppression. If these three novels project a gradual "baring of the device," we may compare the two extremes of *Coronación* and "Taratuta" to further clarify the intention of Donoso's language with regard to social and historical contexts.

There is no question that from the very beginning of his works Donoso has depicted class confrontation. The concluding scene in *Coronación* fully uses visual, melodramatic techniques to mark the clear silencing by the maids, who in this case, speak the mute language of hyperbolic gesture of bourgeois rhetoric as espoused by Misiá Elisa. The spoken voice still belongs to the classes in power, all others must gesture silently. In *Coronación,* Andrés is the creator of his own madness, and, as such, becomes a "narrator" of his destiny. The creation of imaginative worlds, that of Omsk specifically, is for him a consequence of wandering away from his grandmother's house and of walking through the streets of the city in order to avoid the stifling effects of the enclosed structure. But Andrés finally succumbs, retreats to the safety of the house, and becomes a prisoner of his own imagination—fashioning his escape in the interior spaces of madness. His newfound voice is that of the creator who looks inward and discovers a personal language.

Taratuta, the illiterate character who commands the stage of the 1990 novella, usurps the voice of no less than José Donoso himself, ushering in the language of the populace through the medium of mass communication. In this novella, the gesture of class confrontation is repeated: a character without the power to write silences the authority of the upper classes, of which Donoso is a member, by resorting to the popular idiom. Although the message has not changed, by now Donoso's house of fiction has become a house of Babel, filled with the constant echo of vernacular dialects that finally displace the hegemonic figure behind the window. He is now made to walk the streets of the city (the move from inhabiting a house to inhabiting a city was already made in *La desesperanza*). The focus of the work, true to the paradigm that we saw in the introduction, however, still remains the observing gaze of the creator, who now at least consents to speak in an integrated dialogue between masculine (Pepe) and feminine (Pepita). Pepita represents the critical reader, who, like Horacio Carlos, has dared to question the logic of a narration now created in collaboration. In the image of Pepita as critical reader, we are in the same place as the narrator, José Donoso: seated outside looking at the scene beyond, at Taratuta and Zonga in the café. At one point in the novella, Horacio Carlos and José Donoso, likewise, were sitting outside looking in at Zonga removing her Morticia disguise. Narrator and character, looking through a window, were represented as voyeurs of a scene inside a house. This in itself marks a radical change from the scene in *El jardín de al lado* with Julio hidden behind a window looking out. But at the end of "Taratuta," the character Horacio Carlos has reentered the scene and joined Zonga, leaving narrator and reader looking in from the outside (this could be seen as a rewriting of the scene where Santelices leaps into the window frame to join the blond girl). Taratuta, as character and as reader of Donoso's journalistic publications, returns the gaze; thus he succeeds in moving the writer out of his protective, fictional space behind the window frame. Pepe and Pepita sit on the outside looking in; this shift in perspective points to a shift from the creative individual's private concerns to the collective public concerns of a nation (both Chile in *La desesperanza* and Argentina in "Taratuta"). The creator still observes, but he is no longer the voyeur safe within the confines of the house. Ultimately, the two characters, Taratuta and Zonga, leave the scene of representation, close the iron curtain of the café, and thus refuse to continue playing out the narrator's script. All players in the representation—characters, narrator and reader—disperse into the streets of the city and disappear from sight.

In these later fictions, starting with *La desesperanza,* the Chilean novelist becomes a participant in the public arena, inhabiting the unprotected spaces outside and inside the dramatic scene, risking both confrontation and censorship. His collaborative dialogue at the end of "Taratuta" leaves us with the multiple sounds of the Donosian Chilean idiom, a language ringing with the voices of myth, history, and dramatic fiction.

NOTES

Introduction: Entering Donoso's House of Fiction

1. In Mexico, Donoso discovered an entire community of novelists, especially at the home of Carlos Fuentes, where he completed *El lugar sin límites* (1966) [*Hell Has No Limits*]. In Spain during the late sixties, Gabriel García Márquez, Mario Vargas Llosa, Julio Cortázar, Carlos Fuentes, and Donoso would meet in Barcelona, the city whose publishing houses brought the Latin American writers together. Donoso lived in Spain from 1967 to 1981. *Mundo Nuevo,* published in Paris, and edited by the Uruguayan critic Emir Rodríguez Monegal, also contributed toward grouping the literature of these novelists and making them visible to European and North American critics.

2. Donoso's response to the Chilean writer Marta Bruntet's statement implying that *Coronación* was a realist novel appears in his *Historia Personal del "boom,"* chapter 1 [*The Boom in Spanish American Literature: A Personal History* 27].

3. It must be noted that neither writers nor critics of the Boom included women writers of the same period whose narratives followed a similar trajectory. Victoria Ocampo (Argentina), Clarice Lispector (Brazil), Rosario Castellanos (Mexico), Luisa Valenzuela (Argentina), Julieta Campos (Cuba and Mexico), and Elena Poniatowska (Mexico) were just a few of the women writing at this time. For a preliminary anthology of these writers, see Sara Castro-Klarén, Sylvia Molloy, and Beatriz Sarlo, *Women's Writing in Latin America: An Anthology.* See also Susan Bassnett, "Coming Out of the Labyrinth: Women Writers in Contemporary Latin America," 247–67, for a brief account of why these women writers were neglected by critics until the eighties.

4. I owe this definition of the Boom to the Cuban critic Roberto González Echevarría in his article "Sarduy, the Boom and the Post-Boom," 57–72.

5. Examples of these include Gabriel García Márquez, *El amor en los tiempos del cólera* (1985) [*Love in the Time of Cholera*]; Carlos Fuentes, *La cabeza de la hidra* (1978) [*The Hydra Head*]; José Donoso, *La misteriosa desaparición de la marquesita de Loria* (1980) [The Mysterious Disappearance of the Little Marquise of Loria]; and Mario Vargas Llosa, *El elogio de la madrastra* (1988) [*In Praise of the Stepmother*].

6. Just to cite a few: Gabriel García Márquez, *La aventura de Miguel Littín, clandestino en Chile* (1986) [*Clandestine in Chile: The Adventures of Miguel Littín*]; Mario Benedetti, *Primavera con una esquina rota* (1982) [Spring With a Broken Corner]; Isabel Allende, *De*

amor y de sombra (1984) [*Of Love and Shadows*]; Ariel Dorfman, *Viudas* (1981) [*Widows*]; and Marta Traba, *Conversación al Sur* (1981) [*Mothers and Shadows*].

7. I quote Ricardo Gutiérrez Mouat, "José Donoso," 8–9, on Donoso's recognition: "In the last few years he has collected several international awards: the Mondello Prize in Italy (1989), the Roger Caillois in France (1991), the INTAR Golden Palm Award for the year's best contribution to theater by a novelist (New York, 1990), and, last but not least, the long-delayed National Prize for Literature in his native country."

8. See Sharon Magnarelli, *Understanding Donoso,* x–xii, for the chronology of his life and works.

9. I am indebted to Peter Brooks for his masterful definition of the melodramatic imagination in his book bearing that name. See also Martha Vicinus in her article in *New Literary History.*

Chapter 1: Setting the Scene

1. Both theater directors and movie producers have noticed the dramatic possibilities of Donoso's works and have adapted them to theatre and film. *Coronación* was adapted for the theater by the Chilean playwright José Pineda and directed by Eugenio Guzmán. The production opened by the Instituto del Teatro de la Universidad de Chile in August of 1966 and was well covered by the Chilean press. Jorge E. Vera of *La Nación* (15) makes a comparison between novel and drama and underlines that:

> En la pieza de teatro nos asaltan los personajes con su corporeidad visible, con sus gestos y expresiones. Aunque nadie hablara de ellos y ellos callaran, están ahí, dentro de la antigua mansión; algunos como fantasmas de una verdadera pesadilla.

> In the play, the characters overwhelm us with their corporeal visibility, with their gestures and expressions. Even when no one speaks of them and when they themselves are silent, they are there, inside the old mansion, some of them like ghosts from a frightening nightmare.

Even though Luis Buñuel became interested in the production of *El lugar sin límites,* the movie was finally directed by Arturo Ripstein in Mexico (Buñuel concluded that censorship in Franco's Spain would make it impossible for him to produce it). Donoso comments on the film in "A Round Table Discussion with José Donoso."

2. For the pertinent definition of melodrama as used throughout this study, especially as it applies to its expressionistic manifestations in the novel, see Brooks, *Melodramatic Imagination,* especially pp. 91, 126, 146, and 177. For a concise, essential definition of melodrama, based on the conception of Victorian melodrama, see Earl F. Bargainnier's "Melodrama as Formula."

3. Julia Przybos, *L'enterprise melodramatique,* 194, maintains that the genre of melodrama serves as a hollow shell that may be used by any ideological construct to deliver its message:

> Le mélodrame, que perçoit le monde en termes de traîtres et de victimes et qui oeuvre à raffermir l'ordre et l'unité du groupe, est une forme esthétique qui peut véhiculer n'importe quelle idéologie. Une fois remontée, la mécanique du mélodrame se met à fonctionner au profit de tout propagandiste habile. Le mélodrame a perpétué et perpétuera sans doute toujours la soumission de l'individu à la famille, à la patrie, à la race, à la classe, à l'humanité.

> Melodrama, which perceives the world in terms of villains and victims, and which works to confirm the order and unity of the group, is an aesthetic form that can advance

any ideology. Once established, the mechanics of melodrama function in favor of any able demagogue. Without a doubt, melodrama has and will perpetuate the submission of the individual to family, country, race, class, humanity.

In this chapter, and throughout the book, I will define just how Donoso uses melodrama as a shell in order to make evident the ideological context of the social and political events he depicts; and more importantly, in order to elucidate a poetics for his creative process.

4. Sharon Magnarelli, *Understanding José Donoso,* 31, observes that Misiá Elisa's pronouncements become other people's reality:

> One of the major issues of the text is the degree to which the other characters accept her rendition of reality, the degree to which their perception of empirical events is formulated by prior discourse, specifically hers. For example, after being called a whore and a thief, Estela corroborates the words by giving herself to Mario and stealing from Misiá Elisa, that is, by assuming both prophesied roles. Thus, metaphorically Misiá Elisa functions much like an omniscient narrator, the oligarchy she represents, or the generic 'they say,' in that her words shape others' perceptions of their empirical experiences in a manner that favors her and her ideological group while maintaining that group in its central, controlling position.

I agree with Magnarelli in that Misiá Elisa dictates reality for both Estela and Andrés; yet, later, when she is "crowned" by her servants at the end of the novel, she is bereft of the power to anticipate reality and the servants take over as scriptwriters and directors of experience within the household. See my analysis below.

5. Estelle Quain, "The Image of the House," 86, writes: "Once a center of family ritual and a protective enclosure from the outside world, the house in Donoso's novels is abandoned by its original inhabitants and ready to be destroyed. In its dilapidated condition it is the chief symbol of social class on the decline."

6. With *Este domingo* Donoso sets up a program for dramatic representation that often mimics pictorial, operatic, or sculptural designs. This penchant for the dialogue of artistic languages reaches its full expression in *Casa de campo* [*A House in the Country*] and *El jardín de al lado* [*The Garden Next Door*]. The Uruguayan critic Hugo Achugar, in "Ideología y estructuras," 217, describes the dramatizations of Mariola Roncafort thus:

> O sea que el modelo a la máscara de Mariola Roncafort es pura palabra, su realidad esencial es la actividad ideológica. Pero la mediación actuante no es sólo del tipo de lo ofrecido por *Vogue* sino que también es "la Traviata" o los "Ballets Joos." . . . Los juegos de estos niños se nutren de la realidad y, sobre todo, de los modelos culturales— por lo tanto ideológicos—que se desarrollan en esa realidad

> In other words, the model for Mariola Roncafort's mask is pure words, its essential reality is ideological action. Yet its mediating gesture is not only of the kind offered by *Vogue* but it is also of the kind found in *La Traviata* or the "Ballets Joos" . . . These children's games are patterned after cultural, and thus ideological, models that are developed in that reality.

7. In *Understanding Donoso,* 46–48, Magnarelli points out that Violeta's acceptance of the pact only represents Alvaro's point of view in the arrangement. Violeta's acceptance, the critic maintains, is a clear projection of the male's desire to maintain the status quo, while the servant is forced to literally bear the consequences of their weekend encounters. Not much later, Violeta gives birth to Mirella, a child she claims is her boyfriend's and not Alvaro's. By imposing his power as master of the house, Alvaro institutes a role-playing game in which Violeta plays the subservient role.

8. The figure of the grandmother here stands in sharp contrast to that formulated by Adrienne Rich in *Of Woman Born: Motherhood as Experience and Institution,* 22. Although both the grandmother and Rich see themselves as monsters for having failed as mothers, there is a radical difference between the two. In a diary entry of March 1966 Rich observes: "Perhaps one is a monster—an anti-woman—something driven and without recourse to the normal and appealing consolations of love, motherhood, joy in others." Rich goes on to explain that this feeling of monstrosity is born out of a desire to define oneself as an individual, independent of the "normal" exigencies of motherhood that require a woman to give herself unconditionally to child rearing. Although in Donoso's novel the grandmother, in fact, abandons her own children in order to care for others, she does not do it as a way of defining herself outside of the traditionally patriarchal norms of motherhood, rather, she abandons her own because they no longer need her as much as she would have them need her. The character of the grandmother is a projection of a male's fears that the mother will not let go and that masculine individuation will become an impossibility.

9. In her article on the Latin American intelligentsia, Jean Franco, "Beyond Ethnocentrism," 510–11, points to male writers' creation of female characters only in terms of their "natural" and "procreative" abilities:

In the eyes of these novelists, women can never separate themselves from nature. . . . In José Donoso's *The Obscure Bird of Night* [sic] (1979), the entire novel is constructed around the writer's futile attempt to take hold of this archaic power that comes from the creation of life, to steal it from the witches who preside over its secrets and assert their power over it. The recurrence of this ideologeme suggests, therefore, both the writer's ambiguous relation to an unconscious that is defined as feminine and, at the same time, a reaffirmation of women's imprisonment in nature, as if this were the only way that the preservation of authorship as a male activity could be justified.

All of Donoso's novels point to this ambivalence between the figure of the nurturing and devouring mother. See Magnarelli, "José Donoso's *El obsceno pájaro de la noche:* Witches Everywhere and Nowhere."

10. This inversion of the maternal act of engulfing to that of being engulfed may be seen as the inversion of the passive role as played by the children when dependent on the mother to that of an active role of children who reject and annihilate the mother. In *Beyond the Pleasure Principle,* Sigmund Freud explains the dynamics of the *fort-da* game, in which the child tries to master a game to deal with the loss of the mother who has left to return at a later hour. Rather than being overpowered by the experience of the mother's leaving, the child invents a game in which an object is made to appear and disappear at will; in the game, the child becomes the active player in the drama of loss. Lacan's reading of the Freudian interpretation conceives of the game as a form of symbolic activity. Barbara Freedman, *Staging the Gaze,* 212, explains: "The infant is playing out not simply his need for the mother but his own capacity for symbolic activity. He finds himself split as a result of the going of the mother, split between himself as the object of the mother, the mother as the missing complement, and the player of games who creates these splits and then closes them up in symbolic form. In effect, the *fort-da* game is the discovery of drama, which needs no formal optical apparatus other than a single body playing out its losses and discoveries as mediated by the gaze."

11. Even though there is a marked ambivalence in Donoso's creation of female characters (they often seem to embody this contradiction of nurturing and devouring functions), there is no question that the primal scene—the recognition of the accomplishment of reading along with the encouragement of the flight of the imagination in the dubious site of the grandmother's bedroom—links a female character, rather than the father as Lacan would

have it, to the acquisition of the language of the symbolic. In her study of Shakespearean comedy in light of psychoanalytical and optical theories, Freedman, *Staging the Gaze*, 150, dictates: "We can therefore theorize the mother's look as that which functions to displace in advance the father as the privileged level of representation—without identifying the woman with panic, confusion, or a space before language and representation."

12. In a brief study of the first three novels by Donoso in "El mundo José Donoso," 79, Emir Rodríguez Monegal classifies the first as social melodrama: "La crónica familiar degenera en melodrama social" [The family chronicle degenerates into social melodrama]. In using this term, the Uruguayan critic sees "social melodrama" in pejorative terms. My reading of the novel as melodrama underlines Donoso's use of the genre in what I think are obvious ironic terms. Furthermore, as I have stated before, Donoso is playing with melodrama as form. *Coronación* clearly fulfils many of the requirements for a Victorian "domestic melodrama" as clearly defined by Martha Vicinus "Helpless and Unfriended," 128: "Domestic melodrama was the working out in popular culture of the conflict between the family and its values and the economic and social assault of industrialization. The clash between good and evil found in all melodrama provided the means for exploring social and political issues in personal terms. The exploration of contemporary concerns about class and gender gave melodrama its immediacy, while the placing of these issues in a personal context gave it emotional force." In the paragraphs that follow, and specifically in my analysis of the coronation scene, I will illustrate how the melodramatic format is effectively used by Donoso in an ironic manner so as to realize a confrontation between classes and mark the demise of the outmoded rhetorical conventions of the bourgeoisie.

13. Achugar's commentary in *Ideología*, 87, is as follows:

Robo no realizado. Ladrón que nada roba. Palabras que afirman o describen hechos inexistentes o imposibles de verificar. El motivo del ladrón o del robo, desarrolla a varias pintas, no sólo la dialéctica espacial, sino además el juego de representaciones y autorrepresentaciones, de conciencia y autoconciencia que se establece en *Coronación*.

Unaccomplished theft. Thief that steals nothing. Words that affirm or describe nonexisting or unverifiable facts. The motif of the theft or the thief develops at different levels, not only the spatial dialectics, but also a game of representations and self-representations, of consciousness and self-consciousness that is well established in *Coronation*.

14. In the chapter that analyzes this novel, Ricardo Gutiérrez Mouat, *José Donoso*, 52, posits the grandmother as a scriptwriter:

Tanto la abuela como René son personajes corifeos en cuanto funcionan como autores de un "guión" dramático (y teatral), o mejor, como *apuntadores:* no es por casualidad que la última alusión a la casa de los Abalos narre una fiesta que está tomando lugar en un escenario iluminado, y que es atestiguada por espectadores que luego pasan a ser actores.

Both the grandmother and René are coryphaeus characters because they function like authors of a dramatic script, or even better, like *prompters:* it is not by chance that the last allusion to the Abalos household narrates a party that is taking place on a lit stage, a party that is observed by spectators who later become actors.

With this statement, the Chilean critic undermines the power of the grandmother as scriptwriter and gives that power to the maids, who in fact, are the agents (actors) of the final scene in the novel.

15. Since humor here is based on a Spanish wordplay, laughter is lost in translation:

"de repente" [suddenly], the object of the preposition "de" [of], is used as a noun denoting a disease.

16. The definition of melodrama finds its realization in eighteenth-century France, "where a dramatic monologue alternates with pantomime and orchestral accompaniment," Brooks, *Imagination*, 87.

17. For a definition of the Furies, I turn to Barbara G. Walker's *The Woman's Dictionary of Symbols and Sacred Objects,* 249: "Sophocles called the Furies 'Daughters of Earth and Shadow.' Aeschylus called them 'Children of Eternal Night.' Either epithet made them off-spring of the female spirit of primal darkness at the creation and linked them to the primor-dial concept of the Mother's Curse whereby the Goddess inevitably ended each life that she brought forth. . . . Psychologically, they were images of the Scolding Mother and projections of the young child's death fears and pangs of conscience." This last sentence serves to inter-pret the maids' actions as projections of Andrés's death fears and desire to do away with his grandmother. When he narrates the scene of the coronation to his friend Carlos Gross, he does so in a positive light, thus reflecting the pangs of conscience he may be feeling in regard to having abandoned his grandmother on her saint's day. If we compare Andrés's feelings to those of the male narrator in *Este domingo,* we can see an equal amount of ambivalence regarding the maternal figure. In *Coronación,* it is the maids in the guise of the Furies who eliminate the grandmother, while in *Este domingo* it is nameless children who dispose of her. In either case, subservient characters fulfill the male child's and male adult's desires. Charac-ters who act as dramatis personae (the maids) realize the protagonist's censored wishes.

18. The word *gaznate* in Spanish literally means gullet. The description of the old wom-an's animal-like mouth is lost in the English translation.

19. Isis Quinteros, *José Donoso,* 110, emphasizes the visual and cinematic aspects of the coronation scene:

La ceremonia de la coronación de misiá Elisa . . . se transforma . . . en la creación de un ambiente que Donoso logra no con la pluma sino con la paleta de un pintor impresio-nista. Lo que se nos presenta a nuestros ojos—porque la escena la visualizamos, olvi-dándonos de las palabras que la hacen inteligible—, es una realidad creada por la luz y por los reflejos de los cuerpos en el momento de ser contemplados.

Misiá Elisa's coronation ceremony . . . is transformed into . . . the creation of an atmo-sphere that Donoso achieves, not with the pen, but with the palette of an impressionis-tic painter. What is being represented before our eyes—because we visualize the scene, forgetting the words that allow it to be perceived—is a reality created by the light and by the image of the bodies, at the same moment that they are being seen.

Although I disagree with Quinteros only in that I see the scene as Expressionist rather than Impressionist, I see her statement as a very accurate description of Donoso's art in general, a novelistic craft that is created essentially for the reader's contemplation.

20. In her study *Melodrama in Latin America,* 6, (both in film and in television), Ana López begins by stating that the genre "often coincides with the logic of the dominant social and political order in most of Latin America." As the critic develops her argument, however, she marks a departure from the traditional forms of melodrama as borrowed from film in the United States, which emphasizes the values of cultural dependence, in favor of a national production, especially in Brazil and Cuba, which emphasizes aspects of their specific popular cultures. According to López 13, these more recent manifestations of melodrama in the mass media may be conceived "as possible sites of hegemonic resistance." Although in his novels Donoso clearly speaks from the point of view of those in power, he does give voice to the popular sector in such characters as Rosario and Lourdes, who act through hyperbolic

gesture. It must be noted that since these women speak through gesture rather than spoken language, they are still relegated to a mute sector of society.

21. According to Ana María Moix in the prologue to *Cuentos,* "Santelices" was written after *Coronación.* In my opinion, the story shows a marked development of the technique of scene setting and the issue of its mastery. In her discussion of theater in *Staging the Gaze,* 142, Barbara Freedman states: "[T]heater is always about the relationship of what is seen and the fact that it is seen, and always renewing the relation of what is seen to the social gaze in which it is inscribed." Donoso's scrutiny of the Chilean upper class and its relationship to the working class is consistently symbolized by a character's ability to hold the controlling gaze.

22. Mónica Flori in "La función," 30, describes the relationship between Santelices and Bertita:

La clave de la relación existente entre Santelices y Bertita radica en que ésta, como Matilde ["Paseo"], ha reprimido sus impulsos sexuales y los ha sublimado en un papel materno, por lo tanto frente a aquélla Santelices se ve reducido psicológicamente a desempeñar un papel infantil. Como madre, Bertita manifiesta las dos facetas de madre benévola y malévola.

The key to the existing relationship between Santelices and Bertita lies in the fact that Bertita, like Matilde ("Paseo"), has repressed her sexual impulses and has sublimated them into the maternal role. Therefore, when faced with her, Santelices is reduced to playing the role of the child in psychological terms.

23. Brooks, *Imagination,* 201–2.

24. See Freedman, *Staging the Gaze,* 117.

25. In "Ana María," (in *Cuentos,* 183–201, *Charleston,* 1–18), Donoso had already begun to develop his conception of the gaze that attracts and repels at the same time. In this short story, the little girl Ana María inhabits a green garden that links femininity in its pure state with nature and a sort of animalistic seduction. Her eyes, blue and transparent, beckon an old man who works nearby and finally pull him into her world of innocent wisdom. In her book on José Donoso, Sharon Magnarelli concurs with my analysis. The critic defines Santelices's role as "the viewer *and* the viewed" (21).

26. Myrna Solotorevsky, *José Donoso,* 75, points out that the novel begins to use masculine adjectives in relation to La Manuela only after La Japonesita addresses her father as such on p. 59 of the novel.

27. When contrasting the two scenes, Philip Swanson in *José Donoso,* 65, underlines the theatrical aspect of the two moments as well as the character's desire to define himself in feminine rather than masculine terms. I quote at length: "Two different types of sexual activity are juxtaposed. Manuela's sexual experience with Japonesa Grande was for him a negative one and he wants to efface the memory of it by substituting it with a homosexual affair with Pancho—that is, something which for him, a sexually inverted creature, will be positive. . . . There is another curiously inverted parallel with the flashback here. His sexual activity with Japonesa Grande was a kind of performance. . . . But this time the performance will demonstrate the opposite—not his masculinity but his femininity." Swanson's interpretation coincides with mine in that La Manuela utilizes the scene of performance to become an active rather than a passive agent in the formulation of his own definition. In his famous essay on the novel, "Escritura/Transvestismo," 72, Severo Sarduy emphasizes that in the scene with La Japonesa, La Manuela had acted like a male, but a passive male: "[E]n el acto sexual el papel de la Manuela, hombre por atribución narrativa, es pasivo. No femenino— por eso se trata de una inversión dentro de otra y no de un simple regreso al travestismo inicial—, sino de hombre pasivo, que engendra a su pesar" [Manuela's role in the sexual act

is a passive one, even though he is the male in narrative terms. His role is not a feminine one—that's why it's all about an inversion within an inversion and not simply a return to the initial act of transvestism—but his is the role of the passive male who begets in spite of himself].

28. Hortensia R. Morell, in "Visión temporal en *El lugar sin límites:* Circularidad narrativa, teatralidad cíclica," 35, extensively studies the theatrical scenes within the novel and establishes a relationship between theatricality and the mythical structure of the novel

> La fiesta en el contexto de la vendimia aparece constantemente retrotraída en la memoria anticipadora y retrospectiva de la Manuela y la Japonesita. Subrayando su carácter genérico híbrido, *El lugar* incurre en el uso de acotaciones teatrales y técnicas de cine al ordenar esas memorias, así como los recuerdos de la infancia de Pancho Vega, dentro del plano de sucesión de la jornada. Historia y presente confluyen y se iluminan en ese montaje cíclico de lo narrado.

> The feast within the context of the harvest appears repeatedly in Manuela's and Japonesita's recollections. These recollections are presented both as flashbacks and foreshadowing of narrative action. Because of the hybrid character of *Hell Has No Limits,* it relies on the use of stage directions and cinematographic techniques to order those memories, as well as those of Pancho Vega's childhood, within the chronological flow of one day. Story and present intertwine and are illumined in the cyclical montage of the story.

Also see her book *Composición expresionista en "El lugar sin límites" de José Donoso,* 59–82.

29. Gutiérrez Mouat, in *José Donoso,* 131, has already observed that, in fact, Don Alejo's dogs become Pancho and Octavio as they persecute La Manuela: "El soltarlos a los cuatro vientos es el último acto de poder del hacendado pero a la vez constituye—en otro nivel—la transgresión de su propia interdicción contra Pancho, porque esos cancerberos desmandados y temidos que nadie puede ubicar *se transforman* en Pancho y Octavio, igualmente móviles y desmandados por el campo en persecución de la Manuela" [Freeing the dogs is the last gesture of power of the landowner, but it also constitutes—at another level—a transgression of his own interdict against Pancho. Those ruthless guardians, impudent and feared because no one can locate them, *become* Pancho and Octavio, who move equally ruthlessly through the fields in search of Manuela].

30. Humberto Peñaloza, the protagonist of *El obsceno pájaro de la noche,* is born to a lower-class family who aspires to rise above mediocrity through the accomplishments of their son. Consequently, Humberto becomes the secretary of Don Jerónimo, a prominent citizen and politician from the upper classes. Due to his unquestioned faithfulness, Humberto is entrusted with the writing of the Azcoitía family history. When the book is published by Don Jerónimo himself, Humberto becomes disgusted with his subservient role and supposedly sets fire to the family library that holds the biography. As the result of his action, Humberto flees and hides in the dilapidated family convent where he feigns to be a deaf-mute called Mudito.

31. Djelal Kadir, "Next Door," 65, among other critics, has pointed out that potency in Donoso is often expressed as a function of the envious gaze of the dispossessed: "Potency, whether sexual, generative, or scriptive, is not a possession but the consequent by-product of dispossession and, as such, its authority lies in the 'powerless' other."

32. See Alicia Borinsky, "Repeticiones y máscaras: *El obsceno pájaro de la noche,*" and Sharon Magnarelli, "Amidst the Illusory Depths: The First Person Pronoun and *El obsceno pájaro de la noche.*"

33. Zunilda Gertel has spoken of the multiple faces hidden behind a fixed image in her article "*El obsceno pájaro de la noche:* Desencarnación, Transformación, Inexistencia," 25,

"La máscara (la cabeza del gigante) no es aquí el parecer que encubre el ser; es lo mismo que el poncho del relato del cacique, una presencia fija que encubre un vacío de múltiples rostros" [The mask (the giant's head) is not the appearance that conceals being; it is the same as the poncho of the landowner's story, a fixed presence that conceals a void of multiple faces].

34. The English translation uses the word *amazing* (158), which does not convey the monstrous nature that the Spanish word *fenómeno* (25) connotes.

35. In *Donoso*, 107, Solotorevsky points to the reciprocal relationship between Humberto and Don Jerónimo based on the power of the gaze: "Don Jerónimo y Humberto—como corresponde a la relación de dobles—recíprocamente se requieren. Don Jerónimo necesita de la mirada envidiosa y estimulante de Humberto, de la cual depende su potencia; dicha mirada condensaría en un comienzo el 'reconocimiento' de Humberto por don Jerónimo. Humberto precisa participar del ser de don Jerónimo para existir" [Don Jerónimo and Humberto—corresponding to the relationship between doubles—require each other. Don Jerónimo needs Humberto's envious and stimulating gaze, his potency depends on it; likewise, such a gaze crystallizes from the beginning Don Jerónimo's recognition of Humberto. Humberto needs to participate in Don Jerónimo's being in order to exist"].

Chapter 2: Battles Between Oral Tradition and Theatrical Representation

1. For a study of the basic opposition between order and chaos in the novel see chapter 4 of Philip Swanson, *José Donoso*, 67–87.

2. By positing the house as a ruinous space in which contradiction and anarchy coexist after having abolished a previously ordained order in the architectural and patriarchal sense, the novel establishes a metaphorical ground, a heterotopia on which to question the linguistic tenets of novelistic discourse. Donoso's house of fiction represents a metaphorical construct not unlike that established by Michel Foucault in his Preface to *The Order of Things,* xviii, in which, by way of analyzing a passage by Borges, the French philospher questions the very linguistic ground on which the Western world defines its order:

> *Heterotopias* are disturbing, probably because they secretly undermine language, because they make it impossible to name this *and* that, because they shatter or tangle common names, because they destroy 'syntax' in advance, and not only the syntax with which we construct sentences but also that less apparent syntax which causes words and things (next to and also opposite one another) to 'hold together.' That is why utopias permit fables and discourse: they run with the very grain of language and are part of the fundamental dimension of the *fabula;* heterotopias (such as those to be found so often in Borges) desiccate speech, stop words in their tracks, contest the very possibility of grammar at its source; they dissolve our myths and sterilize the lyricism of our sentences.

The myths that Donoso will destroy in this house of fiction not only concern language at its grammatical and syntactical level, but also concern the nature of novelistic discourse as it opposes the preestablished order of the nineteenth-century novel.

3. This theme is further developed in the novella "Sueños de mala muerte" [Second Rate Dreams] found in the collection *Cuatro para Delfina* [*Four for Delfina*]. In addition to the novella, the story was produced for video by the Chilean Silvio Caiozzi and televised in Chile in 1982, and staged by ICTUS both in Chile and Venezuela in 1982 and 1983 with the title "Historia de un roble solo" [Story of a Lonely Oak]. For reviews of these productions see Rosario Larraín; Jorge Vera, "José Donoso al video tape."

4. Magnarelli, "Illusory Depths," 267–68, defines the use of the first person pronoun

in the novel thus: "The *I* here is not posited in relation with an external reality; it is recognized as the absence which Julia Kristeva has suggested it always represents. . . . Thus, the *I* of *El obsceno pájaro* emerges as a fluctuating entity, a compendium of voices, and appears to corroborate Benveniste's theory that the *I* has never had a referent apart from the moment of discourse." Magnarelli devotes most of her article to demonstrating the displacement of the pronominal referent in a ludic manner. She defines the play of the signifier in terms of her readings of Jacques Derrida's formulations of sign and play.

5. See Alicia Borinsky, "Repeticiones y máscaras," which centers around the problematics of displacement in Donoso's novel.

6. By offering a reading of Freud's *Beyond the Pleasure Principle,* Brooks, "Freud's Masterplot," 296, suggests a masterplot for narratives in which the "life" of narrative plot begins and ends from a point of quiescence; the middle constituting a *détour* of a straight line that strives toward the "death" of the narrative. The middle repeats with the intent of postponing the end. The play in the narrative works toward "recognition and the retrospective illumination which will allow us to grasp the text as total metaphor, but not therefore to discount the metonymies that have led to it." The activity of the women's telling through displacement of facts and narrators, and Mudito's showing through dramatic representation, keep transforming, "repeating," the original tale found in chapter 2. Both modes of narration postpone the end, Mudito's death—a moment in the narrative that necessarily returns us to another moment of quiescence, Brígida's death at the beginning. The whole process of displacement can be seen as a metonymic chain that yields the image of death at the end, giving the reader metaphors that illuminate the workings of the text: life as displacement and death as beginning and end.

7. According to Borinsky, "Repeticiones," 281, the first person singular in today's fiction does not refer to a privileged narrator who pretends to occupy a place outside the fiction itself. The narrator is not the author but a character who places himself at a distance from the other characters and from a discrete text within the narrative.

8. In his interview with Donoso, Rodríguez Monegal "Donoso," considers the tale as "un emblema alegórico de la narración" (523) [an allegorical emblem of narration]. In answer to the critic's comment, Donoso jokingly states that the legend is not an authentic Chilean legend, and that readers might consider him a liar for having given it an impression of authenticity. I quote Donoso, 518: "Estoy seguro que en Chile van a decir: bueno, estas leyendas no existen en Chile, jamás han existido, esto es una mentira de Donoso, no conoce Chile." [I'm sure that in Chile people are going to say: well, these legends don't exist in Chile, and have never existed in Chile. This is a lie on the part of Donoso, he doesn't know Chile]. Other critics, such as George McMurray, *José Donoso,* 128; Quinteros, *Donoso,* 216; and Hernán Vidal, *Surrealismo y rebelión,* 123, propose the legend as a paradigm for the novel's development. It is also quite telling that when Donoso's novel was adapted for the theater by Darrah Cloud and directed for the Trinity Repertory Company (Providence, Rhode Island) by Molly Smith, the production opened with the scene of the girl-witch and the father's poncho. The play was performed February 28 through April 1, 1990. A review of the performance by Kevin Kelly, "Obscene Bird of Night," 42, states: "The legend is a conceit meant to inform the development of the novel, like the first whispery breath of an echoing horror." In "A Small Biography of *The Obscene Bird of Night,*" 21, Donoso discusses how the novel "happened to me." Also see Donoso's memoir "The Old House."

9. For the classical definition of telling and showing, see Wayne C. Booth, *The Rhetoric of Fiction.*

10. The "dicen" [they say] of the women functions very much like the mindless dialogues between Rosario and Lourdes in *Coronación.* Mudito's directing of dramatic scenes recalls Santelices's expressionistic projections.

11. Following Roland Barthes's *The Pleasure of the Text* in his reading of both *El*

obsceno pájaro de la noche and *Casa de campo,* Enrique Luengo, "Inteligibilidad, coherencia y transgresión," 84, postulates Donoso's writing as "la noción de escritura como una lectura que profiere *vocalmente* ("vocally writing") el texto que está siendo escrito" [the notion of writing as a reading that expresses orally ("vocally writing") the text that is being written]. Presumably, Mudito's changing version of the tale, which we now read, was first told orally by the women, then retold by Mudito to Madre Benita, the listener/reader of the revised tales. All of these orally transmitted tales are woven together (as the sack that later envelops Mudito) to constitute Donoso's writing.

12. The collaboration between the women and Mudito in the fashioning of new characters is grounded in the mixing of contexts, an action which desacralizes religion, history, and social hierarchies so that they all coexist on the same plane.

13. The antecedent for this scene is that of the coronation in Donoso's first novel. If in that first work the maids were the directors and actors, here the male figure takes those roles.

14. For a careful analysis of the package as metaphor in the novel, see Borinsky, "Repeticiones," and Magnarelli, *"El obsceno pájaro de la noche."*

15. At the end of the novel, the sack that Mudito has become as the consequence of being wrapped and tied by the ladies of the house, is dragged out of the ruins by an old witch. Since she gets cold by the river, she burns the large bundle and Mudito's ashes are scattered by the wind into the river.

16. Magnarelli, "The Baroque, the Picaresque, and *El obsceno pájaro de la noche,"* 85–86, classifies the novel as a neobaroque novel, basing her argument on Severo Sarduy's definition of the baroque:

Now, as Severo Sarduy has noted, the principal figure of rhetoric used in the baroque is the ellipsis (Barroco, p. 67), a figure which indirectly includes many of the other rhetorical figures and tropes. The ellipsis, of course, is based on a missing element, and thus, the result of the ellipsis is a displacement, a shift of attention; that is, rather than detecting the 'original' element, we tend to perceive its substitute. Thought of in these broad terms, the ellipsis is the basis of the metaphor, the synecdoche, the metonymy, and the allusion. In each case, the meaningful element which has been alluded to is missing, and our attention is shifted, either to a substitute element, or as I believe is the case in the neo-baroque, to language itself, since dialectically, once we recognize that there has been a substitution, we seek the 'original' element and its point of contact with its substitute. Thus, our attention is overtly drawn away from both elements and shifted to the very fact of the substitution, i.e. rhetoric and language. In this respect, it is totally correct to suggest that the baroque is a continual 'searching for' that something which is necessarily always missing.

This paragraph is a superb summary of the way that Mudito, and interpretation in general, proceeds in regard to other narrations in the novel. My only disagreement with the statement, however, is that Mudito, as creative interpreter, possesses the means to transform absence into presence at the end of the novel by becoming the metaphor of the burning package, which signifies a new narrative mode. In this article, Magnarelli has gone beyond the grammatical analysis of the language in the novel (see "Illusory Depths") to an interpretation of it at the rhetorical level of language. I agree with the critic's suggestion that ellipsis as figure can help the reader understand Donoso's work, and I believe that metaphor predominates in his novels as the receptacle of literary meaning to be deciphered by interpretation. In the prologue to *Poemas de un novelista,* 12, Donoso admits to the hermetic nature of his prose and compares an incident described realistically in a poem and metaphorically in *Casa de campo:* "Pero en la novela—en la prosa—el hecho parece transubstanciado, metaforizado, lleno de disfraces y máscaras, mechado de significaciones, parte del mundo de la fantasía, episodio y vértebra de una secuencia" [But in the novel—in the narrative—the fact appears transubstantiated, expressed in metaphors, full of disguises and masks, laden with meaning, part of the world of fantasy, an episode and a link in a sequence]. Magnarelli develops further the notion of ellipsis in the novel in chapter 7 of *The Lost Rib: Female Characters in the Spanish American Novel*, 147–68.

17. In the novel, witches such as the nursemaid turn children into *imbunches*, 41: "[P]orque para eso, para transformarlos en imbunches, se roban las brujas a los pobres inocentes y los guardan en sus salamancas debajo de la tierra, con los ojos cosidos, el sexo cosido, la boca, las narices, los oídos, todo cosido, dejándoles crecer el pelo y las uñas de las manos y de los pies, idiotizándolos, peor que animales los pobres, sucios, piojosos, capaces sólo de dar saltitos cuando el chivato y las brujas borrachas les ordenen que bailen" [*(B)ecause that's the reason witches steal poor innocent children, to turn them into* imbunches *and keep them in their underground grottoes, with their eyes sewed up, their sex organs sewed up, their anuses sewed up, their mouths, nostrils, ears, everything sewed up letting their hair and their fingernails and their toenails grow long, turning them into idiots, making the poor things worse off than animals, filthy, ridden with lice, able only to hop around when the goat and the drunken witches command them to dance* (29)]. The most succinct definition of an *imbunche* is provided by McMurray, in *Donoso*, 166n12: "Based on a myth of the Araucanian Indians of Chile, the *imbunche* refers to a child that has been stolen by witches and transformed into a monster with all its orifices sewed shut." Other definitions of the *imbunche* also appear in Rodríguez Monegal, "José Donoso," 523; Achugar, *Ideologia*, 274; Adriana Valdés, "El 'Imbunche',", 125–60; and Quinteros, *Donoso*, 244.

18. With the image of the imbunche and the subsequent burning of Mudito, Donoso has transformed "the ultimate (Gothic) nightmare of burial alive, loss of mobility and identity" (Brooks, *Melodramatic Imagination*, 50) into a discourse on the production of the novel.

19. In her book *Understanding José Donoso*, 97, Magnarelli points to the coincidence of Mudito's shrinking size until he becomes a baby (content), and the shrinking number of pages as we approach the end of the novel (form): "In the final chapter of the novel, Mudito is miraculously (re)born as an incarnation of the long-awaited savior baby. Then, wrapped and sewn into a burlap sack, he becomes smaller and smaller. In this respect, the fictional space of the novel—the burlap sack that contains the ostensible narrator and was earlier figured as an oppressive creation or creative space of the mind (199/245)—becomes smaller as the physical space of the novel (the number of pages to be read) becomes smaller. Thus content and form mirror each other."

20. Bloom's statement, from *The Anxiety of Influence*, 141, reads as follows: "In this observation I want to distinguish the phenomenon from the witty insight of Borges, that artists *create* their precursors, as for instance the Kafka of Borges creates the Browning of Borges. I mean something more drastic and (presumably) absurd, which is the triumph of having so stationed the precursor, in one's own work, that particular passages in *his* work seem to be not presages of one's own advent, but rather to be indebted to one's own achievement, and even (necessarily) to be lessened by one's greater splendor. The mighty dead return, but they return in our colors, and speaking in our voices, at least in part, at least in moments, moments that testify to our persistence, and not to their own."

21. For the historical development of the novel from the epic, see George Lukács, *The Theory of the Novel;* and for the nature of oral narratives, see Albert B. Lord, *The Singer of Tales.*

22. In his book on Cervantes and Donoso, *Conciencia y lenguaje en el Quixote y El obsceno pájaro de la noche*, 192, Héctor Calderón points to the formulaic nature of oral narration in Donoso's novel:

En resumen, estos son los elementos básicos de la tradición oral que Donoso utiliza en su obra: 1) el anonimato de la tradición; 2) la ausencia de registros permanentes; 3) la repetición habitual o ritualística de los temas; 4) la ausencia del pensamiento "racional" o de investigación deliberada que acompaña a la expresión formulaica.

In conclusion, these are the basic elements of oral tradition that Donoso uses in his work: 1) the anonymous tradition, 2) the absence of permanent records, 3) the habitual and ritualistic repetition of themes, 4) the absence of "rational" thought or deliberate investigation that accompanies formulaic expression.

Lord *Singer of Tales,* 36, describes the function of memory in the formulaic thus: "When we speak a language we do not repeat words and phrases that we have memorized consciously, but the words and sentences emerge from their habitual usage. He [the bard] does not 'memorize' formulas, any more than we as children 'memorize' language. He learns them by hearing them in other singers' songs, and by habitual usage they become part of his singing as well." This description is apt for the childlike narrative ("dicen" [they say]) of the old ladies in Donoso's novel.

23. In her excellent reading of the women's role in the novel, Magnarelli, *Lost Rib,* 166–68, also provides us with a very convincing interpretation of the epigraph in which both wolf and obscene bird revert back to the image of the witch and her dog.

Chapter 3: Casa de campo

1. Pamela Constable and Arturo Valenzuela detail these historic events in *A Nation of Enemies: Chile Under Pinochet.* On September 11, 1973, Chile's military made an air attack on the presidential palace (La Moneda) where President Salvador Allende had refused an unconditional surrender to General Augusto Pinochet. After the air attack, he was found dead, "his head had been demolished by machine-gun fire" (17). After the fall of Allende, there were mass raids, "over 45,000 people were held for interrogation in army barracks, navy training camps, air force hospitals, soccer stadiums, and even merchant ships anchored off Valparaiso. . . . By December, at least fifteen hundred civilians were dead . . . and a reign of professional state terror had begun" (20). Soon after Pinochet's rise to power, in June of 1974, the Dirección de Inteligencia Nacional (DINA), was formed to "produce the intelligence necessary to formulate policies and planning, and to adopt measures to procure the safeguarding of National Security and development of the country" (91). DINA created interrogation and detention camps in which former members of Allende's socialist government and the Movimiento de Izquierda Revolucionario/Movement of the Revolutionary Left (MIR) were detained and tortured. According to estimates by the Catholic legal aid office, which tried to expose the extreme human rights abuses, 668 prisoners vanished between 1973 and 1978; a less conservative count put the figure at 1,000. Also during that time, in September 1976, Orlando Letelier, a foreign minister and former ambassador to the United States under Allende, was killed by a car bomb in Washington, D. C. A lengthy investigation tied the murder of Letelier to DINA. The reign of terror that Pinochet established through DINA during these five years finds an echo in *Casa de campo* through allegorical means. (Pinochet's dictatorship lasted until 1990.)

2. Maria A. Salgado devotes a good part of *Casa de Campo o La realidad de la apariencia"* to the definition of both house and narrative as labyrinth. The story by Borges may be found in *Labyrinths: Selected Stories and Other Writings.*

3. For a detailed reading of the novel's allegorical subtext in relation to Chile's history see Luis Iñigo Madrigal, "Alegoría, historia, novela"; see Lucille Kerr, "Conventions of Authorial Design"; Marie Murphy, "Authorizing Fictions: José Donoso's 'Casa de campo'";

and Z. Nelly Martínez, "*Casa de Campo* de José Donoso" for their discussion of narrative and authorial concerns in the text.

4. In his book *Donoso,* 235, Gutiérrez Mouat clearly states: "El relato se abre con la instauración en la casa de un vacío de poder que se va a ir llenando de diversos modos" [The narrative opens with the establishment of a power void in the house which is going to be filled in several ways]. Kerr, "Conventions of Authorial Design" 142, concentrates on the issue of authority at the narrative level: "[T]he novel explores how authority is legitimized or challenged, how power is exercised or eliminated in the real world as well as in narrative fiction. One of the conclusions, as it were, to such conflicts is that no single system or individual, group or leader, emerges as entirely legitimate or finally authoritative."

5. Salgado, "*Casa de campo,*" 288, states that the center of the house in the country lies not in the kitchen or the bedrooms, but rather in Hermógenes's business office, thus marking its emphasis on economics as the "glue" that brings all members to the family:

> El paralelismo casa-negocio se refuerza irónicamente cuando el narrador sugiere que el "tabernáculo" de la casa no es el dormitorio o la cocina (símbolos tradicionales del amor y la comunión hogareñas), sino el despacho del padre. . . . El narrador hace hincapié en que el sistema de valores de los Ventura es puramente material al referirse a esta habitación como "el tabernáculo de la riqueza de la familia." (p. 288)

> [The parallelism house/business is reinforced ironically when the narrator suggests that the "tabernacle" in the house is neither the bedroom nor the kitchen (traditional symbols of love and home communion), but the father's office. . . . The narrator emphasizes that the Ventura value system is purely material when it refers to this room as "the tabernacle of the family's wealth."]

6. Alfred J. MacAdam, "José Donoso: *Casa de campo,*" 259, emphasizes that individual identity and morality in the family are directly related to the ownership of private property: "Una ficción, la propiedad privada y la necesidad de conservarla, engendra otra—los nativos por ser caníbales merecen ser esclavos—y así los Ventura construyen una moralidad y una justificación. La historia y la tradición apoyan estas costumbres: cualquier cambio sería inmoral" [Private property and the necessity to conserve it, a fiction, engenders another fiction—because the natives are cannibals they deserve to be slaves. Thus the Venturas construct their morality and its justification. History and tradition support these rituals: any change would be immoral]. René Jara, *El revés de la arpillera: Perfil Literario de Chile,* 217, affirms that "*Casa de campo* (1978), más que una imagen del golpe militar es la deconstrucción de la fantasía fundadora del sistema patriarcal y burgués de la clase dominante" [More than an image of the military coup, *A House in the Country* is the deconstruction of the founding fantasy of the patriarchal and bourgeois system of the dominating class].

7. In *El osbceno pájaro de la noche,* chapter 2 is key in setting up the interpretive mechanism that Mudito will employ as he displaces listening with dramatic representation. Chapter 2 provides the seed from which all other forms of representations will proliferate. In *Casa de campo* that chapter is 3. In this respect, the two novels mirror each other.

8. Baker, in "Perfil del narrador," 39, points to the rhetorical similarities between the language of the children as they play their game and that of the parents: "Igual que sus progenitores, los niños desarrollan un 'idioma marquesal' (436) que compite en preciosidad y vacuidad con el habla decimonónica de sus padres" [Just like their parents, the children develop an "aristocratic language" that competes in exquisiteness and emptiness with the nineteenth-century speech of their parents].

9. In *Coronación,* the maids use the language of melodrama to liberate themselves from the tyranny of Misiá Elisa. In "Santelices," the dramatic language of the protagonist has a liberating effect, the scenes framed by the office window facilitate the resolution of

Santelices's internal conflicts. In *El obsceno pájaro de la noche,* likewise, Mudito uses the language of theater in order to carve out a space for himself in the house as well as in the narrative. He goes from a marginal to a central position in both. Thus, dramatic language is placed at the service of self-definition. In *Casa de campo,* however, theatrical language obfuscates.

10. Gutiérrez Mouat, "José Donoso," Martínez, "*Casa de campo,*" have pointed to the carnavalesque nature of the novel.

11. Donoso's model for this scene is clearly that of grand opera. *The New Harvard Dictionary of Music,* 565, defines grand opera as follows: "Grand opera, as it developed in the second and third quarters of the 19th century, produced significant works in its own right and influenced the course of Italian and German opera as well. . . . These works derive their energy from large-scale conflicts—not just of individuals but of whole national or religious groups—that are frozen at climactic moments into striking, massed tableaux in which all possible aural and visual forces—soloists, chorus, orchestra, ballet, costumes, scenery—contribute to achieve a maximum effect." The production of a maximum effect to highlight the inauguration of Allende's period is used to bring together forces of past and present, myth and history with aural and visual grandiose gesture.

12. Brooks, *Melodramatic Imagination,* 28, defines the functioning of melodrama as follows: "The articulation of melodrama's messages in this kind of sign language [visual representation]—and in verbal language which strives toward the status of sign language in its use of a vocabulary of clear, simple, moral and psychological absolutes—suggests the extent to which melodrama not only employs but is centrally about repeated obfuscations and refusals of the message and about the need for repeated clarifications and acknowledgments of the message."

13. For allegorical readings of the novel see the essays by Guitiérrez Mouat, *José Donoso;* Kerr, "Conventions"; Iñigo Madrigal; Jorge Campos, "'Casa de campo' de José Donoso"; Pamela Bacarisse, "Donoso and Social Commitment"; and Balmiro Omaña, "De *El obsceno pájaro de la noche* a *Casa de campo.*" Beatriz Urraca, "El concepto de personaje," 114, points to the emblematic nature of the characters in the novel:

> En primer lugar, la búsqueda de la propia identidad es una constante en personajes que sólo están definidos con relación al grupo en que pertenecen. . . . En segundo lugar, a nivel alegórico estos grupos forman un microcosmo de la sociedad actual, constituyéndose en representates de las clases que la forman. . . . [L]a lucha de cada personaje estará marcada tanto por fines individuales como por un designio colectivo.

> In the first place, the search for one's own identity is a constant in characters that are defined only in relationship to the group to which they belong. . . . (T)he struggle of each character will be defined as much for its individual ends as for its collective designs.

Martínez, 446, goes further and sees the development of characters in a much more significative way, both within the novel and as representatives of clearly historical events:

> El existir auténtico se postula en CC desde diversas perspectivas. En un sentido, existir auténticamente implica la noción de hacerse en la historia: en la nuestra individual y también en la otra. Hacerse en el juego de los signos que escriben la historia. Escribirla, en suma: protagonizarla.

> Being, in authentic terms, is defined in *A House in the Country* from several perspectives. On the one hand, to be, in real terms, implies the notion of becoming in history: in one's individual history as well as in the other. It implies becoming through the play of signs that write history. To write history, is, in short, to become a player in it.

14. I am indebted to the writings of Mikhail Bakhtin, specifically those found in *Rabelais* and his essay "Discourse in the Novel." For a cultural analysis of Bakhtin's works see Stallybrass and White, *Politics and Poetics.*

15. Both Wenceslao and Mudito represent the male authoritative figure who, within the walls of the labyrinthine house (Donoso's fiction), describes wandering paths in the development of fictional story (in the case of Mudito) and history (in the case of Wenceslao).

16. In her article on the role of women in Donoso's novel, Maria A. Salgado, "On Mothers and Power," 94, points to the positive and negative aspects of Malvina's strength as a character: "Malvina's success in wresting the power away from her relatives suggests a double reading: on the negative side, her triumph is reprehensible since it is evident that she plays by the Venturas' rules. That is, in order to attain her ends she abides by the materialistic values of the spiritually bankrupt Venturas' patriarchal system; on the plus side, she may be said to establish a new literary role model for female characters, since it is also evident, that although a female, Malvina plays one of the most active and aggressive roles in the novel."

17. See Kerr, "Conventions of Authorial Design," for an analysis of the narrator and his designs.

18. Carlos Cerda, *Casa de campo,* 126, makes the link between time and political resistance: "También la resistencia es aludida alegóricamente en relación con el tiempo. Resistir es no olvidar que éste existe, que hay día y noche, que hubo un pasado que no se puede olvidar y un futuro posible y diferente" [Resistance is also alluded to in allegorical terms in relation to time. To resist is not to forget that time exists, that there is day and night, that there was a past that cannot be forgotten and a future that is possible and that will be different].

19. If we establish a parallel between the fictional and historical pairs of Adriano Gomara/Wenceslao (man of action/creator of languages), and Allende/Donoso, we can conclude that faced with the historical reality of a failed progressive government, the writer Donoso opts for the production of a novel that pinpoints the ideological struggle at the linguistic level.

20. Brooks, *Melodramatic Imagination,* 63, 65, defines tableaux as follows: "Subjects are evidently conceived for their plastic figurability, the dramatic interplay of posture and gesture. The spoken word is rarely used toward the formulation of significant messages; it is largely confined to emotional utterance, outburst, expressive cadenzas." Also: "He develops a full theory of the use of tableaux, arguing for the grouping of persons in postures and gestures that show their reactions to a strong emotional peripety."

21. Brooks' definition of tragedy, *Melodramatic Imagination,* 205, seems to be very apt in the context of Donoso's novel: "Tragedy generates meaning ultimately in terms of orders higher than one man's experience, orders invested by the community with holy and synthesizing power. Its pity and terror derive from the sense of communal sacrifice and transformation." In a novel of emblematic characters, Wenceslao rises above the others as legendary figure (see the narrator's theorizations about Wenceslao, p. 391). He becomes a heroic character as he recognizes his place as creator of new languages within the context of the new repressive society. His heroic stance, however, is elliminated at the end of the novel, as he joins the rest of the faceless figures in a gesture of "communal sacrifice and transformation."

Chapter 4: The Androgynous Narrator in El jardín de al lado

1. When analyzing Balzac's and James's novelistic form, Brooks uses the rubric of melodramatic imagination to describe the genius of both. What Brooks has to say in conclusion, *Melodramatic Imagination,* 200, applies as well to Donoso's imagination: "And we realize how much what we have been calling melodrama constitutes the very conditions of

possibility of the novel, in Balzac and James's understanding of the form. Melodrama offered a complete set of theatrical signs, words, and gestures, corresponding to heightened meanings." This quotation serves to describe Julio's specific means of narrating, as he projects through the window a highly theatrical scene that in turn reflects back his subjectivity.

2. The English translation omits the last part of the sentence, which associates creativity ("the world that I engendered in the garden") with a fusion of past and present.

3. Kerr, "Writing Disguises," 116, offers a masterful analysis of the hidden shift in narrative/authorial voice that occurs between chapters 5 and 6. At one point she summarizes the exchange of voices as a series of contests at the thematic and discursive levels:

> In fact, to read the final chapter is to see the apparent outcome of several contests involving these two narrators, these potential or 'real' authors, who are also partners in parallel plays for authority within the novel's story. In both the thematic and textual relations of significance the woman who first seems to occupy a less important position is transformed into, as she is also revealed to have been, the 'real' power behind the man who has formerly seemed to control the text, and also her. As he moves from the position of subject to that of object of the narration, this apparently dominant male figure seems to have to surrender his privileged place to the woman beneath whom he is ultimately resituated.

4. Priscila Meléndez, "Writing and Reading the Palimpsest," 210, proposes that Gloria's novel is a rewriting of Julio's, after a silent reading of it while Gloria is depressed: "As the creator of Julio's narrative voice, she (to some extent out of envy) impersonates his discourse, codes, and sufferings, but only to free herself from anonymity. She happens to be the observer, the *reader* of the next-door garden which, as she suggests at the end, inspired the *writing* of her novel." Further, the critic contends that the end of the novel is Núria Monclús's reading of Gloria's inconclusive novel. See also Kerr, "Writing Disguises," who proposes that all three characters, Julio, Gloria, and Núria, occupy the position of narrator/author in the novel.

5. In his comparative study of the novel, Gutiérrez Mouat, "Aesthetics, Ethics, and Politics," 69, considers such a topic and concludes: "*El jardín de al lado* is a successful exploration of the contradictory ground that separates politics from the autonomous work of art, an exploration carried out by the transference of the notion of crisis from the political realm to the aesthetic."

6. Language as palimpsest stands as a linguistic device used by "male" writers to invite the reader's involvement in the act of recovery of the hidden message, or voice. Gilbert and Gubar, 534, describe the power of the commentary in male literary fantasies by pointing to James Joyce's mastery: "But of course, if we have space to consider only one example, the twentieth century's greatest master of linguistic transformation—the man who definitely converted comment into the charm—was James Joyce, whose 'densest condensation, hard,' with its proliferation of puns and parodies, tranforms what Hélène Cixous calls the 'old single-grooved mothertongue' into what we are calling a 'patrius sermo' only comprehensible by those who, like Merlin and like Joyce himself, can translate what has been 'scribbled, crost, and cramm'd' on the margins of literature into a spell of power." It must be emphasized that a masculine voice as described by Gilbert and Gubar is not necessarily exclusive to writers who are men, neither is a feminine voice exclusive to writers who are women. Catharine R. Stimpson, "Gertrude Stein and the Transposition of Gender," 15, concludes that Stein often adopts the traditional "masculine" voice as she assumes the role of the husband in her poems regarding her relationship with Alice B. Toklas. Furthermore, Gertrude Stein's often hermetic language resembles more closely a "patrius sermo" than the "old single-grooved mothertongue." More often than not, Stein vacillated from the use of a language

that is gender charged to one that has no gender or supplies the possibility of being all: male, female, neuter; "Yet, even *Tender Buttons* cannot, will not, wholly erase the heterosexual patterns that Stein and Toklas followed and that helped Stein to write. Because of this, the text is a cautionary fable about two Utopian dreams: an agenda of scarcity that would do away with gender altogether, and an agenda of plenty that would permit everyone to be he, she, or it as one pleased" (15). Donoso's discourse is not unlike Stein's in that it allows the narrator to be both he (Julio), she (Gloria), and it (the superimposition of the two), as well as to provide a linguistic arena where both the power of commentary and of referentiality cohabit. Stimpson underlines the fact that Stein's discourse presented a tension between language as representative and as a self-reflexive system. *El jardín de al lado* struggles with the question of whether a novel about exile should use a self-reflexive or referential language. Its discourse juxtaposes one and the other, but never chooses between the two.

7. Gilbert and Gubar, 523, point to one of Virginia Woolf's contributions to the redefinition of a feminine voice: "Provisionally, therefore, we want to suggest that Woolf used what was essentially a *fantasy* about a utopian linguistic structure—a 'woman's sentence'—to define (and perhaps disguise) her desire to revise *not woman's language but woman's relation to language.*"

8. For an incisive study of the carnavalesque and the play of the text in Donoso's works up to *La misteriosa desaparición de la marquesita de Loria,* see Gutiérrez Mouat, *Donoso.*

9. For a very extensive analysis of the relationship between art and linguistic expression in *El jardín de al lado,* see Rosemary Geisdorfer Feal, "Veiled Portraits: Donoso's Interartistic Dialogue in *El jardín de al lado.*"

10. Magnarelli has written several essays on *El obsceno pájaro de la noche* that deal with the polyphonic and neobaroque nature of the text. She dedicates a chapter of *Lost Rib* to this novel to elucidate the function of the feminine voice in Donoso.

11. Kadir, "Next Door," 68, points to the androgynous nature of Donoso's text by referring to the two novels that frame *El jardín de al lado: Middlemarch* and *The Spoils of Poynton:* "The first, authored by a woman writer, Marian Evans, with a male persona, George Eliot, becomes incorporated into *The Garden Next Door,* a novel with a male author and an ostensibly male narrator but with a female scriptor. The second, an equally androgynous script scripted by a Henry James whose authorial gender has its animus in the ambiguities of his own sexual otherness. This too, subsumed by Donoso into the equivocal ruse of his graphic figures and into the ambiguity of Donoso's/Gloria's revising and 'revised' scriptor."

Chapter 5: Political and Personal
Transformations in La desesperanza

1. It is important to note that the word *historia* in Spanish means both story and history and that for this moment in the novel I choose to emphasize the second definition.

2. For an analysis of the role of "New Song" in Latin American political movements, see Fernando Reyes Matta, "The 'New Song' and Its Confrontation in Latin America."

3. Refer to Magnarelli, "Illusory Depths"; Kerr, "Authority and Play"; and Flora González, "Androgynous Narrator," for the function that desire, authority, and play have in Donoso's works.

4. In his short essay, Fernando Alegría, "Good-bye to Metaphor," 78, asserts that although the characters in the novel could be identified with specific members of the Chilean "social and literary menagerie," "it is not the *who* that matters but the *what* they represent."

5. See Guitiérrez Mouat, *Donoso,* and Kerr, "Conventions," for an analysis of *Casa de campo,* and n.3 above for literature on *El jardín de al lado.* Alegría, 77, states: "For those who wonder if Donoso finally makes a pronouncement in this novel on the bleak record of

Pinochet's military dictatorship, the answer is loud and clear: not only does he take a stand but states it in the harshest terms."

6. I am indebted to Stallybrass and White for their formulation of the private/public within bourgeois mentality.

7. One wonders whether in this sentence the male author/narrator is not, like Mañungo, projecting his fantasies onto the female character. Her desire, rather than being hers, tends to be an ideological construct imposed upon her by male definitions of female desire. When speaking about the effects of ideology on women's experience, and specifically about sexual fantasies and roles as projected in literature, Margaret Higonnet, "Speaking Silences," 77, states regarding Flaubert's Emma Bovary: "Though sensuous in appearance, her desires are ideological constructs that have little to do with instinctuality: they have been fostered by the trivial wish-fulfillment novels she consumed at the convent." It is questionable that a woman in Judit's circumstance of terror would have been able to indulge in sexual fantasies. My conclusion is that the character's insistence on that desire and the resulting guilt has been imposed on her by male desires at the representational level within the novel and at the discursive level by the male author.

8. Women involved in underground work are exposed to a double vulnerability: that suffered under police detention and that endured by the rejection of male colleagues who see women's bodily functions (menstruation, pregnancy, and sexual desire itself) as impediments to their functioning in political work. For a brief study of the association of women with nature in Latin American literature see Franco, 512, who quotes Ana Maria Auraujo, a former Tupamara (Uruguay): "Feminine sexuality, desire to have children or not to have them, the disposition of our bodies was not taken into account. For instance, maternity was lived by us as an obstacle that prevented us from continuing the struggle, especially the military struggle." In her novel about a woman's participation in the Sandinista struggle in Nicaragua, *La mujer habitada,* Gioconda Belli represents the concerns expressed by Franco at a critical level.

9. Jane Gallop, "The Bodily Enigma," 18, is helpful in the interpretation of Donoso's novel. Judit feels she must be forgiven for being female, she realizes that suppressing her sexuality in the public sphere constitutes in itself a kind of repression imposed by the male authoritarian order: "Defensive suppression is another form of violent domination, but one which if successful passes under the guise of calm and order rather than violence."

10. Bakhtin, *Rabelais,* 89, stresses laughter's "indissoluble and essential relation to freedom." He goes on to underline the relativity and brevity of that freedom within the medieval stratified society (not unlike Pinochet's Chile), where its expression was permitted only during carnival time: "The very brevity of this freedom increased its fantastic nature and utopian radicalism, born in the festive atmosphere of images."

11. Gutiérrez Mouat, "Review," 142, asserts regarding the carnivalesque: "Pero en *La desesperanza* el discurso liberador del carnaval, que modela la producción entera de Donoso, figura sólo como detrito o resto" [But in *Curfew* the liberating discourse of carnival, which models Donoso's entire novelistic production, appears only as detritus or residue]. Although I agree with Gutiérrez Mouat that this novel must be classified as an example of critical realism, I would not go so far as to state that the carnivalesque as discourse is present only as "detritus." In agreeing with McMurray, "Review," 120, who states that *La desesperanza* is "perhaps the author's most optimistic to date," I contend that Donoso's optimism can best be discerned in scenes such as that of the funeral, where despair and song go hand in hand and where the people's spirit of freedom can still be shared in public, even though its song is brief.

12. For an excellent evaluation of the role that the opposition has played in Chile since 1970, see Brian Loveman.

13. In *La desesperanza,* Donoso infuses history with myth so as to counteract the nega-

tive forces of the current political reality. Gutiérrez Mouat, "Donoso," 8, described the novel thus: "*Curfew* is Balzacian in its voracity, in the multiplicity and variety of its characters, and in its attempt to graft legend onto the fabric of history."

Chapter 7: Masking History in "Taratuta"

1. The young Russian industrialist, Schmidt, dies in jail and leaves his fortune to the Bolshevik Revolution. He is survived by two sisters whose husbands must also donate their share of the inheritance. One of the two sisters is involved with the anarchist Taratuta at the time of her brother's death and he becomes the financial manager for the Bolsheviks.

2. Brooks, *Melodramatic Imagination,* 29, describes the plot trajectory of the melodrama thus: "Yet, typically, the first exchanges of the play, or even the title . . . suggests mysteries or ambiguities hovering over the world, enigmas unresolved. And there swiftly supervenes a threat to virtue, a situation—and most often a person—to cast its very survival into question, obscure its identity, and elicit the process of its fight for recognition." In Donoso's novella this fight for recognition gets played out at the level of characterization, and as we shall see later in this essay, at the discursive level as well.

3. At this time I should remind the reader that in Borges's "El jardín de senderos que se bifurcan" ["The Garden of Forking Parths"], there is a similar encounter between a British researcher of Asian literature who spent his life in the study of one novel and the descendant of that Asian writer, who before his untimely death comes to understand the significance of being an Asian spying for Nazi Germany.

4. With the exception of "Borges y yo" ["Borges and I"], which appears in *Antología personal,* and "Deutsches Requiem" in *El Aleph,* the remainder of the stories mentioned in this essay are found in *Ficciones.* Translations of all stories mentioned in this chapter appear in *Labyrinths.*

5. See "El Milagro Secreto" ["The Secret Miracle"] and "Deutsches Requiem" for the two most obvious parallels. For the definition of literary anxiety of influence see Harold Bloom's book of the same name.

6. For antifascist essays by Borges see *Borges: A Reader,* particularly "A Comment on August 23, 1944," 153–54; "Portrait of the Germanophile," 127–29; and "I, A Jew," 64–65. This last short essay could have been a point of departure for Donoso's novella since in the essay Borges declares his dismay at not being able to find his own Jewish ancestry. Both Borges and Horacio Carlos Taratuta wish to be Jewish and go about defining that identification through a genealogical search. Also see "The Old House," for Donoso's experience with anti-Semitism in Chile.

7. Linda Hutcheon, *Poetics of Postmodernism,* 5, posits contradiction as being at the crux of contemporary art: "While all forms of contemporary art and thought offer examples of this kind of postmodernist contradiction, this book (like most others on the subject) will be privileging the novel genre, and one form in particular, a form that I want to call 'historiographic metafiction.' By this I mean those well-known and popular novels which are both intensely self-reflexive and yet paradoxically also lay claim to historical events and personages.

8. Donoso, *Historia personal del "boom,"* 43; [*The Boom in Spanish American Literature* (45–46)]:

> Mis abundantes lecturas de novelas de todas partes, mi estudio con cierta profundidad de autores como Henry James (gusto adquirido en la Universidad de Princeton y jamás abandonado), Marcel Proust, Faulkner, me aportaron entusiasmo y cierta medida de sabiduría técnica, de teoría; pero siempre ejercieron una influencia a nivel de conocimiento, no irrumpieron en mi mundo, hermanándose conmigo para que al competir con ellas tratara de emularlas.

My voracious reading of novels from all over the world, my study in some depth of writers like Henry James (a taste acquired at Princeton and never abandoned), Marcel Proust, and Faulkner, contributed an enthusiasm and a certain measure of technical skill, of theory; but these authors always exercised an influence at the level of knowledge: they did not invade my world, they did not harmonize with me to the extent that in competing with them I would be trying to emulate them.

See also "El tiempo perdido" ["Time Lost"], a novella published in *Cuatro para Delfina* [Four for Delfina], which is a bittersweet rendering of the Proustian theme.

9. The Summer 1992 issue of *The Review of Contemporary Fiction* published a short story by Donoso that deals with the subject of the disappeared in Chile. "Nobody Wears Fedoras Anymore" first appeared in Spanish in *La Epoca* (Santiago), in its September 2, 1990, issue. The story was written initially in 1983.

Conclusion: Cast Out of Donoso's House of Fiction

1. Even though Josefina Delgado, like José Donoso, is a real person, and in her case, a noted journalist and critic, I will treat her in this discussion as a character in Donoso's fiction.

WORKS CITED

Primary Sources

Donoso, José. *Coronación.* Barcelona: Seix Barral, 1968. [1957]

———. *Coronation.* Trans. Jocasta Goodwin. New York: Knopf, 1965.

———. *El lugar sin límites.* México: Joaquín Mortiz, 1966.

———. *Hell Has No Limits.* In *Triple Cross,* trans. Suzanne Jill Levine and Hallie D. Taylor. New York: Dutton, 1972.

———. *Este domingo.* Barcelona: Seix Barral, 1976. [1966]

———. *This Sunday.* Trans. Lorraine O'Grady Freeman. New York: Knopf, 1967.

———. *El obsceno pájaro de la noche.* Barcelona: Seix Barral, 1970.

———. *The Obscene Bird of Night.* Trans. Hardie St. Martin and Leonard Mades. Boston: David Godine, 1979.

———. *Cuentos.* Barcelona: Seix Barral, 1971.

———. *Charleston and Other Stories.* Trans. Andree Conrad. Boston: David Godine, 1977.

———. *Historia personal del "boom."* Buenos Aires: Sudamericana/Planeta, 1984. [1972]

———. *The Boom in Spanish American Literature: A Personal History.* Trans. Gregory Kolovakos. New York: Columbia University Press and Center for Inter-American Relations, 1977.

———. *Casa de campo.* Barcelona: Seix Barral, 1978.

———. *A House in the Country.* Trans. David Pritchard with Suzanne Jill Levine. New York: Knopf, 1984.

———. *La misteriosa desaparición de la marquesita de Loria.* Barcelona: Seix Barral: 1980.

———. "A Round Table Discussion with José Donoso." In *The Creative Process in the Works of José Donoso,* ed. Guillermo I. Castillo-Feliú, 14–34. Rock Hill, S.C.: Winthrop Studies on Major Modern Writers, 1982.

———. *El jardín de al lado.* Barcelona: Seix Barral, 1981.

———. *The Garden Next Door.* Trans. Hardie St. Martin. New York: Grove/Atlantic, Inc., 1992.

———. *Poemas de un novelista.* Santiago: Ganymedes, 1981.

———. *Cuatro para Delfina.* Barcelona: Seix Barral, 1982.

———. "Lenin." *El Mercurio* (April 7, 1985): E1.

———. *La desesperanza.* Barcelona: Seix Barral, 1986.

———. *Curfew.* Trans. Alfred MacAdam. New York: Grove/Atlantic, Inc., 1988.

189

————. "The Old House." *Wilson Quarterly* 11.4 (Autumn 1987): 152–63.

————. *Taratuta/Naturaleza muerta con cachimba*. Madrid: Mondadori, 1990.

————. *Taratuta/Still Life With Pipe*. Trans. Gregory Rabassa. New York: W. W. Norton, 1993.

————. "A Small Biography of *The Obscene Bird of Night.*" *Review of Contemporary Fiction* 12.2 (1992): 18–31.

————. "Nobody Wears Fedoras Anymore." *Review of Contemporary Fiction* 12.2 (1992): 32–38.

Secondary Sources

Achugar, Hugo. *Ideología y estructuras narrativas en José Donoso.* Caracas: Rómulo Gallegos, 1979.

Alegría, Fernando. "Good-bye to Metaphor: Curfew." *Review of Contemporary Fiction* 12.2 (1992): 77–79.

Bacarisse, Pamela. "Donoso and Social Commitment: *Casa de campo.*" *Bulletin of Hispanic Studies* 60.4 (1983): 319–32.

Baker, Rilda L. "Perfil del narrador desenmascarado en *Casa de campo.*" *La Chispa '81: Selected Proceedings* (February 26–28, 1981). Ed. Gilbert Paolini, 35–41. New Orleans: Tulane University Press, 1981.

Bakhtin, Mikhail. "Discourse in the Novel." In *The Dialogic Imagination: Four Essays,* ed. Michael Holquist, trans. Caryl Emerson and Michael Holquist, 257–422. Austin: University of Texas Press, 1981.

————. *Rabelais and His World.* Trans. Helene Iswolsky. Bloomington: Indiana University Press, 1984.

Bargainnier, Earl F. "Melodrama as Formula." *Journal of Popular Culture* (Winter 1975): 726–33.

Barthes, Roland. *The Pleasure of the Text.* Trans. Richard Miller. New York: Hill and Wang, 1975.

Bassnett, Susan. "Coming out of the Labyrinth: Women Writers in Contemporary Latin America." In *On Modern Latin American Fiction,* ed. John King, 247–67. New York: Hill and Wang, 1987.

Belli, Gioconda. *La mujer habitada.* Tafarroa, Navarra: Taxalaparta, 1990.

Bloom, Harold. *The Anxiety of Influence: A Theory of Poetry.* New York: Oxford University Press, 1982.

Booth, Wayne C. *The Rhetoric of Fiction.* Chicago: University of Chicago Press, 1961.

Borges, Jorge Luis. *El Aleph.* Buenos Aires: Emecé, 1957.

————. *Antología personal.* Buenos Aires: Editorial Sur, 1966.

————. *Borges: A Reader: A Selection from the Writings of Jorge Luis Borges.* Ed. Emir Rodríguez Monegal and Alastair Reid. New York: E. P. Dutton, 1981.

————. "The Garden of Forking Paths." In *Labyrinths. Selected Stories and Other Writings,* ed. Donald A. Yates and James E. Irby, 19–29. New York: New Directions 1962.

————. "El jardín de senderos que se bifurcan." In *Ficciones,* 101–16. Madrid: Alianza, 1988.

————. *Labyrinths: Selected Stories and Other Writings,* eds. Donald A. Yates and James E. Irby. Pref. André Maurois. New York: New Directions, 1962.

Borinsky, Alicia. "Repeticiones y máscaras: *El obsceno pájaro de la noche.*" *Modern Language Notes* 88 (1973): 281–94.

Brooks, Peter. "Freud's Masterplot: Questions of Narrative." *Yale French Studies* 55/56 (1977): 280–300.

————. *The Melodramatic Imagination: Balzac, Henry James, Melodrama and the Mode of Excess.* New York: Columbia University Press, 1985.

Works Cited

Calderón, Héctor. *Conciencia y lenguaje en el Quijote y El obsceno pájaro de la noche.* Madrid: Pliegos, 1987.

Campos, Jorge. "'Casa de campo' de José Donoso." *Insula* 389 (1979): 11.

Canto, Monique. "The Politics of Women's Bodies: Reflections on Plato." In *The Female Body in Western Culture: Contemporary Perspectives,* ed. Susan Rubin Suleiman, 337–53. Cambridge, Mass.: Harvard University Press, 1985.

Castro-Klarén, Sara, Sylvia Molloy, and Beatriz Sarlo, ed. *Women's Writing in Latin America: An Anthology.* Boulder: Westview Press, 1991.

Cerda, Carlos. *José Donoso: Originales y metáforas.* Santiago de Chile: Planeta, 1988.

Constable, Pamela, and Arturo Valenzuela. *A Nation of Enemies: Chile Under Pinochet.* New York: W. W. Norton, 1991.

Felman, Shoshana. "Women and Madness: The Critical Phallacy." *Diacritics* 5.4 (1975): 2–10.

Flori, Monica. "La función de los personajes femeninos en 'Paseo' y 'Santelices' de José Donoso." *Explicación de Textos Literarios* 14.1 (1985–86): 25–32.

Foucault, Michel. "Las Meninas." In *The Order of Things. An Archaeology of the Human Sciences,* ed. R. D. Laing, 3–16. New York: Vintage Books, 1973.

———. "Preface." In *The Order of Things: An Archaeology of the Human Sciences,* ed. R. D. Laing, xv–xxiv. New York: Vintage Books, 1973.

Franco, Jean. "Beyond Ethnocentrism: Gender, Power and the Third-World Intelligentsia." In *Marxism and the Interpretation of Culture,* eds. Cary Nelson and Lawrence Grossberg, 503–15. London: MacMillan Education, Board of Trustees of the University of Illinois, 1988.

Freedman, Barbara. *Staging the Gaze: Postmodernism, Psychoanalysis and Shakespearean Comedy.* Ithaca: Cornell University Press, 1991.

Freud, Sigmund. *Beyond the Pleasure Principle.* Trans. C. J. M. Hubback. London: Hogarth Press and the Institute of Psycho-analysis, 1992.

Gallop, Jane. *Thinking Through the Body,* 11–20. New York: Columbia University Press, 1988.

Geisdorfer Feal, Rosemary. "Veiled Portraits: Donoso's Interartistic Dialogue in *El jardín de al lado.*" *Modern Language Notes* 103.2 (1988): 398–418.

Gertel, Zunilda. "*El obsceno pájaro de la noche:* Desencarnación, Transformación, Inexistencia." *Chasqui* 6.1 (1976): 17–29.

Gilbert, Sandra M., and Susan Gubar. "Sexual Linguistics: Gender, Language and Sexuality." *New Literary History* 16.3 (1985): 515–43.

González, Flora. "The Androgynous Narrator in José Donoso's *El jardín de al lado.*" *Revista de Estudios Hispánicos* 23.1 (1989): 99–113.

González Echevarría, Roberto. "Sarduy, the Boom and the Post-Boom." *Latin American Literary Review* 15.29 (1987): 57–72.

Gutiérrez Mouat, Ricardo. "Aesthetics, Ethics, and Politics in Donoso's *El jardín de al lado.*" *PMLA* 106.1 (1991): 60–70.

———. "José Donoso: An Introduction and Checklist." *Review of Contemporary Fiction* 12.2 (1992): 7–10.

———. *José Donoso: Impostura e impostación. La modelización lúdica y carnavalesca de una producción literaria.* Gaithersburg, Md.: Hispamérica, 1983.

———. "Review of *La desesperanza* by José Donoso." *Hispamérica* 16.48 (1987): 142.

Higonnet, Margaret. "Speaking Silences: Women's Suicide." In *The Female Body in Western Culture: Contemporary Perspectives,* ed. Susan Rubin Suleiman, 68–83. Cambridge, Mass.: Harvard University Press, 1985.

Hutcheon, Linda. *A Poetics of Postmodernism: History, Theory, Fiction.* New York and London: Routeledge, 1988.

191

Iñigo Madrigal, Luis. "Alegoría, historia, novela (a propósito de *Casa de Campo,* de José Donoso)." *Hispamérica* 9.25–6 (1980): 5–31.

James, Henry. *The Art of the Novel.* Intro. R. P. Blackmur. Boston: Northeastern University Press, 1984.

Jara, René. *El revés de la arpillera: Perfil literario de Chile.* Madrid: Hiperión, 1988.

Jurado, María Cristina. "José Donoso: Tiempo de volver." *Bravo* 4.7 (1980): 4–9.

Kadir, Djelal. "Next Door: *Writing* Elsewhere." *Review of Contemporary Fiction* 12.2 (1992): 60–69.

Kelly, Kevin. "'Obscene Bird of Night' is a confusing, horror-filled trip to hell." Review of "The Obscene Bird of Night." *Boston Globe* 2 March 1990: 42.

Kerr, Lucille. "Authority and Play: José Donoso's *El jardín de al lado.*" *Criticism* 25.1 (1983): 41–65.

———. "Conventions of Authorial Design: José Donoso's *Casa de campo.*" *Symposium* 42.2 (1988): 133–52.

———. *Reclaiming the Author: Figures and Fictions from Spanish America.* Durham: Duke University Press, 1992.

Larraín, Rosario. "Dos funciones extras hará el ICTUS en Caracas." *El Mercurio* 29 April 1983.

———. "José Donoso escribe guiones para el Ictus y Anthony Quinn." *El Mercurio* 5 November 1982: 6–7.

———. "'Sueños de mala muerte': Obra de José Donoso llena de bocinazos la sala La Comedia." *El Mercurio* 31 October 1982.

———. "Ultimas funciones de la obra de José Donoso." *El Mercurio* 6 April 1983.

López, Ana. "The Melodrama in Latin America: Films, *Telenovelas* and the Currency of a Popular Form." *Wide Angle* 7.3 (1985): 5–13.

Lord, Albert B. *The Singer of Tales.* Cambridge: Harvard University Press, 1960.

Loveman, Brian. "Military Dictatorship and Political Opposition in Chile." In *Chile: Dictatorship and the Struggle for Democracy,* ed. Grinor Rojo and John J. Hassett, 17–52. Gaithersburg, Md.: Hispamérica, 1988.

Luengo, Enrique. "Inteligibilidad, coherencia y transgresión en *El obsceno pájaro de la noche* y *Casa de campo* de José Donoso. *Hispanófila* 108.3 (1993): 75–87.

Lukács, Georg. *The Theory of the Novel.* Cambridge: MIT Press, 1971.

MacAdam, Alfred J. "José Donoso: *Casa de campo.*" *Revista Iberoamericana* 47.116–17 (1981): 257–63.

McMurray, George R. *José Donoso.* Boston: Twayne, 1979.

———. Review of *La desesperanza* by José Donoso. *Chasqui* 17.1 (1988): 120.

Magnarelli, Sharon. "Amidst the Illusory Depths: The First Person Pronoun and *El obsceno pájaro de la noche.*" *Modern Language Notes* 93 (1978): 267–84.

———. "The Baroque, the Picaresque, and *El obsceno pájaro de la noche.*" *Hispanic Journal* 2.2 (1981): 81–93.

———. *The Lost Rib: Female Characters in the Spanish American Novel,* 147–168. Lewisburg: Bucknell University Press, 1985.

———. *"El obsceno pájaro de la noche:* Fiction, Monsters and Packages." *Hispanic Review* 45.4 (1977): 413–19.

———. *Understanding José Donoso.* Columbia: University of South Carolina Press, 1993.

Martínez, Z. Nelly. *"Casa de campo* de José Donoso: Afán de descentralización y nostalgia del centro." *Hispanic Review* 50.4 (1982): 439–48.

Meléndez, Priscila. "Writing and Reading the Palimpsest: Donoso's *El jardín de al lado.*" *Symposium* 41.3 (1987): 200–13.

Moix, Ana María. "Prólogo" to *Cuentos* (José Donoso), 9–21. Barcelona: Seix Barral 1971.

Montero, Oscar. *"El jardín de al lado:* La escritura y el fracaso del éxito." *Revista Iberoamericana* 49.123–24 (1983): 449–67.

Works Cited

Morell, Hortensia R. *Composición expresionista en "El lugar sin límites" de José Donoso.* Río Piedras: Universidad de Puerto Rico, 1986.

———. "Visión temporal en *El lugar sin límites:* Circularidad narrativa, teatralidad cíclica." *Explicación de textos literarios* 11.2 (1982–83): 29–39.

Murphy, Marie. *Authorized Fictions: José Donoso's "Casa de campo."* London: Tamesis Books Limited, 1992.

The New Harvard Dictionary of Music. Ed. Don Michael Randel. Cambridge: Belknap Press of Harvard University Press, 1986.

Omaña, Balmiro. "De *El obsceno pájaro de la noche* a *Casa de campo.*" *Texto Crítico* 7.22–23 (1981): 265–79.

Pérez-Blanco, Luciano. "*El jardín de al lado* o del exilio al regreso." *Cuadernos Americanos* 239.6 (1981): 191–216.

Przybos, Julia. *L'enterprise melodramatique.* Paris: Jose Korti, 1987.

Quain, Estelle. "The Image of the House in the Works of José Donoso." In *Essays in Honor of Jorge Guillén on the Occasion of his 85th Year,* 85–96. Cambridge, Mass.: Abedul Press, 1977.

Quinteros, Isis. *José Donoso: Una insurrección contra la realidad.* New York: Hispanova, 1978.

Reyes Matta, Fernando. "The 'New Song' and Its Confrontation in Latin America." In *Marxism and the Interpretation of Culture,* ed. Cary Nelson and Lawrence Grossberg, 503–15. London: MacMillan Education, Board of Trustees of the University of Illinois, 1988.

Rich, Adrienne. *Of Woman Born: Motherhood as Experience and Institution.* Tenth Anniversary Edition. New York: W. W. Norton, 1986.

Rodríguez Monegal, Emir. "José Donoso: La novela como Happening." *Revista Iberoamericana* 37.76–77 (1971): 517–36.

———. "El mundo de José Donoso." *Mundo Nuevo* 12 (1967): 77–85.

Salgado, María A. "*Casa de campo* o La realidad de la apariencia." *Revista Iberoamericana* 51.130–31 (1985): 283–91.

———. "On Mothers and Power and How Not to Run A House in the Country." In *Studies on the Works of José Donoso: An Anthology of Critical Essays,* ed. Miriam Adelstein, 77–99. Lewiston, N.Y.: The Edwin Mellen Press, 1990.

Sarduy, Severo. "Escritura/Transvestismo." *Mundo Nuevo* 20 (1968): 72–74.

Solotorevsky, Myrna. *José Donoso: Incursiones en su producción novelesca.* Valparaíso: Ediciones Universitarias de Valparaíso, 1983.

Stallybrass, Peter and Allon White. *The Politics and Poetics of Transgression.* Ithaca, New York: Cornell University Press, 1986.

Stanton, Domna C. "Difference on Trial." In *The Poetics of Gender,* ed. Nancy Miller. 155–82. New York: Columbia University Press, 1986.

Stimpson, Catharine R. "Gertrude Stein and the Transposition of Gender." In *The Poetics of Gender,* ed. Nancy Miller, 1–18. New York: Columbia University Press, 1986.

Swanson, Philip. *José Donoso: The "Boom" and Beyond.* Liverpool: Francis Cairns, 1988.

Urraca, Beatriz. "El concepto de personaje en *Casa de campo:* Entre la tradición y la innovación." *Revista chilena de literatura* 31 (1988): 105–24.

Valdés, Adriana. "El 'Imbunche.' Estudio de un motivo en *El obsceno pájaro de la noche.*" In *La destrucción de un mundo,* 125–60. Buenos Aires: Fernando García Cambeiro, 1975.

Vargas Llosa, Mario. "En torno a la nueva novela latinoamericana." In *Teoría de la novela,* ed. Agnes and Germán Gullón, 113–32. Madrid: Taurus, 1974.

Vera, Jorge E. "Coronación" de José Pineda (Adaptación teatral de la novela de José Donoso)." *La Nación,* 28 Agosto 1966. 15.

———. "José Donoso al video tape." *Bravo* 60 (11 Mayo 1982): 59–61.

193

Vicinus, Martha. "'Helpless and Unfriended': Nineteenth-Century Domestic Melodrama." *New Literary History* 13.1 (1981): 127–43.

Vidal, Hernán. *Surrealismo y rebelión de los instintos.* Barcelona: Aubí, 1972.

Walker, Barbara G. *The Woman's Dictionary of Symbols and Sacred Objects.* San Francisco: Harper and Row, 1988.

Walter, Gérard. *Lénine.* Paris: René Julliard, 1950.

INDEX